# Inflation, stagflation, relative prices, and imperfect information

# Inflation, stagflation, relative prices, and imperfect information

ALEX CUKIERMAN
*Associate Professor of Economics*
*Tel Aviv University*

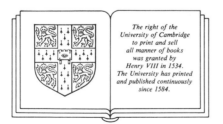

The right of the
University of Cambridge
to print and sell
all manner of books
was granted by
Henry VIII in 1534.
The University has printed
and published continuously
since 1584.

## CAMBRIDGE UNIVERSITY PRESS

*Cambridge*
*London   New York   New Rochelle*
*Melbourne   Sydney*

WILLIAM MADISON RANDALL LIBRARY UNC AT WILMINGTON

Published by the Press Syndicate of the University of Cambridge
The Pitt Building, Trumpington Street, Cambridge CB2 1RP
32 East 57th Street, New York, NY 10022, USA
10 Stamford Road, Oakleigh, Melbourne 3166, Australia

First published 1984

Printed in the United States of America

*Library of Congress Cataloging in Publication Data*
Cukierman, Alex.
Inflation, stagflation, relative
prices, and imperfect information.
Includes bibliographical references and index.
1. Inflation (Finance) 2. Unemployment – Effect
of inflation on. 3. Phillips curve. 4. Rational
expectations (Economic theory) I. Title.
HG229.C83   1984   332.4′1   84–5825
ISBN 0 521 25630 5

*In memory of my parents
and to Israel A.*

# Contents

vii

x    **Contents**

# Preface

The past decade witnessed a substantial reevaluation by economists of previously established views concerning inflation and its interaction with real phenomena. In particular the stable inflation–output trade-off view popularized during the sixties was strongly shaken both by new theoretical developments and by the stagflation of the mid-seventies. The behavior of inflationary expectations was recognized as a prime determinant of the real effects of inflation. New evidence and theory suggested that the distribution of relative prices is not independent of the distribution of inflation in direct contradiction to the neutrality of money paradigm. Simultaneously the idea that expectations are formed rationally with all the available relevent information being used became a major element of macroeconomic thinking and modeling.

Those changes, which were spawned by the relative failure of Keynesian policy prescriptions during the seventies, reopened the age-old question regarding money, inflation, and their interaction with real phenomena. Two families of theories, both grounded in rational expectations, were developed during the seventies to explain those interactions. One following the Keynesian tradition relies on price rigidities created by implicit or explicit contracts. The other is based on imperfect information.

This book is a summary of the imperfect information approach to macroeconomic modeling. Two types of informational limitations are considered. One involves models in which individuals have asymmetric information about the current general price level and consequently suffer from the aggregate–relative confusion. The other considers models in which individuals cannot distinguish permanent from transitory shocks as soon as they occur, thus creating a temporary but persistent confusion between permanent and transitory changes.

Part I of the book explores the implications of the confusion between aggregate and relative price changes for various effects of inflation within a *unified* rational expectations equilibrium framework of the type pioneered by Robert Lucas (1973). The focus of this part of the book is on the interrelationships among the following phenomena: monetary variability, the magnitude of the trade-off coefficient between output and unanticipated inflation, the degree of divergence between the inflationary expectations of different individuals, inflation uncertainty, inflation variance, and the variability of relative prices. Although most of the discussion is at the conceptual level, relevant empirical evidence is summarized when available. Recognition of the fact that even at one time different individuals have different views about the future course of inflation has important implications for the behavior of investors in the bond market. Chapter 5 traces those implications for the allocative efficiency of the bond market, Fisher's theory of interest, and the volume of trade in bonds. The aggregate–relative confusion is a prominent example but by no means the only one in which asymmetric information plays a fundamental role in economic theory. Chapter 2 provides perspective on this by discussing the role of asymmetric information in microeconomic models of signaling and screening and in finance-oriented models that focus on the information content of prices. Chapter 7 compares and contrasts the finance-oriented literature on the information content of prices with the macroeconomics-oriented aggregate–relative confusion.

Part II explores the implications of the inability of individuals to distinguish perfectly between permanent and temporary changes in the economic environment for stagflation, relative price variability, and the efficiency of the price system. Unlike the aggregate–relative confusion, the confusion between permanent and transitory changes does not disappear with the publication of aggregate price statistics. In the presence of the permanent–transitory confusion, erratic monetary policies have persistent effects on the composition of output. Producers' expectations and decisions adjust gradually to actual changes in relative prices. Chapter 9 shows that the symptoms of stagflation – decrease in output and investment, increase in unemployment and interest rates, and a temporary increase in measured inflation – all occur when individuals in the economy are slow to detect permanent reductions in productivity. For the sake of perspective, other persistence-creating mechanisms besides the permanent–transitory confusion are surveyed in Chapter 8.

The reader's mathematical training need not go beyond standard calculus and elementary statistical theory. In order not to break continuity, long mathematical arguments are relegated to a series of appendixes. Besides professional economists, the main audience for the book is the advanced undergraduate or the first-year graduate student. The book may be used as a supplementary text in a first-year graduate course in macroeconomics or as a main text in a self-contained course on inflation and its real effects. I have used it in courses on inflation at both the graduate and the undergraduate levels.

Some of the material appearing in this volume has been adapted from articles that appeared originally in journals. In particular I am grateful to the editors and publishers of the *American Economic Review, Journal of Monetary Economics, Journal of Political Economy,* and *Economics Letters* for their permission to include material that was originally published in their journals. Some of those articles constitute joint work with Paul Wachtel and with Karl Brunner and Allan Meltzer. In particular, Chapter 4 on differential expectations and to a lesser extent Chapter 6 draw on joint work with Wachtel (Cukierman and Wachtel 1979, 1982a, 1982b). Chapter 9 on stagflation is based on joint work with Brunner and Meltzer (Brunner et al. 1980).

In undertaking a project of this size one necessarily incurs many debts. David Folkerts-Landau read the entire manuscript and made suggestions that led me to write Chapters 2, 7, and 8. I also benefited from discussions with Avraham Beja, Martin Hellwig, Ephraim Kleiman, Chester Spatt, and John Taylor. The Foerder Institute for Economic Research and the faculty of social sciences at Tel Aviv University provided partial financial support. Some of the ideas in the book were developed while I was on leave at GSIA, Carnegie–Mellon University. I am also grateful to Maria-Teresa Salvemini, who first got me interested in writing this book. Connie Wilsack thoroughly edited the entire manuscript. Jan Detisch and Stella Padeh typed several versions of the manuscript skillfully and efficiently. Finally I am indebted to my family, who gave me the means, the disposition, and the freedom to write books such as this one.

*Note:* Address all correspondence for author dated before June 1985 to Prof. Alex Cukierman, Graduate School of Industrial Design, Carnegie–Mellon University, Schenley Park, Pittsburgh, PA 15213.

# CHAPTER 1

# General overview

## 1 Introduction

The past decade has witnessed a substantial change in the field of macroeconomics. Fixed price and wage models of the simple Keynesian variety have been displaced by flexible price and wage models. The Phillips curve, which until the end of the 1960s was viewed as representing a stable trade-off between inflation and unemployment, has come to be regarded as a temporary phenomenon that lasts only as long as inflationary expectations differ from actual inflation.

In a world with a stable trade-off, the government could pick, at least within some range, any desired combination of inflation and employment. Recognition that the trade-off is temporary altered this view drastically: The consensus became that in the long run there is no policy-exploitable trade-off between inflation and unemployment. Monetary policy may temporarily boost employment, but after a while employment will return to its original level and the rate of inflation will be higher. Moreover, if policy makers try to use monetary policy to maintain employment *systematically* at a level higher than it would otherwise be, the Phillips trade-off will become more biased toward inflation and ultimately vanish even in the short run.

Because many modern explanations of the Phillips curve rely on the relationship between actual and expected inflation, the modeling and empirical measurement of inflationary expectation have become important tasks for macroeconomics. Initially expectations were considered adaptive: Yesterday's expectation is altered partially in response to the current forecast error. This and similar ways of modeling expectations were strongly criticized by the so-called rational expectations school, whose leading figure is Robert Lucas.[1] The view advanced by this school is that the formation of expectations should be consistent with the actual behavior of the economy. This does not mean that in the presence of stochastic shocks individuals do not make forecast errors. It means that individuals use all their systematic knowledge about the deterministic and stochastic structure of the economy to form an optimal forecast of inflation and possibly other variables that are relevant to their behavior.

1

Adaptive expectations that do not use all the information available on the functioning of the economy are therefore not rational. Recognition of this has forced modern macroeconomic model builders to specify more carefully who knows what, and when, and to formulate mechanisms for forming expectations that are consistent with this information structure.

The implication that systematic monetary policy cannot affect real economic variables is a direct consequence of the "rational" modeling of expectations. As a result the rational expectations school came to be associated with the methodological precept that expectations formation has to be consistent with the structure of the economy, as well as with the statement that systematic monetary policy cannot affect the rate of unemployment and other real economic variables.

It is fair to say that there is broad consensus on the first element, whereas the second is still controversial. Some economists think it is possible to accept the notion that individuals use the information available to them in an optimal manner without having to accept the policy conclusion that systematic monetary policy is powerless. Both groups agree that *unpredictable* monetary policy has real effects but disagree on whether such unpredictable monetary policy is desirable on general welfare grounds.

Economists who favor policy activism are often labeled "Keynesian," whereas those who favor stable rules rather than discretionary policy are often identified as "monetarist." Affinities with other methodological elements may also be used to characterize the two groups. For example, Keynesians prefer to model the economy as being in disequilibrium, with at least one price fixed exogenously. The slow adjustment of wages is explained within this framework by "stickiness," or the existence of contracts. Monetarists usually prefer to view the economy as always adjusting to equilibrium rather quickly; wages and prices move swiftly to equilibriate markets, so perfectly anticipated changes in the money supply have no or little effect on real variables.

According to the monetarist approach, a doubling of the quantity of money doubles all individual prices, leaving relative prices and therefore real variables unchanged. On the other hand, within the framework of the Keynesian model with its sticky variable, often taken to be the nominal wage rate, a change in the quantity of money affects employment and output by changing the real wage rate and therefore the demand for labor. The effect on real variables holds in this case because some nominal variables (like prices) adjust to the change in the quantity of money, while others (like the nominal wage rate) do not.[2]

## 2    Equilibrium versus disequilibrium views of the economy

Modern formulations of disequilibrium models specify prices in some markets as being fixed from the outside and then work out the implications for the behavior of other markets (Barro and Grossman 1976). The trouble with such formulations is that there is nothing in the model to explain why the fixed prices are fixed, why they are fixed at some levels rather than at others, and what, if anything, would change them.

Some of those questions are partially answered by the contract literature in macroeconomics. In this literature the nominal wage rate is fixed in advance to achieve a real wage rate that would clear the labor market in an ex ante sense. Because the price level depends on a variety of stochastic factors, some of which are not known with certainty when the terms of the contract are set, the actual real wage and actual employment end up being different from their ex post market-clearing values.[3] This formulation of disequilibrium behavior is more complete, since it provides an explicit hypothesis about the factors that determine the temporarily fixed value of the nominal wage. However, it is still open to the objection that any level of employment different from the ex post market-clearing level involves forgone mutually beneficial trades by both workers and employers. Any level of employment other than at the ex post equilibrium of the labor market dominates any other (disequilibrium) levels because the welfare of some individuals can be improved without decreasing the welfare of others (Barro 1977).

At the other extreme are models in which all markets including the labor market clear, so that prices, wages, and quantities are always at their equilibrium levels. Models incorporating rational formation of expectations are usually specified as equilibrium models, but nothing compels the two to appear together always (Taylor 1980). Monetarist policy prescriptions are usually supported by equilibrium models, however, whereas Keynesian policy prescriptions are normally implied by a disequilibrium view of some markets in the economy. One criticism of equilibrium models is that the level of unemployment fluctuates a great deal more than real wages, making it hard to believe that the labor market is usually in equilibrium (Hall 1977). This phenomenon can be explained within an equilibrium framework as well, however (Brunner et al. 1983).

The view taken in this book is that as a matter of *modeling strategy*, equilibrium is preferable to disequilibrium for two reasons: First, equilibrium models yield more complete hypotheses about the behavior of important economic variables like wages, relative prices, and inflation.

Second, most of the technical apparatus of modern economics has been developed for equilibrium rather than disequilibrium situations. It is therefore likely that, at the current state of knowledge, equilibrium modeling of the economy will come up with stronger and more specific predictions than disequilibrium modeling will.

More insights are to be gained from modeling slow adjustments of prices and wages as a succession of temporary market-clearing values of those variables than from just specifying the movements of these variables exogenously, as is often done in the disequilibrium literature. Within an equilibrium framework, reasons for the slow adjustment of wages (e.g., imperfect information and costs of adjustment) can be treated explicitly rather than implicitly. In consequence it becomes possible to investigate the effects of the structure of information and other costs of adjustment more explicitly than in disequilibrium models. Finally it should be stressed that an equilibrium view of the economy does not always lead to monetarist policy prescriptions. Adoption of the equilibrium paradigm as a modeling tool does not imply the automatic acceptance of rules such as a constant rate of money growth.

## 3    Neutrality of money, the Phillips curve, and the aggregate–relative confusion

A basic tenet of classical economics is that real economic behavior depends only on relative prices. A change in the general price level accompanied by an equiproportional change in all prices should not change the real equilibrium of the economy because real behavior responds to relative prices rather than to absolute prices.

An immediate corollary is that a doubling of the quantity of money, which doubles all prices and therefore also the general price level, does not affect the equilibrium values of real economic variables. Money is neutral in the sense that it affects the absolute price level but not relative prices or other real variables that are independent of the quantity of money. In more technical terms, the economy is dichotomized; real variables, including the *real* quantity of money, are determined independently of the *nominal* quantity of money, which affects only the general price level. A classic description of such a model of the economy appears in Patinkin (1965).

The existence of a Phillips curve, expressing a relation between the rate of inflation and the rate of unemployment, is a clear violation of the neutrality of money because it involves a systematic relationship between the rates of change of a nominal variable (inflation) and a real variable. Similarly, there is evidence that relative price variability is not independent of the distribution of the general rate of inflation (Glejser 1965, Vining and Elwertowski 1976, Parks 1978, Padoa-Schioppa 1979). This evidence raises the following fundamental question: Must the view that money is neutral be abandoned, or can the observed facts be reconciled with classical theory?

In a series of influential papers, Lucas (1972a, 1972b, 1973) suggested that the Phillips curve may be reconciled with monetary neutrality by proposing that individuals temporarily confuse aggregate and relative price movements. Typical individuals have more timely information on the price of the good they sell than on the general price level. Knowing that their price partially reflects movements in the general level of prices, they use it to improve their estimate of the current general price level. This in turn affects their view about the relative price of the good they sell and the supply of that good. When an unexpected increase in the rate of growth of the money supply pushes up the rate of inflation, suppliers of different goods partially interpret the increase in the prices of their respective products as relative price increases and react by producing more. This creates a temporary positive relationship between unexpected inflation and the level of employment and output even though money is neutral in the absence of this aggregate–relative confusion. Thus the Lucas hypothesis makes it possible to reconcile the neutrality of money $+$ with the existence of a Phillips curve.

The same hypothesis can also explain the observed relationship between relative price variability and the variance of the general rate of inflation.[4] As the general rate of inflation becomes more variable, individuals attribute more of the fluctuations in actual relative prices in their own markets to fluctuations in the general price level. As a result, their supply curves become less responsive to actual relative prices. A given distribution of relative demand shocks across markets thus causes more relative price dispersion across markets. On the other hand, when the variance of inflation is low, the typical market-specific supply curve is highly sensitive to the actual relative price in the market. In consequence, a given distribution of demand across markets creates large differences in production and small differences in relative prices across markets. Thus the observed relationship between general monetary variability and relative price variability can be explained by the aggregate–relative confusion even if the underlying economic system is basically neutral. The aggregate–relative confusion is also useful in explaining the cross-sectional distribution of inflationary expectations.

A basic implication of the aggregate–relative confusion is that, ceteris paribus, an increase in monetary uncertainty increases the variability of inflation, the relative price variability, the cross-sectional variance of inflationary expectations, and the extent of inflation uncertainty. Provided these different variabilities change mostly because of changes in monetary uncertainty, they should all be positively related.[5]

## 4      Confusion between permanent and transitory changes

The confusion between aggregate and relative price movements usually lasts as long as it takes for the publication of figures on the general price level. There may be a further delay if part of the public does not assimilate the new information immediately, but this confusion probably cannot last more than several months. Obviously by the time past confusions have been resolved, new ones arise, but any given confusion is relatively short lived.

There is an additional confusion that does not wither away so quickly: Whenever changes occur in the economy, the public (even with full current information) is uncertain about their permanence. The published statistics do not reveal how much of a given change is here to stay and how much is a temporary aberration.

Because most current decisions about employment, production, savings, and consumption depend on expectations concerning the future, individuals have to guess how much of the current changes will last before they commit themselves. Those guesses, even when formed rationally, are usually imperfect. Permanent changes are initially interpreted as being partly transitory, and transitory shocks are initially interpreted as being partly permanent. Individuals can learn about the permanence of a given shock only by observing how long it persists.

The permanent–transitory confusion is instrumental in explaining various economic phenomena. In particular, the symptoms of stagflation – a combination of inflation and unemployment – can be generated by a large reduction in productivity that is temporarily misperceived as being transitory (Brunner et al. 1980). Because of this misperception, individuals initially believe that they are almost as rich as before and continue to consume at the previous relatively high level. Workers demand the previous relatively high real wage rates. When they discover that the market offers only lower real wage rates, some of them, believing that this is a temporary phenomenon, wait for better days and do not accept employment. The measured rate of unemployment thus increases. Production decreases because of both the decrease in productivity and the decrease in employment, so aggregate supply decreases. Since aggregate demand remains nearly the same, this causes an excess demand, which is resolved by a temporary increase in the rate of inflation. Thus an imperfectly perceived decrease in permanent productivity temporarily increases both inflation and unemployment.

The permanent–transitory confusion is also useful in explaining relative price variability, whether induced by real or monetary reasons. A differing persistence of shocks across markets combined with the permanent–transitory confusion leads to different interpretations of their permanence and hence to different supply responses and price changes in different markets (Cukierman 1982a).[6]

## 5 Welfare costs of inflation

The past decade has also witnessed a substantial reevaluation of the costs of inflation. These were previously believed to be largely due to the decrease in real money balances induced by inflation (Friedman 1969). It has now become apparent, however, that many of the social costs of inflation are related to its uncertainty and to the concomitant increase in relative price variability.[7]

As stressed by Friedman (1977), relative price uncertainty makes it more difficult for the price system to perform its allocative function in an efficient manner. Some recent evidence suggests that increased inflation uncertainty reduces output and/or increases unemployment (Blejer and Leiderman 1980, Levi and Makin 1980, Mullincaux 1980). Cukierman and Wachtel (1979) show that an increase in the variability of inflation is associated with an increase in the cross-sectional variance of inflationary expectations across individuals. As a result, opinions about future inflation and current real rates of interest become more divergent.

An important consequence of differential inflationary expectations is that different savers and investors in the bond market make their decisions on the basis of differently perceived real rates of interest. As a result, rates of return on investments are not equalized at the margin, thus causing a misallocation of capital (Cukierman 1978). The larger inflation uncertainty and the divergence of inflationary expectations are, the more serious those costs become. More generally, when uncertainty (whether caused by real or by monetary factors) increases, the decision errors made by producers become larger and more costly. The policy implication is that a stable political and monetary environment is conducive to greater efficiency.[8]

## 6 Guide to the topics and layout of the book

This book discusses many of the issues mentioned here within a rational expectations equilibrium framework. No attempt is made to cover exhaustively the voluminous literature that has developed on macroeconomics and the business cycle during the past decade. Instead the book focuses on phenomena that are explainable in terms of incomplete information like the Phillips curve, relative price variability, differential inflationary expectations, and stagflation.

The discussion is organized around two basic types of incomplete information or confusions: the aggregate–relative confusion and the permanent–transitory confusion. Part I deals with the implications of the aggregate–relative confusion for various macroeconomic issues. Part II deals with the implications of the permanent–transitory confusion. To bring out the role of the aggregate–relative confusion within the general context of asymmetric information in economics, the first and last chapters of Part I (Chapters 2 and 7) discuss some of the broader implications of differential information. Readers who are mostly interested in macroeconomic issues can go directly to Chapters 3-6.

Chapter 2 is a selective survey of the literature on signaling, screening, and the information content of prices. Chapter 3 presents a simplified and modified version of Lucas's (1973) multimarkets equilibrium model and uses it to derive the basic Lucas hypothesis on the slope of the Phillips curve. This is followed by a review of some related empirical evidence. The same framework is used in Chapter 4 to investigate the conceptual and empirical relationships among inflation variance, differential inflationary expectations, and inflation uncertainty. Chapter 5 focuses on the bond market to investigate the implications of heterogeneous expectations for Fisher's theory of interest, the allocative efficiency of the bond market, and the volume of trade in bonds.

The implications of the aggregate–relative confusion for relative price variability and its relationship to inflation variance and unanticipated inflation are presented along with supporting empirical evidence in Chapter 6. The analytical framework of this chapter is the same as that of Chapters 3 and 4. This chapter also considers the effects of unanticipated monetary shocks on relative price variability in the presence of differing supply elasticities across markets. Readers who are more interested in analytical continuity than in topical continuity may want to read Chapter 6 immediately after Chapters 3 and 4. These three chapters deal with the interactions among monetary uncertainty, the Phillips curve, inflation variance, relative price variability, the variance of inflationary expectations, and inflation uncertainty within a unified framework.

Chapter 7 concludes the first part of the book with a comparison between the macroeconomic and finance models that are both based on differential information. This chapter also features a discussion of the consequences of the introduction of an economy-wide bond market into a Lucas–Phelps multimarkets equilibrium model.

Part II focuses on the permanent–transitory confusion as a mechanism that creates persistence in the behavior of economic variables. Chapter 8 briefly surveys the various explanations for persistence and serial correlation in the time paths of economic variables. The remaining three chapters of this part focus on the effects of the confusion between permanent and temporary shocks in various areas.

The implications of the permanent–transitory confusion for stagflation and the persistence of unemployment following large permanent shocks are developed in Chapter 9. The framework used is anchored on an extended version of the IS–LM model. Chapter 10 investigates the effects of this confusion on the allocative efficiency of the price system and monetary policy within the framework of a multimarkets equilibrium model. The same analytical framework is used in Chapter 11 to investigate the effects of the permanent–transitory confusion on aggregate and relative price variability.

An attempt has been made to make the book more readable by omitting long proofs from the text and putting them in appendixes to certain chapters.

# PART I

# Aggregate–relative confusion

# Asymmetric information in economics and the information conveyed by prices and other signals

## 1    Introduction

This part of the book is based on the notion that individuals do not have perfect current information on the general price level. They have timely information on prices in their own markets but are unable to distinguish perfectly between price changes that are caused by adjustments in the general price level and changes that reflect adjustments in relative prices. This is because individuals have current access to only the price in their own market. The representative individual thus observes only one component of the vector of current prices in the economy. Because this component is correlated in equilibrium with the general price level, it conveys information about the current general price level. The information conveyed is not exact, however, because the general price level and individual prices are not perfectly correlated. As a result, no individual in the economy knows the current general price level with certainty, and movements in the aggregate price level are to some extent confused with relative price changes.

We refer to this as the *aggregate–relative confusion*. The informational setup that characterizes the aggregate–relative confusion can be viewed as a particular instance of asymmetric information in economics: Different individuals have different information sets.

The notion of asymmetric information in the form of different information sets for different individuals has been used extensively in the microeconomic and finance literature. In particular, the asymmetric possession of information about characteristics of certain nonhomogeneous goods (such as labor) by the buyers and sellers of these goods is the basis for the signaling and screening literature. Differences in information sets are also at the root of the finance literature that explores the information content of prices. Individuals come to the market with different notions about the prospective returns of assets. These beliefs are then reflected in the market prices of the assets, which reveal part or all of the private information possessed by individuals to all other individuals in the market.

To highlight the role played by the aggregate–relative confusion within the more general context of incomplete information in economics, this chapter surveys some of the extensive literature on signaling, screening, and the information content of prices. The unifying theme of all this literature, including the literature based on the aggregate–relative confusion, is that different agents possess, at least initially, different information sets. The focus of analysis varies, however. The signaling and finance-oriented literature is mostly microeconomic in nature, whereas the aggregate–relative confusion paradigm has been devised to deal with mostly macroeconomic phenomena.

A discussion of asymmetric information and its transmission through signaling and screening appears in Section 2. The role that prices play in the transmission and aggregation of private information is discussed in Section 3. The incentives to collect information and the limits to the aggregation of information by prices are discussed in Section 4. Section 5 concludes the chapter with a discussion of the aggregation of information in the presence of costly information and of conditioning on past prices.

## 2     Asymmetric information and its transmission through signaling and screening

In many situations the buyers and sellers of nonhomogeneous goods have different information about the quality of the good being sold. For example, workers are usually better informed about their own productivity and their propensity to quit than are their prospective employers. Sellers of used cars have better information about the quality of their cars than buyers do. Buyers of health insurance and other personal insurance have better information about their health or about their propensity to be involved in an accident than the company that insures them against those risks. Borrowers usually have better knowledge about their repayment ability and honesty than the lenders who accommodate them. The common feature of all these examples is that one side of the market is better informed prior to the transaction about some relevant characteristic of the good being exchanged.

For concreteness, but without loss of generality, we focus on the used cars example developed by Akerlof (1970). Suppose there are two types of cars: good cars and bad cars or "lemons." Owners know whether they have a good car or a lemon, but prospective buyers have no way of knowing which is which. As a result, the market price for both types of cars is the same. Assuming buyers know the distribution of good and bad cars in the population, the market price that emerges is an appropriately weighted average. As a result the owners of good cars withdraw their cars from the market, leaving only the lemons in it. A possible consequence is that the used car market will dry up altogether; sellers of good cars are willing to sell only at a higher price, but buyers are not willing to buy at the higher price because they are unable to distinguish good cars from lemons prior to purchase.

Clearly, owners of good cars have an incentive to set up a credible mechanism through which they can convey information about the quality of their cars to prospective buyers. Such a mechanism is known as a *signal* when viewed by the seller who sends it and a *screening device* from the point of view of the buyer who uses it to distinguish between owners of good and bad cars. A possible signaling mechanism in this example is a contingent contract that offers buyers the following deal: "Buy the car at the price of a good car. If, after the purchase, the buyer finds out that the car is indeed good, the deal becomes final. If the car turns out to be a lemon, the seller will refund the difference between the price of a good car and the price of a bad car plus a positive fine." The owners of good cars will find it worthwhile to offer such a contract because they will end up selling good cars at the appropriate high price. The owners of lemons will not find it worthwhile because they will end up selling their lemons below market value. The contract is a credible signal because buyers know that only owners of good cars will find it advantageous to offer it. More generally, signals or screening devices make it possible to execute mutually advantageous deals that would not have occurred in the absence of signals.

Note that the crucial feature of a credible and therefore good signal is that it is in the self-interest of only good car owners to send it. This generalizes to many other situations as well.

### 2a     *Education as a screening device for productive ability*

An important example is education used as a signal for productive ability, which has been investigated by Spence (1973, 1974), Arrow (1973), and others.[1] The basic premise is that labor is heterogeneous in terms of productive ability and employers do not know the productivity of individual workers before hiring them. In the absence of screening devices, employers will pay all workers a wage equal to the average marginal productivity of workers in the population. If productivity is negatively correlated with the costs of getting education,[2] however, employers can use the level of education as a screening device to distinguish among workers with different productivities.

Such a screening device works because individuals with low costs of education (and higher productivity) find it worthwhile to obtain higher educational levels. By structuring wages as an appropriately increasing function of the level of educational certification of individuals, the firm screens them by productive ability. This structure of rewards naturally affects the propensity of individuals to invest in the signal by acquiring more education, which in turn has to be consistent with what employers believe about the relationship between the level of education and productive ability.

Spence (1973) formulates this mutual relationship between employers' beliefs and offered wage schedules on one hand and the actual correlation between education and productive ability on the other in terms of self-fulfilling expectations. More precisely, the wage schedule offered by employers induces a pattern of education that is consistent with employers' beliefs about the relation between productive ability and education. Spence shows that many such self-fulfilling equilibriums are possible and that some are more efficient than others.[3]

## 2b     Self-selection and turnover in the labor market

Salop and Salop (1976) consider the case of positive turnover costs. Whenever a firm hires a new worker, it incurs a fixed training cost $T$. There is a fixed pool of workers who supply their services to the market perfectly inelastically. These workers are identical in every respect except their probability of quitting. There are two groups of workers: those with a relatively high probability of quitting, the "fast quitters," and those with a lower probability of quitting, the "slow quitters." Each worker knows the quit group to which he or she belongs, but the firms do not. Because firms have positive turnover costs, they are interested in attracting the slow quitters. In the absence of a device to distinguish slow from fast quitters, however, a competitive labor market will clear at a uniform wage rate for both types of workers.

Starting from such an undifferentiated equilibrium, a single firm can increase its profits by devising a self-selection screening mechanism that will differentiate between the two types of workers. This can be done by offering workers two alternative wage schedules. One is a fixed wage for all the time periods during which the worker is employed at the firm. The other is a two-part wage (TPW), which is lower than the fixed wage in the first period of employment and then higher than the fixed wage by a constant amount for all employment periods from the second on. By choosing the wage differentials between the flat wage schedule and the TPW schedule appropriately, the firm can create a situation in which only the slow quitters will choose the TPW; fast quitters will prefer the flat wage structure because the likelihood that they will be around to get the higher wage rate is small. Thus the worker's choice of wage schedule will reveal the quit group to which an employee belongs.

If only one firm uses this screening device, it will reduce its turnover costs and increase its profits. This firm will expand while others will be forced to contract as their average quit rate rises. The "smart" firm advantage will be eroded, however, as other firms follow its lead in instituting the screening device. In long-run equilibrium, competition among firms causes the first period's wage differential between the flat and the TPW schedules to be exactly equal to the training costs $T$. All firms achieve perfect screening of all workers, but the two-part wage structures make firms indifferent at the margin between hiring a slow or a fast quitter. In terms of present value, the wage rate of the slow quitters is higher than that of the fast quitters. In long-run equilibrium the scarce factor, slow quitters in this case, appropriates all the benefits from the full introduction of the screening device. The screening device, in effect, transforms an initial position of asymmetric information into one of full information.

## 2c     *Asymmetric information in the insurance and credit markets*

In the insurance market, information about risks is usually asymmetric because individuals who buy insurance have a better evaluation of their own accident probability than the company that insures them. Rothschild and Stiglitz (1976) consider the case of high-risk and low-risk individuals who differ in their accident probabilities. Individuals know to which group they belong, but the insurance company does not. The insurance company knows the proportion of high- and low-risk individuals in the population and the probability of accident to each. In the absence of a screening device, the insurance company may choose to offer a single contract on which it breaks even on average. With such a contract, low-risk individuals subsidize high-risk individuals and may withdraw from the market altogether. Like the case of the market for lemons, bad risks drive good risks out of the market.

Rothschild and Stiglitz show that with a uniform contract, equilibrium does not exist in the insurance market. Equilibrium *may* exist if the insurance company can find a self-selection device that separates high-risk from low-risk individuals. This is achieved by offering two insurance contracts: one at a high price without any limitations on the amount to be paid by the insurance company if an accident occurs, and the other at a low price but with an upper limit. Provided the upper limit is appropriately chosen, high-risk individuals will prefer the first contract, whereas low-risk individuals will opt for the lower rate offered in the second contract. These choices create a self-selection mechanism that makes information in the market symmetric.

Two features of this setup are of particular interest: First, an equilibrium may not exist even in this case. Whether an equilibrium exists or not depends on the relative sizes of the two groups of individuals, their degree of risk aversion, and the probabilities of accident. Second, equilibrium is characterized by a quantity constraint for some insurance contracts even though the insurance market is competitive. The quantity constraint is needed to screen the two types of risk. In practice, such constraints may take the form of a large deductible or an upper limit on the insurance payment when an accident occurs.

Competitive rationing as a device that induces self-selection in the presence of asymmetric information is not limited to the insurance market. When lenders are uncertain about the honesty of borrowers, credit rationing may be used as one component of a self-selection device to separate honest from dishonest borrowers. The size of the loan and the interest rate in the contract chosen by the individual convey information about his or her honesty and point to the "correct" loan contract from the point of view of the lender (Jaffee and Russell 1976).

The screening and incentive-creating properties of the interest rate also explain why in a group of borrowers who appear to be identical, some receive credit and others do not, and why those denied credit do not receive it even if they offer a higher interest rate or more collateral. Stiglitz and Weiss (1981) explain this phenomenon by showing that in the presence of uncertainty about the riskiness of the projects undertaken by its borrowers, a bank will, by raising the interest rate, increase the average riskiness of the projects undertaken by its borrowers and therefore the possibility of default. One way to limit the detrimental effects of this mechanism is to deny credit to some of those who apply for it at the interest rate set by the bank. Under such circumstances there is an excess demand for loans even when the bank is in equilibrium. An obvious way to eliminate this disequilibrium would be to raise the interest rate. If the detrimental effects of this increase because of the increase it causes in the probability of default outweigh the direct positive effects of the increase on the bank's objective function, however, it will pay the bank to maintain the interest rate at the lower level and under some circumstances to grant credit to only some of the applicants, thus rationing credit.

The increase in the average riskiness of the projects financed by the bank's loans caused by an increase in the interest rate occurs through two channels. First, at higher rates the fraction of borrowers with more risky projects who apply for the bank's loans increases. Second, at higher rates each borrower finds it worthwhile to undertake more risky projects. The first channel works because the interest rate acts as a screening mechanism, and the second by triggering incentive effects. Both increase the average probability of default to the bank.

The bank could eliminate an excess demand for its loans also by raising collateral requirements. When the collateral individuals put down acts as a screening device that reveals some information about the riskiness of the projects undertaken by them, however, raising collateral requirements may not be profitable either. This will be the case, for example, when wealthier individuals who can afford to put up more collateral are also less risk averse. Stiglitz and Weiss (1981) present conditions under which the increase in the risk of default caused by the decrease in the average degree of risk averseness of the borrowers' pool as a result of an increase in collateral requirements may outweigh the direct benefits of such an increase to the bank. The upshot is that in the presence of asymmetric information, credit rationing may be an equilibrium situation.

## 2d    *Other examples of signaling and self-selection devices*

In general the sellers of high-quality products or services are interested in conveying the message that their product is of higher quality. Because all sellers are motivated to signal that their product is of high quality, the signal of the true high-quality producer will be recognizable only if it is sent in a way that would not be rational for the low-quality producer. As stressed by Hirschleifer and Riley (1979), any activity is a potential signal if the sellers of higher-quality products can engage in it at higher marginal returns. Nelson (1974, 1975) offers a similar argument to justify advertising for high-quality goods when repeat purchases are prevalent. By acquiring a pool of satisfied customers, the seller of high-quality goods will achieve lower marginal advertising costs per unit of sales. Even if the information content of the advertising message itself is zero, a message is nevertheless being conveyed: The product is worth promoting.

An original self-selection mechanism is presented by Salop (1977). Salop considers a monopolist who is interested in discriminating against individuals with higher search costs because these individuals also happen to have less elastic demand curves. The monopolist does not know a priori which individual belongs to the first group and which to the second. To discover who belongs to each group, the monopolist simply allows price dispersion. Those who search less end up paying higher prices on average. In Salop's words, "The very presence of disperson both splits the market and charges a higher purchase price to the sub-market of inefficient searchers" (1977: 393). By confronting customers with price uncertainty the monopolist reduces his or her own uncertainty about the customers' characteristics.

## 3    Asymmetric information and its transmission through market prices

In the presence of asymmetric information, market prices fulfill two functions. First, as in the presence of symmetric information, they serve as guides for consumption and production decisions. Second, they convey part or all of the information available to some agents in the economy to all other agents. The resultant observation of equilibrium prices by all individuals tends to make beliefs symmetrical or homogeneous. In some important cases market prices even transmit *all* the relevant private information to all agents in the economy, thus leading to the full uniformity of relevant information in equilibrium. The transmission of private information to the public is a function that prices fulfill only when there is some privileged information to start with or, in other words, when information is initially asymmetric.

An example that illustrates how prices disseminate private or "inside" information may be useful at this stage. Following Grossman (1977), consider a market for an agricultural product that is produced only in the current period and consumed both in the current and in the next periods. Demand in the next period is stochastic, and price in each period is determined by market clearing. Because demand is distributed over both periods whereas supply appears only in the first, it usually pays to store part of the output for the second period. There are firms that can store output at a cost.

Firms are identical in all respects except that some have more information than others about the next period's demand. Both types of firms know the distribution of the shock to demand in the next period, but the informed firms have access in the current period to an observation on a random variable, $\theta$, which is correlated with the demand shock of the second period. They can therefore estimate the next period's price with more precision than the uninformed firms.

Suppose now that the informed firms get an observation of $\theta$ that suggests that the next period's demand and price will be higher than average.

They respond by buying more of the current output for storing. As a result the current price increases. Uninformed firms that observe this price and know that it is positively correlated with the information that informed firms get about next period's demand infer the information of the informed traders from this price. In particular they infer from the fact that the current price is higher than average that informed traders believe that the next period's price will be higher than average. When the only stochastic variable in the market is the second period's demand shock, the current price fully reveals the information of the informed to the uninformed. When there is some additional uncertainty, such as when the current level of output is unknown by the uninformed, however, the current price reveals some but not all the information of the informed to the uninformed. The information transfer is, in this case, not perfect because when the current price increases, the uninformed are not sure whether it increases because the informed have become more bullish about future demand or because current production is unusually low.

This example illustrates how equilibrium prices transfer privileged information to all participants in the market. It also suggests that there is a fundamental difference between the usual Walrasian equilibrium under symmetric information and the equilibrium that results when information is asymmetric (Grossman 1981: Sect. 3). When all individuals have the same information, the demand and supply of each trader can be derived as functions of exogenously given prices *independently* of what the equilibrium prices will ultimately be. When information is asymmetric, however, demand and supply functions are not independent of the realization of *equilibrium* prices. This is because equilibrium prices convey some of the information of the informed to the uninformed, which alters the demand and supply functions of the latter. Thus under asymmetric information, an observation of equilibrium prices affects the positions of the demand and supply schedules. As a result the price vector that would clear all markets when the informational feedback from equilibrium prices is not taken into consideration is different from the market-clearing price vector that holds when this feedback is recognized.

Given a certain distribution of information across agents in the economy, it is possible to find market-clearing prices that correspond to the usual Walrasian equilibrium. These prices reflect the information available to different agents, however. If agents know the structure of the economy, the observation of these prices transmits private information into the public domain and causes changes in demands and supplies. Thus, after observing the Walrasian equilibrium price vector, individuals desire to recontract because they have additional information. Hence with asymmetric information the usual Walrasian equilibrium is not a stable equilibrium; a stable equilibrium will hold if, after observing the equilibrium price vector, individuals have no desire to recontract.

More precisely, suppose we find the demand and supply schedules that are conditional on a certain distribution of information that includes each individual's own private information plus a given vector of equilibrium prices that is the same for all individuals. Next we find the market-clearing prices for those demand and supply schedules. If those prices are identical to the initial price vector and their distributions are identical too, the equilibrium is stable and there is no incentive to recontract. Following Grossman (1981), we refer to such an equilibrium as a "rational expectations equilibrium." This equilibrium notion is fairly general and applies both in the finance literature surveyed in this subsection and in the macroeconomic literature discussed in the remaining chapters of the book.

Note that with symmetric information prices do not convey any new information so that the rational expectations equilibrium reduces to the usual Walasian equilibrium.

### 3a    *Price as an indicator of quality or inside information*

Consider a good whose quality is not perfectly known; however, some individuals have had prior experience with the good so their information is better than that of others. Because the demand of the informed individuals affects the market price of the good, uninformed individuals can learn something about the quality of the good simply by observing the market price.

Kihlstrom and Mirman (1975) consider the case in which there is uncertainty about the quality of a consumption good and individuals are expected utility maximizers in the von Neumann–Morgenstern sense. The uncertainty takes the form of a random multiplicative parameter $a$, that augments or shrinks the utility gained from consuming one unit of the commodity whose quality is unknown. The expectations of agent $i$ about $a$ are represented by a subjective probability distribution $PR^i$. One individual, denoted by 1, has more information than others through an observation of a random variable $y$ that is correlated with $a$. Before observing $y$, the individual has a prior probability distribution $PR^1$. After having observed $y$, the individual's beliefs are represented by a posterior distribution $u_y$ that depends on the realization of $y$. The equilibrium price depends on the subjective beliefs individuals have about the quality of the good. In particular, it depends on the posterior distribution of the informed agent. Kihlstrom and Mirman show that if the function that describes the relationship between the equilibrium price and the subjective probability distribution of the first agent is invertible, the equilibrium price is a sufficient statistic for the privileged information $y$. Intuitively, when the market price is known, knowledge of $y$ is redundant. Thus, with invertibility, the market price reveals the information of the experienced consumer to all other consumers. Another intepretation of the same model is that the random variable $a$ represents an unknown return on a risky asset and $y$ represents imperfect but relevant inside information about the return on the risky asset. For this interpretation the main result is, analogously, that if the price function is invertible, the equilibrium price reveals the inside information to all uninformed individuals.[4]

More generally, different individuals may have different bits of inside information on the future return of a risky asset. The current price of the risky asset reflects, in this more general case, the private information of many traders. Such a case is considered in the following section.

## 3b    *Prices as aggregators of information*

Grossman (1976) considers the case in which many traders, each with a constant but different degree of risk aversion, invest their respective initial endowments in a riskless and in a risky asset. Because the utility function is assumed to be exponential in wealth, investors care about only the mean and the variance of wealth. Investment decisions are made in period 0, and returns are realized and appropriated in period 1. In period 0 the yield of the risky asset $P_1$ is unknown, but the $i$th trader has an observation as early as period 0 of a variable $y_i$ where

$$y_i = P_1 + \epsilon_i$$

where $\epsilon_i$ is a white noise process with a standard normal distribution. Thus the $i$th trader knows the future realization of the risky asset yield up to a random shock. We refer to $y_i$ as the private information of individual $i$. The equilibrium price of the risky asset in period 0, $P_0$, is affected in general by the private information of all the traders in the market. Thus $P_0$ is a function of the vector $y$, where $y \equiv (y^1, \dots, y^H)$ is the vector of all private information. Hence it is reasonable to expect that the observation of the current equilibrium price by all individuals in the market transmits some of the private information to the public domain. The remarkable result that Grossman finds is that the market price $P_0$ transmits all *relevant* private information to the public domain. In more technical terms, he shows that $P_0$ is a sufficient statistic for the vector of private information $y$. This does not mean that $P_0$ reveals all the components of $y$. It does mean that once $P_0$ is known to all traders in the market, the additional information in the vector $y$ is redundant.

This is an example of the more general principle that prices aggregate the information of different traders. The aggregation of information by prices does not always have to reveal all relevant information to everybody, but in this particular instance it does. The proof of this result is obtained by deriving an explicit expression for the rational expectations equilibrium solution of $P_0$ in terms of $y$ and showing that $P_0$ depends only on the mean of the elements of $y$. Because traders' expected utility in this framework depends on only the conditional mean and variance of wealth, they need to know only the mean of the components of $y$. Grossman shows that price is an invertible function of the mean of the components of $y$ so that an observation of $P_0$ is equivalent to an observation of the mean of the $y_i$ values.

The result that equilibrium prices transmit all relevant private information to the public domain also holds in the presence of full contingent markets. In particular, Grossman (1981) shows that with full contingent markets and disparate information sets across individuals, there is a sense in which prices transmit all relevant information to the public domain. To make this notion more precise, we briefly sketch the model used by Grossman. There are $H$ individuals, indexed by $h$, each with a Von Neumann–Morgenstern utility function and private information. There are $n$ states of nature $s_1, \dots, s_n$. Each individual has a state-dependent utility function that is defined over the current (certain) consumption and the next period's state-contingent consumption.[5] Each individual has an initial endowment of current consumption and a state-dependent endowment of future consumption. The private information of individual $h$ about the next period's state takes the form of an observation $y^h$ of a random variable $\bar{y}^h$ that is correlated with the distribution of the state. Consumer $h$ observes $y^h$ in the first period and uses it to make inferences about the probability that state $i$ will occur. Let $\Pi_i^h(y^h)$ be the probability that individual $h$ assigns to state $i$ given that he observes $y^h$ in the first period.

Consider alternatively all the information that is available in the economy in the first period. This information can be summarized by the vector $y \equiv (y^1, \dots, y^H)$, a realization of the random vector $\bar{y} \equiv (\bar{y}^1, \dots, \bar{y}^H)$. Let $\Pi_i(y)$ be the conditional probability that state $i$ realizes given $y$. The difference between $\Pi_i^h(y^h)$ and $\Pi_i(y)$ is fundamental. The term $\Pi_i^h(y^h)$ summarizes the beliefs of individual $h$ about the next period's states given only private information. The term $\Pi_i(y)$, on the other hand, summarizes the *homogeneous* beliefs that would prevail in the economy if all individuals had access to all the information available in the economy in the first period.

It is instructive to consider first the full information equilibrium in the $n$ state-contingent markets that operate in the first period. In this equilibrium each individual chooses a vector of consumption to maximize expected utility subject to a personal budget constraint, using $\Pi_i(y)$, where $i = 1, \ldots, n$, as the probability weights. Market clearing then determines $n$ relative prices – that is, the prices of one unit of consumption in each state of nature in the future in terms of current consumption. We denote this equilibrium price vector by $P^a(y)$. Note that these prices do not transmit any information because all the information available in the economy in the first period is known by everybody at the beginning. Grossman (1981) refers to $P^a(y)$ as the Walrasian equilibrium price vector under conditions of symmetric information. The superscript "a" indicates that it is an artificial equilibrium based on the assumption that all private information is publicly available.

We come back now to the main case in which each individual has access to only private information. Each individual's demands are derived by maximizing expected utility using $\Pi_i^h(y^h)$, where $i = 1, \ldots, n$, as probability weights. As before, the $n$ relative prices of contingent consumptions are determined by market clearing. The equilibrium price vector that emerges in this case is a Walrasian equilibrium under asymmetric information. It is not a stable equilibrium, however, because a moment after the publication of market prices, individual demands change owing to the additional information they obtained.

As explained at the beginning of this section, only a rational expectations equilibrium will be stable in the sense that excess demand functions are not revised after the publication of market prices. In this case a rational expectations equilibrium is a mapping $P^0(y)$, such that if each individual's demands are derived by maximizing her expected utility given her private information *and* an observation $P^0(y)$ on prices, the market-clearing prices that emerge are precisely $P^0(y)$.

Grossman (1981) shows that if the utility functions of individuals are strictly concave in their arguments and if they are additively separable in the initial period's consumption, then if there exists a Walrasian equilibrium $P^a(y)$ in the fully informed artificial economy, this equilibrium is also a rational expectations equilibrium for the economy in which each trader $h$ observes only $y^h$ and market prices.[6]

This result implies that the equilibrium allocations that hold under rational expectations when individuals have access to only private information are the same as those that would have arisen if all privately available information was made public. Thus, prices aggregate information in the sense that the decisions made by all individuals in the economy when information is private but when they are allowed to extract the information available in market prices are identical to the decisions they would have made if all the available information was publicly available. This does not mean that prices fully reveal the beliefs $\Pi_i^h(y^h)$ of each trader to all other traders. To decide how much to consume and invest in future state-contingent consumptions, however, this information is redundant. Traders need to supplement their private information with only the information available in market prices.

An important element that contributes to this rather strong result is that there are as many relative prices as there are states of nature – a fact that is directly traceable to the assumption of complete contingent markets.

### 3c    *Futures markets as transmitters of information*[7]

Futures markets are usually thought of as institutions devised to permit a more efficient exchange of risks. Once the information transmission role of prices is acknowledged, it has to be recognized that prices in futures markets also transmit information.

The information transmission function of futures markets is illustrated here by extending the discussion of the agricultural product that appears at the beginning of this section. This good is produced in the current period only but consumed in both the current and the next periods. There are two types of firms: those that have some privileged information $\theta$ about the second period's demand and those that do not. We saw that when the only uncertainty is about the second period's demand, the current market price of the good reveals all the relevant information of the informed to the uninformed.[8] When there is additional uncertainty, however, as when the current output is not known with certainty, the current price reveals some but not all the relevant information of the informed to the uninformed. As a result, differences in expectations about price in the next period persist even in the rational expectations equilibrium. Under these circumstances, one type of firm desires to take "long" positions in the product, whereas the other desires to take "short" positions, so there is an incentive for the opening of a futures market. In addition, the expected value of profits of informed firms exceeds that of uninformed firms, giving an incentive to acquire privileged information even at a cost. The difference in expected profits is an increasing function of the conditional variance of the information of the informed, given that the information of the uninformed is restricted to the current price. Hence the incentive to spend resources to become informed increases when this variance increases.

When a futures market opens, two prices transmit information from the informed to the uninformed. One is, as before, the spot price of the good; the other is the futures price. Together these two prices reveal all the privileged information of the informed (including total current output and the conditional expected value of the next period's spot price given $\theta$). As a result the beliefs held by both types of firms become identical. In addition the incentive to collect costly information to become informed disappears because all the relevant information is costlessly disseminated by prices.

Thus the addition of unknown stochastic shocks prevents prices from fully revealing all information, while the addition of markets increases the ability of the price system to transmit privileged informaton. This general principle can explain why we do not observe markets for the delivery of commodities contingent on all possible states of the world. If such markets did exist, all inside information would immediately have been transmitted to everybody, thus nullifying the incentive to collect costly information. Hence equilibrium in a costly information market requires that there be fewer prices than random events; otherwise there is no incentive to become informed. This notion is discussed more fully in Section 4.

To maintain some incentive for becoming informed, Grossman introduces an additional source of uncertainty in the form of a stochastic (for the uninformed) risk-aversion parameter for informed firms. As a result the price system no longer perfectly transmits the information of the informed to the uninformed and the incentive to collect costly information is retained. Under these circumstances there are two motives for taking positions in the futures market. One is the hedging motive, which is positively related to the physical quantity of the good that is stored for the second period. The other is positively related to the conditional variance of the relevant information of the informed given the current spot price and the futures price. Because this variance measures the dispersion of the information of the informed given the information of the uninformed (which includes only current market prices), it is a natural measure of the divergence in information between the informed and the uninformed. The volume of trade in the futures market is positively related to the divergence in information between the informed and the uninformed. A similar phenomenon will be discussed in Chapter 5 in the context of traders in a bond market who face an uncertain rate of inflation.

## 4    Implications for the incentive to collect information and the limits of price information

When prices fully aggregate information or fully transmit private information to the public domain, individuals have no incentive to collect information because they get all they need from market prices. If they get their information costlessly as a by-product of their normal activities, individuals will possess some private information when they come to the market. If individuals have to incur a cost to obtain this private information, however, they will abstain from collecting it because all the relevant information available to *all* participants in the market is costlessly revealed by market prices.[9] The models of the previous section provide examples of this general principle. In the case of the agricultural product discussed in Section 3c we saw that when there are two shocks (a shock to future demand and a shock to current supply) and two currently observed market prices (the spot and the futures price), all inside information is revealed by prices. If a cost is incurred in the original acquisition of such information, traders will refrain from paying because it will no longer be worthwhile to come to the market with inside information. Prices in this case will no longer reflect inside information. A similar phenomenon arises in the full contingent markets model discussed in Section 3b. Because the prices of contingent consumptions perfectly aggregate all information in the market and each individual trader has no effect on prices, the incentive to collect private information disappears if such an activity is costly. Thus the transmission of information through prices bestows a public good aspect on the collection of information. The full aggregation of information creates an externality that makes it impossible for the providers of information to appropriate the benefits from doing so. This externality implies that nobody in a competitive market with costly information and the full aggregation of information by prices will collect information. Because prices will therefore no longer reflect information, it will pay the individual trader to buy information. As soon as the information is bought, however, it is transmitted to everybody and the incentive to buy information disappears. This suggests that a competitive equilibrium with costly information and the full revelation of information by prices does not exist. To have an equilibrium in which some effort is invested in securing information, the number of markets must not be so large as to allow market prices to perfectly aggregate information. Prices may convey some, but not all, information so that individuals who spend resources on information get compensated for their efforts. Grossman and Stiglitz (1980) present a framework in which this is the case. The proportion of people who decide to obtain information directly is determined endogenously by the condition that at the margin the difference in benefits between being informed and not being informed is equal to the cost of acquiring information. For this condition to be satisfied, some difference between the information of the informed and the uninformed must persist in equilibrium. A framework in which this is the case is discussed in the following section.

4a    *Rational expectations equilibrium with costly private information*[10]

As in Section 3b there are many individuals with different initial endowments of a risky asset and a riskless asset. All traders have the same exponential utility function of wealth with a constant coefficient of absolute risk aversion $d$. Each individual's demands for the risky and the riskless asset are derived by maximizing expected utility subject to the individual's budget constraint given the information available to him or her. The information of all individuals includes the current market prices of both assets. In addition each individual can at a cost $c$ obtain an observation on a random variable $\theta$ that differs from the random return $u$ on the risky asset by a white noise process $\epsilon_t$. An observation of $\theta$ does not fully reveal the return $u$, but it does improve the information of those who buy it compared to those who do not. The quality of this information is conveniently measured by the ratio $r \equiv \sigma_\theta^2/\sigma_\epsilon^2$, where $\sigma_\theta^2$ and $\sigma_\epsilon^2$ are the variances of $\theta$ and $\epsilon$, respectively. The higher $r$ is, the better is the information held by the informed because $r$ is positively related to the coefficient of correlation between $u$ and $\theta$.

The aggregate current supply of the risky asset $S$ is stochastic, too. As a result an observation of the market price does not fully reveal the information of the informed to the uninformed. The reason is that uninformed individuals cannot perfectly distinguish between movements in price that are caused by changes in the information of the informed about future returns and changes that are caused by changes in the current supply of the risky asset. Let $\lambda$ be the proportion of informed individuals in the economy. Assuming that all stochastic variables are normally distributed, Grossman and Stiglitz show that the current self-fulfilling equilibrium price of the risky asset is a linear function of the information variable $\theta$ plus noise. The parameters of the price function also depend on the proportion of informed individuals $\lambda$, on the risk-aversion parameter $d$, and on the variances of $\theta$, $\epsilon$, and $S$. For an arbitrary given $\lambda$, the information market is not necessarily in equilibrium because the difference between the equilibrium expected utilities of the informed and the uninformed is not necessarily equal to the cost of information. Whenever there is a divergence between this difference and the cost of becoming informed, there is an incentive for more individuals to become informed, or vice versa, thus inducing changes in $\lambda$. The equilibrium value of $\lambda$ is, therefore, determined by the condition that the difference between the expected utilities of the informed and the uninformed is equal to the cost of becoming informed. When this equilibrium occurs in the range $0 < \lambda < 1$, there is some difference in information between the informed and the uninformed. There is no incentive to alter this, however, because when the cost of collecting information is taken into account, the expected utilities of informed and uninformed individuals are equal. This notion of equilibrium resolves the nonexistence of equilibrium that arises when prices reveal all relevant information and there are positive costs of becoming informed.[11] Furthermore it suggests that when an equilibrium exists, the market cannot be "fully efficient" in the sense that price reveals *all* relevant information. Some difference in information persists even with full equilibrium; otherwise equilibrium would not exist.

The model can be used to investigate the effects of various exogenous parameters on the informativeness of the price system and on the volume of trade. The informativeness of the price system is measured by the squared coefficient of correlation $\rho_\theta^2$ between the market price and the information of the informed $\theta$. In the limit when $\rho_\theta^2$ tends to 1, price reveals all the information of the informed to the uninformed. At the other extreme when $\rho_\theta^2 = 0$, price does not reveal any information about $\theta$. Grossman and Stiglitz show that $\rho_\theta^2$ is an increasing function of $r$ and a decreasing function of the cost of becoming informed and of the risk-aversion parameter of informed individuals. The first result just states that an increase in the quality of information of the informed also increases the quality of information carried through price. Changes in all other exogenous parameters do not affect $\rho_\theta^2$ because they trigger two conflicting effects that cancel each other. For example, by increasing the level of noise, an increase in the variance of the supply of the risky asset $\sigma_s^2$ decreases $\rho_\theta^2$ for a given $\lambda$. When $\sigma_s^2$ increases, however, the equilibrium proportion of informed individuals increases, too. The increase in $\lambda$ taken alone increases $\rho_\theta^2$ by an amount that exactly offsets the direct negative impact of $\sigma_s^2$ on $\rho_\theta^2$.

As the costs of becoming informed become very large or very small, the proportion of informed individuals becomes, respectively, very small or very large. Thus in both cases information is not far from being homogeneous. As a result both the mean and the variance of trade among individuals tend toward zero. A similar phenomenon occurs when the precision of the information of the informed becomes perfect ($r$ tends toward infinity). The theory of efficient markets in finance claims that the market prices of assets reflect all the relevant information [see Fama (1970), for example]. More precisely, a market is said to be efficient with respect to the union of the information sets of all individuals in the market if the prices it generates when each agent has access to only the individual information set are identical to those generated in an otherwise identical economy in which all individuals have access to the information sets of all taken together. In the present case the market need not be efficient in this sense. First, because beliefs differ in equilibrium, prices cannot reflect all the information available to all traders in the market. Second, if all the information available in the economy was available to every trader, the equilibrium price would normally not be the same. The upshot is that in general, in the presence of costly information, markets cannot be fully efficient.

## 4b     The limits of price information in market processes

In all the literature on the revelation of information by prices discussed to this point, a rational expectations equilibrium is defined as a function that maps the information of all traders in the economy into market prices subject to the following conditions:

1.  Each individual maximizes his (or her) objective function subject to appropriate constraints given his private information and the information he has on market prices.
2.  The model used by each individual to interpret the information content of prices is identical to the true model.
3.  The prices generated by the price function or mapping are market clearing.

This notion of self-fulfilling or rational expectations equilibrium permits equilibrium prices to depend directly on the union of the information sets of all individuals in the economy. One way to conceptualize the mechanism underlying this notion of equilibrium is through the fictitious but useful institution of the auctioneer. Each individual transmits the information set to the auctioneer, and the latter uses the union of these sets to choose a price vector that fulfills requirements 1–3 above. It is important to note that individuals transmit *all* their private information to the auctioneer. Beja (1977) argues that in genuine market processes individuals transmit only their excess demands, rather than all their private information. The implication of this is that the price function can depend on the set of private information in the economy only through excess demands, since these are the only bits of information communicated to the auctioneer. Let $y_i$ be the information of individual $i$, where $i = 1, \ldots, H$. Let $y = (y^1, \ldots, y^H)$ be the information of all individuals in the economy. Beja's approach implies that if two prices differ in equilibrium because the underlying information sets $y$ differ, this is possible only if some excess demands differ. With genuine market processes, information affects prices only through individual excess demands. Beja shows that when the mapping from $y$ into prices is a genuine market process, prices reveal less information than when the mapping from $y$ to prices is unrestricted. More specifically, with genuine market processes prices cannot be sufficient statistics. Intuitively, because with genuine market processes two different excess demand vectors may generate the same prices, the observation of these prices is not sufficient for the underlying information set $y$. The general implication is that even in the absence of information costs, individuals will in many cases find it profitable to use their private information in addition to market prices.

Recent papers by Hellwig (1980), Diamond and Verrecchia (1981), Anderson and Sonnenschein (1982), and Verrecchia (1982) incorporate the restriction that private information affects equilibrium prices only through excess demand functions [see also Section 6 of Jordan and Radner (1982)]. The model presented in Diamond and Verrecchia (1981) is similar in structure to that of Grossman (1976) used in Section 3b, with two main differences: First, it fulfills the restriction that market prices are affected by information only through excess demands. Second, it incorporates an additional source of noise in the form of a random current supply of the risky asset. As a result prices reveal part but not all of the relevant information in the market. Some differences in information persist in equilibrium. When the variance of the noise term tends to the extreme values of zero and infinity, the model displays, respectively, full revelation and no information transmission through prices. In the first case the model becomes qualitatively similar to that of Grossman (1976), in which price reveals all relevant information. In the second case it resembles Lintner's (1969) model in which prices do not transmit information.

## 5    Recent extensions: costly information with aggregation of information and conditioning on past prices

An extension of the model of Grossman and Stiglitz (1980) (from the previous section) has been developed by Verrecchia (1982). It involves two main elements: First, each agent is allowed to observe a noisy signal of the return on the risky asset at a cost that is an increasing convex function of the precision of the signal. Second, the information of the $i$th trader takes (as in Section 3b) the form of an observation on a signal

$$y_i = P_1 + \epsilon_i$$

where $y_i$ is the signal observed by the $i$th trader, $P_1$ the return on the risky asset, and $\epsilon_i$ a white noise process. The first element allows each individual to choose the level of precision that maximizes the expected utility net of the cost of becoming informed. The second element makes it possible to discuss the aggregation of information by price in the presence of costly information. (By contrast, Grossman and Stiglitz consider the particular case in which there is a single piece of information to acquire.)

As in Grossman and Stiglitz, there is an additional source of noise that takes the form of random endowments of the risky asset. The resulting rational expectations equilibrium is characterized by the *partial* aggregation of information through the price of the risky asset. The paper generalizes and extends some comparative static results of Grossman and Stiglitz. In particular, as traders become more risk tolerant, they acquire more costly information. For related reasons the informativeness of the price system becomes a nondecreasing function of the group risk tolerance. Intuitively, more risk-tolerant investors take larger positions in the risky asset. They therefore demand more information to protect their riskier positions. Hence with a higher group risk tolerance, the precision of the information that is acquired is higher and so is the precision of the information that is aggregated by the price of the risky asset.

A basic assumption that is shared by all the literature on asymmetric information surveyed to this point is that individuals need no time to extract the information that is available in market prices. Prices clear markets and individuals learn information from prices simultaneously. There is no delay between the observation of a price and the formulation of excess demands based on the information extracted from those prices. Hellwig (1982) suggests that there usually is a delay between the publication of market prices and the formulation of excess demands that use the information conveyed by these prices. More precisely, he considers the rational expectations equilibrium that holds when agents can learn only from past but not from current prices. He shows that even if the lag between current and past prices is very short, the informed agents retain an information advantage over the uninformed. As a result there is always a positive incentive to collect some costly information even in the absence of noise.

In contrast, the rational expectations equilibrium described by Grossman and Stiglitz (1980) (see Section 4a) breaks down in the absence of noise because no trader is able to appropriate the returns from investing in information, since this information is costlessly and instantaneously disseminated by the price to all other traders. When there is a lag, however small, between transactions and the latest observed price, there is always an incentive to collect costly information because noninformed traders can use the information available in current market prices only in the next trading period. As a result an informed trader manages to retain an advantage during the current trading period. Basically, the preservation of the incentive to collect information that is achieved in Grossman and Stiglitz (1980) and Verrecchia (1982) through noise is achieved in Hellwig (1982) by preventing traders from using currently the information learned from the current price.

Using a Wiener process formulation of uncertainty, Hellwig shows that even when the lag between trading periods tends toward zero, the return to being informed remains bounded away from zero, yet the market tends toward full informational efficiency. Intuitively, as the interval between trading periods shrinks, the difference in information between informed and uninformed traders becomes negligible. This does not destroy the incentive to become informed, however; as uncertainty decreases with the length of the period, traders take larger positions so that even a small information advantage remains important. The upshot is that with conditioning on past prices, almost full informational efficiency may coexist with a positive incentive to collect costly information.

# CHAPTER 3

# Aggregate–relative confusion: implications for the Phillips curve

## 1    Phillips trade-off from Phillips to Lucas: overview

Until the end of the 1960s, most Western economists believed in a stable trade-off between inflation and unemployment. The policy implication was that the government could choose a menu of inflation and unemployment rates along a given stable Phillips curve [see, for example, Samuelson and Solow (1960)].

This view was strongly shaken by Friedman (1968) in his presidential address to the American Economic Association. Friedman's basic challenge to a stable Phillips trade-off was theoretical: In an economy without money illusion, no significant real decisions should depend on the general level of prices. [Similar arguments were raised by Phelps (1967).] If all prices double, neither consumption, production, nor labor supply decisions should be affected. In particular, the rate of unemployment (a real variable) and the rate of inflation (the rate of change in a nominal variable) should not be systematically related.

Acceptance of this view raised the obvious question why empirically estimated Phillips curves displayed a systematic negative relationship between inflation and unemployment – at least until the end of the sixties. [See, for example, Phillips (1958) and Lipsey (1960) for the United Kingdom and Perry (1966) for the United States.] Friedman gave the following answer: When the rate of monetary growth accelerates and prices follow suit, employers realize that the price level is higher sooner than workers do. As a result, while nominally raising wages they can offer what amounts to a reduced real wage rate. Workers mistakenly view this increase in nominal wages as a boost to their real wage and are willing to work more. This results in a new labor market equilibrium in which there is more employment because both the quantity demanded and the quantity supplied are greater. Thus employment increases (and unemployment decreases) concurrently with an acceleration in the rate of monetary inflation.

— However, says Friedman, this boost to employment can last only as long as workers do not realize the full extent of the change in the price level. As soon as they do, the effective labor supply shrinks and employment decreases back to its full information level (Friedman's "natural rate"). Thus the Phillips curve exists only as long as workers are fooled about the price level: Once they realize what the price level is, the levels of employment, unemployment, and other real variables become independent of the rate of monetary expansion.

In the long run, then, inflation and unemployment are independent. Here "long run" does not mean chronological time but rather the length of time it takes workers to comprehend the new price level. The chronological meaning of "long run" will vary with the characteristics of the inflationary process and the previous experience workers and employers have had with inflation. Friedman's view implies that empirically estimated Phillips curves should be interpreted as short-run relationships between the rate of unemployment and *unanticipated* inflation. The observed negative relationship between inflation and unemployment is, in this view, the result of a positive short-run correlation between actual and unanticipated inflation coupled with the negative effect of unanticipated inflation on the rate of unemployment.

Although it sounds plausible, Friedman's explanation of the short-run Phillips curve rests on a postulated asymmetry: Employers catch on to price level changes quicker than employees do. Evidence on whether this is so is hard to come by, and what little evidence there is suggests that it is not always the case.[2]

A theory to explain the short-run Phillips curve without relying on systematic asymmetries in perceptions between workers and employers was provided by Lucas (1973). Lucas considers an economy with many markets. Individuals in each market have instantaneous information on the equilibrium price in their own market but only delayed information about the general price level. Because production decisions are made on the basis of relative prices, individuals in any given market must predict the current general price level in order to decide how much to supply. The different markets of the economy are affected by two types of random shocks: (1) an aggregate shock, which affects demand in all markets in the same manner, and (2) a market-specific demand shock. The former reflects the effects of economy-wide changes in some nominal aggregate such as the quantity of money, whereas the latter reflects changes in relative demands across markets.

The price in each market is determined by market clearing. Because the supply in each market depends on the relative price as perceived at the time by individuals in that market, the equilibrium price in the market depends on the perceptions that individuals in it have about the general price level. Individuals know that the price movements they observe in their own market reflect movements common to all prices as well as changes in the relative price in their own market. Knowing that, they *partly* use their own price to guess the current general price level. As a result, a current unanticipated increase in the stock of money (which will ultimately increase all prices in the same proportion) is temporarily partly interpreted as an increase in relative prices. This causes a temporary increase in production. Thus, a short-run positive relationship emerges between unanticipated changes in the money supply and the general price level on the one hand and the level of economic activity on the other – which is a Phillips-type relationship.

This, in a nutshell, is Lucas's theory of the short-run Phillips curve. Like Friedman's explanation, it implies that only unanticipated changes in the money supply or the general price level affect economic activity. Unlike Friedman's explanation, however, it is completely symmetric. All sectors of the economy are subject to the confusion between aggregate and relative movement in demands and prices. The crucial element here is that individuals obtain information on the price in their own market quicker than they do about the general price level.[3] This corresponds rather well to the actual state of affairs in Western countries; data on the general price level are usually published with a one- to two-month lag, whereas prices in individual markets can be observed daily by participants in those markets.

Lucas's model incorporates three additional elements:

1. Expectations about the general price level are "rational" in the Muth (1961) sense. This means that the formation of perceptions about the current general price level fulfills two conditions: First, individuals use their knowledge about the structure of the economy in conjunction with all currently available information to form an optimal forecast of the current general price level. Second, the actions they take on the basis of this forecast generate the same structure they use in forming their perceptions.
2. Subject to informational limitations, all markets are always in equilibrium. This is in marked contrast to Lipsey's (1960) original explanation of the Phillips curve, which was based on a disequilibrium view of markets.[4]
3. When full information is available in all markets, an increase in the relevant nominal aggregate increases prices in all markets by the same proportion and does not affect economic activity. Thus money is neutral when full information is available but not in the short run when there is still confusion between absolute and relative changes in prices.

The next two sections present a more explicit account of Lucas's (1973) theory, although some of the analytical detail follows Cukierman and

Wachtel (1979) more closely than Lucas. For pedagogic reasons the model is presented first under the assumption that full current information is available; that is, individuals in all markets know the current general price level with certainty and therefore know their relative price with certainty. Section 2 shows that in this case money is neutral even in the short run. In Section 3 the aggregate–relative confusion is reintroduced by preventing individuals from having full current information, and it is shown that this generates a temporary trade-off between unanticipated money and economic activity.

## 2      Lucas's (1973) model with full current information about the general price level

The economy is composed of a large number of markets. Each is characterized by a supply function and a demand function. The quantity supplied in each market is the product of a *normal* or secular component common to all markets and a *cyclical* component that varies from market to market. Letting $v$ index markets and using $y_{nt}$ and $y_{ct}(v)$, respectively, to denote the logs of these components, the supply in market $v$ is

$$y_t^s(v) = y_{nt} + y_{ct}(v) \tag{3.1}$$

The secular component follows the trend line

$$y_{nt} = \alpha + \beta t \tag{3.2}$$

The cyclical component is an increasing function of the relative price in market $v$:

$$y_{ct}(v) = \gamma[p_t(v) - Q_t], \qquad \gamma > 0 \tag{3.3}$$

where $p_t(v)$ and $Q_t$ denote, respectively, the log of the actual price in market $v$ at time $t$ and the log of the (geometric) average price level at time $t$. $\alpha$, $\beta$, and $\gamma$ are constant parameters. Equation (3.3) states that the supply in market $v$ is an increasing function of the relative price of good $v$.

The demand in each market is stochastic. The stochastic component has two parts: one common to all markets and the other specific to the particular market. The demand function is

$$y_t^d(v) = x_t + w_t(v) - p_t(v) \tag{3.4}$$

where $x_t$ is an exogenous random shift variable common to all markets, and $w_t(v)$ is a random shock whose realization is specific to market $v$ but whose distribution is common to all markets. Because $x_t$ can be interpreted as the log of the quantity of money,[5] its (stochastic) first difference $\Delta x_t$ is the rate of change in the quantity of money. It is assumed that the random shocks are distributed normally and are independent of each other:[6]

$$\Delta x_t \sim N(\delta, \sigma_x^2) \tag{3.5a}$$

$$w_t(v) \sim N(0, \sigma_w^2) \tag{3.5b}$$

where $w_t(v)$ represents shifts in relative demands across markets, given the total level of aggregate nominal demand as summarized by $x_t$.

The general price level $Q_t$ is defined as a fixed-weight index of the (logs of) prices in individual markets, with weight $u(v)$ assigned to market $v$:

$$Q_t \equiv \sum_v u(v) p_t(v) \tag{3.6}$$

where $\sum_v u(v) = 1$ and $u(v) \geq 0$ for all $v$. It is further assumed that each of the individual weights is not too large in comparison to the sum of the weights.

At the risk of repetition, it should be pointed out that we assume, in this section only, that the current general price level $Q_t$ is known with certainty in all markets in period $t$. This assumption is expressed in Equation (3.3) through the fact that the cyclical component of output depends on the actual general price level rather than on the perception of the general price level. Hence, in this section the aggregate–relative confusion has been assumed away.

We now show that without this confusion, money is neutral in the sense that it does not affect output even in the short run; an increase in the money supply raises all prices by the factor by which the money supply increased without changing any relative prices. This case will serve as a useful benchmark against which to compare the effects of money when the aggregate–relative confusion is introduced.

Equating demand and supply in market $v$ and solving for the equilibrium price in that market, we get

$$p_t(v) = \frac{1}{1+\gamma}[-(\alpha+\beta t) + x_t + \gamma Q_t + w_t(v)] \tag{3.7}$$

Formally, this result is obtained by substituting Equations (3.2) and (3.3) into (3.1), equating the result with Equation (3.4), and solving for $p_t(v)$.

Substituting Equation (3.7) into (3.6), we get

$$Q_t = -\alpha - \beta t + x_t \tag{3.8}$$

from which it can be seen that the general price level $Q_t$ is directly proportional to the quantity of money and is inversely related to productivity as measured by $\alpha + \beta t$. Substituting Equation (3.8) into (3.7) and rearranging give

$$p_t(v) - Q_t = w_t(v)/(1 + \gamma\theta) \tag{3.9}$$

which suggests that the relative price in market $v$ depends on only real *relative* shocks to demand and *not* on the quantity of money $x_t$.

It follows from Equation (3.3) that output does not depend on money at all, even in the short run. Furthermore it follows from Equations (3.8) and (3.9) together that any increase in $x_t$ increases all prices and therefore the general price level equiproportionally.

## 3    Reintroduction of the aggregate–relative confusion into Lucas's model: rational expectations and equilibrium[7]

We now assume that information about the current general price level is available with only a one-period lag, meaning that people have to guess the current general level of prices. Denoting the optimal forecast of the current general price level as computed at time $t$ by individuals in market $v$ by $E[Q_t/I_t(v)]$, the cyclical component of output is now respecified as

$$y_{ct}(v) = \gamma\{p_t(v) - E[Q_t/I_t(v)]\}, \qquad \gamma > 0 \tag{3.3a}$$

That is, because the actual relative price is unknown, suppliers decide how much to produce currently on the basis of the perceived relative price. In each market $v$, this perception is formed by making optimal use of the information currently available in that market $I_t(v)$.

Because expectations are rational, individuals use the information available to them as well as what they know about the structure of the economy to derive a forecast of the current general price level. Those perceptions influence, in turn, the cyclical component of output in Equation (3.3a). This changes the equilibrium price in market $v$, causing in turn a change in the perceived relative price.

This suggests that the actual and the perceived relative prices are determined *simultaneously*. The perceived relative price affects the actual relative price, and the actual relative price affects the perception of the relative price. Because expectation formation is rational, the systematic behavior of the economy induced by those expectations has to be identical to what individuals assume about the economy when forming those expectations.

We now assume that the beliefs of market participants are described by the set of equations that follows [(3.10)–(3.12)] and show that when individuals in all markets act on those beliefs, the actual systematic behavior of the economy is identical to the postulated beliefs. This is needed to establish that expectations are indeed rational.[8]

$$p_t[w_t(v)] = Q_t + z[w_t(v)] \tag{3.10}$$

$$Q_t \sim N(\bar{Q}_t, \sigma^2), \qquad z[w_t(v)] \sim N(0, \tau^2) \tag{3.11}$$

$$E[Q_t / I_t(v)] = (1-\theta)p_t[w_t(v)] + \theta \bar{Q}_t \tag{3.12}$$

where

$$\theta \equiv \sigma_w^2 / (\sigma_w^2 + \sigma_x^2) \tag{3.12a}$$

Equation (3.10) states that people believe that the price in any individual market can be decomposed into the sum of the general price level $Q_t$ plus a deviation $z$ that depends on only the realization of the market-specific demand shock $w_t$ in that market. Because all prices are measured in logarithms, $z[w_t(v)]$ is approximately equal to the percentage deviation of the price in market $v$ from the general price level. It will therefore be referred to as the *relative price* of market $v$.

Equation (3.11) states that people believe that both the general price level and the relative price of market $v$ are distributed normally. The value $\bar{Q}_t$, which is the mean of the distribution of the general price level, is based only on information pertaining to past periods up to and including period $t-1$. It varies over time as new information accumulates.

Equation (3.12) states that the perception of the current general price level in market $v$ is formed as a weighted average of the currently observed equilibrium price in that market and of the current mean of the distribution of the general price level. As can be seen from (3.12a), the weight assigned to the price in market $v$ is a function of the ratio of the variance of relative demand shocks to the variance of the rate of change in the quantity of money.

3a    *Demonstration of the rationality of expectations*

This section is devoted to demonstrating that Equations (3.10)–(3.12) represent not only what people believe but also the actual behavior of the economy. The proof yields some insight into the technical aspects of specifying rational expectations models. It is therefore recommended for the serious student of the topic; it does not require more than simple algebra and some knowledge of conditional probabilities. Those who are more interested in results and interpretation, however, can take this result on faith and proceed to the next section.

Equating demand and supply in market $v$, substituting Equation (3.12) into the resulting expression, and solving for the equilibrium price in that market [or, more precisely, equating the sum of Equations (3.2) and (3.3a) with (3.4), substituting (3.12) into the resulting equation and solving for $p_t(v)$], we get

$$p_t(v) = \frac{1}{1+\gamma\theta}[x_t - \alpha - \beta t + \gamma\theta\bar{Q}_t + w_t(v)] \tag{3.13}$$

for all $v$. Substituting Equation (3.13) into the right-hand side of (3.6), we obtain the following expression for the general price level:

$$Q_t = \frac{1}{1+\gamma\theta}[x_{t-1} + \delta - \alpha - \beta t + \gamma\theta\bar{Q}_t + \epsilon_t] + \frac{\sum_v u(v)w_t(v)}{1+\gamma\theta} \tag{3.14}$$

where use has been made of (3.5a) and the identity

$$x_t \equiv x_{t-1} + \delta + \epsilon_t \tag{3.15}$$

which defines $\epsilon_t$ as the (stochastic) deviation of the rate of growth of the money supply $\Delta x_t$ from its mean $\delta$. Provided there is a large number of markets, none of which is "large" in comparison to the sum total of the other markets, the last term on the right-hand side of Equation (3.14) converges in probability to zero. [This is formulated and demonstrated rigorously in Appendix A of Cukierman and Wachtel (1979).] Of the remaining elements on the right-hand side of Equation (3.14), the only one not known in period $t$ is $\epsilon_t$, whose expected value conditional on information up to and including period $t-1$ $(I_{t-1})$ is zero. [This follows directly from (3.5a) and (3.15).] Because $\bar{Q}_t$ is defined as the mean of the distribution of the general price level conditional on $I_{t-1}$, it can be calculated by taking the conditional expected values on both sides of Equation (3.14) and by solving for $\bar{Q}_t \equiv E[Q_t/I_{t-1}]$. The result is

$$\bar{Q}_t = x_{t-1} + \delta - \alpha - \beta t \tag{3.16}$$

Noting that the sum of the first four terms inside the brackets on the right-hand side of Equation (3.14) is equal, from (3.16), to $\bar{Q}_t$, we can rewrite (3.14) as

$$Q_t = \bar{Q}_t + \frac{\epsilon_t}{1+\gamma\theta} \tag{3.17}$$

Using Equation (3.14) without its last right-hand-side term (which is zero) in (3.13), this last equation can be rewritten:

$$p_t(v) - Q_t = w_t(v)/(1+\gamma\theta) \equiv z[w_t(v)] \tag{3.18}$$

Because [from (3.5a)] $\epsilon_t$ is normally distributed and the variance of $\epsilon_t \equiv \Delta x_t - \delta$ is equal to $\sigma_x^2$, Equation (3.17) implies that

$$Q_t \sim N(\bar{Q}_t, \sigma^2) \tag{3.19a}$$

where $\sigma^2 \equiv \sigma_x^2/(1+\gamma\theta)^2$, and Equation (3.18) together with (3.5b) implies that

$$z[w_t(v)] \sim N(0, \tau^2) \qquad (3.19b)$$

where $\tau^2 \equiv \sigma_w^2/(1+\gamma\theta)^2$.

The results in Equations (3.19a) and (3.19b) establish that Equation (3.11) characterizes the actual behavior of the economy. Moreover, Equations (3.19a) and (3.19b) characterize $\sigma^2$ and $\tau^2$ in terms of the underlying exogenous variance of Equation (3.5). Equation (3.18) establishes that the actual behavior of the economy is also characterized by Equation (3.10).

So far we have established that Equations (3.10) and (3.11) represent the behavior of prices in the economy both as they actually are and as they are believed to be. To finish the proof, it remains to show that under these conditions Equation (3.12) is indeed the optimal predictor of the general price level from the point of view of individuals in market $v$. The mean of the distribution of the general price level $\bar{Q}_t$, which is known in all markets, will be used to compute an optimal forecast of the current general price level; in addition, individuals in market $v$ have an observation of the current price in their own market $p_t(v)$, which they know, through Equation (3.18), to partially reflect movements in the actual general price level $Q_t$. Because $p_t(v)$ is the sum of two normal variates, it is also distributed normally. It follows that $Q_t$ and $p_t(v)$ have a joint normal distribution. The problem of finding an optimal forecast for $Q_t$ in market $v$ can therefore be reduced to the following statistical problem: Find the expected value of $Q_t$ conditional on $\bar{Q}_t$ and $p_t(v)$. As is well known, the conditional expected value is both an unbiased and a minimum mean square error estimator. For normal variates the conditional expectation is a linear function of the conditioning variable and its explicit form is [see, for example, Brunk (1965: 212–18)]

$$E[Q_t/I_t(v)] = E[Q_t/\bar{Q}_t, p_t(v)]$$

$$= \rho_{Q_t p_t(v)} \frac{p_t(v) - E p_t(v)}{\sigma_{p_t(v)}} \sigma_{Q_t} + E Q_t \qquad (3.20)$$

where $\rho_{Q_t p_t(v)}$ denotes the correlation coefficient between $Q_t$ and $p_t(v)$, $\sigma_{p_t(v)}$ denotes the standard deviation of the price in market $v$, $\sigma_{Q_t}$ is the standard deviation of the general price level, and $E$ without a conditioning sign stands for the expected value conditioned on only information up to and including period $t-1$. Using Equations (3.17)–(3.19) in (3.20), we can show that (3.20) is equivalent to (3.12). The details of the calculation appear in the Appendix to this chapter.

3b        *Confusion between relative prices and the absolute price level revisited*

So far we have shown that the equilibrium of the model is "rational" or self-fulfilling in the sense that Equations (3.10) and (3.11) describe both the actual and the perceived behavior of the economy, and that Equation (3.12) is an optimal predictor of the general price level given those perceptions and the information currently available in market $v$. Equation (3.13) suggests that $p_t(v)$ differs across markets only to the extent that $w_t(v)$ differs across markets because all the other terms on the right-hand side of (3.13) are identical for all markets. It is therefore convenient to parametrize prices in individual markets by the realization of the shock $w_t$ in those markets and delete the market index $v$. Hence, Equations (3.10)–(3.12) may be rewritten as follows:

$$p_t(w_t) = Q_t + z(w_t) = Q_t + w_t/(1+\gamma\theta) \tag{3.10*}$$

$$Q_t \sim N(\bar{Q}_t, \sigma^2), \qquad z(w_t) \sim N(0, \tau^2) \tag{3.11*}$$

$$Q_t^*(w_t) \equiv E[Q_t/I_t(w_t)] = (1-\theta)p_t(w_t) + \theta\bar{Q}_t \tag{3.12*}$$

where from Equations (3.19a), (3.19b), and (3.12a),

$$\sigma^2 = \sigma_x^2/(1+\gamma\theta)^2, \qquad \tau^2 = \sigma_w^2/(1+\gamma\theta)^2, \qquad \theta = \tau^2/(\tau^2+\sigma^2) \tag{3.19c}$$

Note that because information differs across markets only if $w$ is different across markets, it is also possible to write the information set $I_t(v)$ as $I_t(w_t)$, where $I_t(w_t)$ should be interpreted as the information available in a market $v$ that has sustained the relative demand shock $w_t$. The notation $Q_t^*(w_t)$ is shorthand for the more cumbersome expected value that follows it in Equation (3.12*), which can also be indexed by the shock realization $w_t$ rather than by the market index $v$. (This notation distinguishes between markets only to the extent that they have different prices, which happens in turn only if they sustain different relative demand shocks. We shall refer to a market that sustains a shock $w$ as "market $w$.")

Equation (3.17) lagged one period is

$$Q_{t-1} = \bar{Q}_{t-1} + \frac{\epsilon_{t-1}}{1+\gamma\theta} = \bar{Q}_{t-1} + \frac{\Delta x_{t-1} - \delta}{1+\gamma\theta} \tag{3.17a}$$

In period $t$ individuals in all markets obtain information about the last period's general price level $\bar{Q}_{t-1}$ from the appropriate statistical agency. Assuming that they knew $Q_{t-1}$ in the previous period, this information amounts, through Equation (3.17a), to an observation on $\Delta x_{t-1}$ and therefore on $x_{t-1} \equiv x_{t-2} + \Delta x_{t-1}$.

By using this information in Equation (3.16), individuals in all markets can compute $\bar{Q}_t$. Thus, knowing the price index for the last period is equivalent to knowing $\bar{Q}_t$. As can be seen from (3.16), however, $\bar{Q}_t$ does not reflect the current unanticipated money supply shock $\epsilon_t$, which also influences the current price level. (The current anticipated money supply shock $\delta$ is taken into account in the computation of $\bar{Q}_t$.) Because $p_t(w)$ partially reflects movements in $\epsilon_t$, it is used together with $\bar{Q}_t$ in Equation (3.12*) to form an optimal prediction of the general price level.

It can be seen from Equations (3.12*) and (3.19c) that the weights assigned to $p_t(w_t)$ and $Q_t$ depend, through $\theta$, on the ratio of the variance of the general price level to the variance of the relative price. This dependence has an appealing interpretation; for a given $\sigma^2$, as the variance of relative prices $\tau^2$ increases, it becomes more likely that changes in $p_t(w_t)$ are caused by changes in $z(w_t)$ rather than by changes in the general level of prices $Q_t$. Because $p_t(w_t)$ becomes a poorer indicator of the general price level, it is given less weight in Equation (3.12*), the optimal prediction equation. Formally, $1-\theta$, the weight assigned to $p_t(w_t)$, decreases as $\tau^2$ increases. At the limit when $\tau^2$ is very large in comparison to $\sigma^2$, the weight given to the individual price is zero, since it carries no information about the general price level. At the other extreme, when $\sigma^2$ is very large in comparison to $\tau^2$, movements in $p_t(w)$ reflect mostly movements in the general price level. In this case, the optimal predictor of $Q_t$ relies mostly on the individual market price ($\theta$ is small).

The relative price as perceived by individuals in a market that sustains a relative demand shock $w_t$ is, from Equation (3.12*),

$$p_t(w_t) - Q_t^*(w_t) = \theta[p_t(w_t) - \bar{Q}_t] \qquad (3.21)$$

where $\theta$ is between zero and one. (It will be zero or one only when the ratio $\sigma_x^2/\sigma_w^2$ assumes the extreme values of infinity or zero. We rule out these extreme cases by assumption, since they do not yield any aggregate-relative confusion.) Hence any deviation of $p_t(w_t)$ from $\bar{Q}_t$ will be only partly interpreted as a deviation of the relative price in market $w$ from zero. In particular, suppose the entire deviation of $p_t(w_t)$ from $\bar{Q}_t$ is caused by an unanticipated shock $\epsilon_t$ to the rate of growth of the money supply. Because $\theta > 0$, it follows from Equation (3.21) that part of this deviation is interpreted as causing a change in the relative price even though the actual relative demand has not changed.

Conversely, suppose that the entire deviation of $p_t(w)$ from $\bar{Q}_t$ is caused by an unanticipated shock to relative demand in the market. Because $\theta < 1$, only part of this deviation is interpreted as a change in relative price, although in fact the entire deviation is really a change in relative demand and therefore in relative price. In both these cases, individuals are subject to the aggregate–relative confusion: They interpret purely monetarily induced shocks to the level of all prices partly as changes in relative prices and underinterpret real shocks to relative demands.

This confusion between the aggregate price level and relative prices is not confined to the polar cases just mentioned. As a matter of fact, there will almost always be some confusion between aggregate and relative price changes. The only case in which the aggregate–relative confusion does not exist is when the actual relative price from Equation (3.18) is equal to the perceived relative price in (3.21). Equating the right-hand sides of these two equations, using (3.17) and (3.18), and rearranging, we find no confusion only when

$$\frac{w_t}{\epsilon_t} = \frac{\theta}{1-\theta} = \frac{\tau^2}{\sigma^2} = \frac{\sigma_w^2}{\sigma_x^2} \qquad (3.22)$$

that is, when the ratio of the relative demand shock to the unanticipated money shock is equal to the ratio of the variances of those two shocks. Stated slightly differently, there will be no confusion only when $w_t/\epsilon_t$ is equal to the ratio of the variance of relative prices to the variance of the general price level. Because both $w_t$ and $\epsilon_t$ are random variables, whereas $\tau^2/\sigma^2$ is a constant, condition (3.22) will usually be violated and there will almost always be some confusion between aggregate and relative changes in prices.

## 4      Implications for the short-run Phillips curve and empirical testing

The discussion of the preceding section suggests that unanticipated monetary shocks are interpreted in the short run as changes in relative prices. Because the cyclical component of output in Equation (3.3a) depends on the perceived relative price, a positive shock to monetary growth will push up the cyclical component of output in all markets.

More precisely, substituting Equation (3.21) into (3.3a) and using (3.10*) and (3.17), we get

$$y_{ct}(v) = y_{ct}[w_t(v)] = \gamma\theta[p_t(w_t) - \bar{Q}_t] = \frac{\gamma\theta}{1+\gamma\theta}[\epsilon_t + w_t(v)] \qquad (3.3b)$$

That is, the cyclical component of output in market $v$ depends on the realization of the relative demand shock $w_t(v)$ in that market as well as on the economy-wide unanticipated shock to the rate of monetary growth

$\epsilon_t$. For a given distribution of $w_t$ across markets, the larger the unanticipated shock $\epsilon_t$, the larger the cyclical component of output will be.

This result can be formalized by computing the weighted (geometric) average cyclical deviation of output in the economy $y_{ct} \equiv \sum_v u(v) y_{ct}(v)$. Because $\sum_v u(v) w_t(v)$ converges in probability to zero (Cukierman and Wachtel 1979: Appendix A), substituting Equation (3.3b) into this expression gives

$$y_{ct} = a(\Delta x_t - \delta) \tag{3.23a}$$

$$a \equiv \frac{\gamma\theta}{1+\gamma\theta} = \frac{\gamma\sigma_w^2}{\sigma_x^2 + (1+\gamma)\sigma_w^2} \tag{3.23b}$$

Equation (3.23a) shows that the average cyclical deviation of output in the economy is positively related to unanticipated monetary growth with a coefficient of proportionality $a$, which is, in turn, from Equation (3.23b), a decreasing function of the variance of the rate of monetary growth $\sigma_x^2$.

This result, which is a central implication of Lucas's (1973) work, indicates that the higher the variance of the rate of growth in the money supply, the less a given unanticipated shock to the rate of monetary growth will affect output. In the limit when this variance becomes very large, $a$ tends toward zero and unanticipated money has no effect on output even in the short run. As $\sigma_x^2$ increases, a larger fraction of the movements in individual prices is attributed to global monetary reasons, as can be seen from Equations (3.21) and (3.3b). As less of any given shock is interpreted as a change in relative prices, the output response is smaller. The negative relationship between $a$ and $\sigma_x^2$ is also the basis for empirical testing of the theory as described in the following section.

The theory also has interesting implications for the effects of monetary growth on the rate of inflation. To see these implications, we again equate the sum of Equations (3.2) and (3.3) with (3.4) to get the market-clearing relation in market $v$ and solve for the equilibrium price in that market:

$$p_t(v) = -(\alpha + \beta t) - y_{ct}(v) + x_t + w_t(v) \tag{3.24}$$

Multiplying both sides of (3.24) by $u(v)$ and summing over markets, using Equations (3.6) and (3.23a), and again making use of the fact that $\sum_v u(v) w_t(v)$ converges in probability to zero, we obtain

$$Q_t = -(\alpha + \beta t) - y_{ct} + x_t \tag{3.25}$$

from which it follows that, ceteris paribus, the higher the average cyclical deviation of output $y_{ct}$, the lower the general price level.

Taking first differences of Equation (3.25) and using (3.23a) to substitute $y_{ct}$ out, we obtain the following expression for the general rate of inflation:

$$\pi_t \equiv Q_t - Q_{t-1} = -\beta + (1-a)\Delta x_t + a\Delta x_{t-1} \qquad (3.26)$$

Because $0 < a < 1$, Equation (3.26) implies that the full effect of an increase in the quantity of money on the rate of inflation is felt within two periods. By contrast, in the case of full current information, the full effect of monetary growth on the rate of inflation is

$$\pi_t = -\beta + \Delta x_t \qquad (3.8a)$$

So in the case of full current information there is a contemporaneous one-to-one relationship between general inflation and monetary growth, and the latter has no effect on output. In the present case, which features some confusion between aggregate and relative changes in prices, there is also a one-to-one relationship between monetary growth and inflation but it is distributed over two periods. The contemporaneous effect of a 1-percent increase in monetary growth is $1 - a$ and the lagged effect is $a$.

It is interesting to note that the higher the short-run trade-off as measured by $a$ in Equation (3.23a), the smaller is the contemporaneous effect of monetary growth on inflation and the larger is the lagged response of inflation to monetary growth. This is not surprising because when $a$ is large, a given rate of monetary expansion causes a higher temporary expansion in the cyclical component of output and temporarily slows the rate of inflation. When this is the case, the lagged response of inflation to money growth, as measured by $a$ in Equation (3.26), is correspondingly higher. So the coefficient $a$ determines both the size of the effect of a given shock on output and the speed with which inflation responds to monetary growth.

In countries where the value of $a$ is high, monetary growth has a strong short-run effect on output and a strong delayed effect on prices. In countries where the value of $a$ is low, the quantity of money has hardly any effect on output even in the short run, and most of the effect of monetary growth is immediately reflected in prices. Because $a$ is a decreasing function of the variance of monetary growth, in countries with stable monetary policies the value of $a$ should be high and in countries with erratic monetary policies the value of $a$ should be low. Following Barro (1976) we will refer to this implication as the Lucas hypothesis on the slope of the Phillips curve. An empirical test of this hypothesis is described in the following section.

Table 1. *Values of $a$, $\sigma_x^2$, and the variance of inflation for selected countries*

| Country | $a$ | $\sigma_x^2$ | Variance of inflation $V(\pi)$ |
|---|---|---|---|
| Argentina | 0.011 | 0.01555 | 0.01998 |
| Paraguay | 0.022 | 0.03450 | 0.03192 |
| Italy | 0.622 | 0.00040 | 0.00044 |
| West Germany | 0.820 | 0.00073 | 0.00026 |
| United States | 0.910 | 0.00064 | 0.00007 |

*Source:* Adapted from Lucas (1973: Tables 1 and 2).

## 4a    *Empirical testing of the Lucas hypothesis*

The empirical test performed by Lucas focuses on the estimation of $a$ from either (3.23a) or (3.26) in a cross section of countries with different values of $\sigma_x^2$. If the hypothesis is to be supported, the estimates of $a$ and of $\sigma_x^2$ should be negatively correlated across countries.

Estimating Equation (3.23a) and $\sigma_x^2$ requires data on $\Delta x_t$ and on the cyclical component of output $y_{ct}$. The choice of an empirical proxy for $\Delta x_t$ rests on the fact that in the model presented, $\Delta x_t$ is equal to both the rate of change in the money stock and the rate of change in total nominal income (Cukierman and Wachtel 1979: Appendix B). The empirical proxy for $\Delta x_t$ is thus taken to be the rate of change in the total nominal gross national product (GNP), and $\sigma_x^2$ for a given country is the variance in this rate of change over time. The second variable needed for the estimation of Equation (3.23a) is the cyclical component of output. This is taken to be the residual from a regression of the log of nominal GNP on a time trend as specified in the model.[9] Lucas's results support the hypothesis that there is a negative relationship between the slope of the Phillips curve and the variability of monetary policy.

Table 1 summarizes the results for a representative subset of Lucas's sample. The countries are arranged by the size of $a$. The most striking fact brought out by the table is the strong negative relationship between $a$ and $\sigma_x^2$ when the countries with a relatively high $\sigma_x^2$ (Argentina and Paraguay) are compared with the countries with a relatively low $\sigma_x^2$ (Italy, West Germany, and the United States). However, within each group the evidence on the negative relationship is somewhat mixed. It is possible that for the countries where the values of $\sigma_x^2$ are similar, the differences in *a* are too small (in comparison to elements not explicitly introduced in the model) to be revealed by the data. In any case, the results obtained in the full country sample used by Lucas support the view that there is a negative relationship between *a* and $\sigma_x^2$.

Another interesting finding suggested by Table 1 is that *a* and the variance of the inflation rate are also negatively related. Again, this is most evident when the countries with the most volatile rates of inflation (Argentina and Paraguay) are compared with those with stable rates of inflation. That this is also an implication of the model can be seen by noting from Equation (3.17) that the variance of the rate of inflation $V(\pi)$ is

$$V(\pi) \equiv E[Q_t - Q_{t-1} - E(\bar{Q}_t - \bar{Q}_{t-1})]^2 = \frac{1+(\gamma\theta)^2}{(1+\gamma\theta)^2}\,\sigma_x^2 \qquad (3.27)$$

Partial differentiation of Equation (3.27) with respect to $\sigma_x^2$ reveals that it is an increasing function of $\sigma_x^2$ (Mitchell and Taylor, 1982: Appendix A).

This leads to the following observation: If the countries in the sample differ mostly because $\sigma_x^2$ is different across countries whereas $\gamma$ and $\sigma_w^2$ are relatively stable across countries, we should expect to observe a negative relationship between the slope of the short-run Phillips relation and the variance of the rate of inflation. [This is because *a* is negatively related to $\sigma_x^2$ and $V(\pi)$ is positively related to $\sigma_x^2$.] This relation too is broadly supported by the full Lucas sample.

4b      *The Phillips–Lucas trade-off: evidence from the 1970s*

A reexamination of data extending up to 1976 (thereby covering a substantial portion of the turbulent seventies, including the supply shocks caused by the quadrupling of oil prices) was recently done by Froyen and Waud (1980). Their main finding, based on both cross-country and over-time (within-country) comparisons, is that there is a negative relationship between *a* and the variance of the rate of inflation. In particular the latter period, which includes the end of the sixties and more than half of the seventies, is typically characterized by lower values of *a* and higher values of $V(\pi)$ than the earlier period. However, neither the negative relationship between *a* and $\sigma_x^2$ nor the positive relationship between $V(\pi)$ and $\sigma_x^2$ implied by the theory is unambiguously supported by the data.

To explain this new evidence, Froyen and Waud suggest a modification that consists of introducing an aggregate stochastic supply shock $u_t$ into the supply functions in the various markets.[10] Thus Equation (3.1), the supply equation in market *v*, is respecified as

$$y_t^s(v) = y_{nt} + y_{ct}(v) + u_t \qquad (3.28a)$$

where

$$u_t \sim N(0, \sigma_u^2) \qquad (3.28b)$$

All other elements of the model remain the same. When solved as in Section 3, we get

$$a = \frac{\gamma \sigma_w^2}{\sigma_x^2 + \sigma_u^2 + (1+\gamma)\sigma_w^2} \qquad (3.29a)$$

$$V(\pi) = \frac{1 + (\gamma\theta)^2}{(1+\gamma\theta)^2}(\sigma_x^2 + \sigma_u^2) \qquad (3.29b)$$

where now

$$\theta \equiv \frac{\sigma_w^2}{\sigma_x^2 + \sigma_u^2 + \sigma_w^2} \qquad (3.29c)$$

Equations (3.29) suggest that for a given $\sigma_x^2$, an increase in the variance of the aggregate supply shock $\sigma_u^2$ decreases $a$ and at the same time increases $V(\pi)$.[11] Thus, changes in the variance of aggregate supply shocks over time or over countries may cause a negative relationship between the slope of the Phillips curve and the variance of the rate of inflation even for a given $\sigma_x^2$. Moreover, if in the seventies the cross-country variation in $\sigma_u^2$ became dominant in comparison to the cross-country variation in $\sigma_x^2$, we should expect to observe a negative relationship between $a$ and $V(\pi)$ without necessarily having to observe the relationship between $\sigma_x^2$ and both $a$ and $V(\pi)$ with equal strength. The results presented by Froyen and Waud seem to be consistent with this view.

### Appendix

A1     *Derivation of the optimal predictor $E[Q_t/I_t(v)]$ in Equation (3.12)*

From Equations (3.17) and (3.18), respectively, it follows that $Ep_t(v) = EQ_t = \bar{Q}_t$. From (3.19a) it follows that

$$\sigma_{Q_t} = \sigma_x/(1+\gamma\theta)$$

Because $w_t(v)$ and $\epsilon_t$ are statistically independent, Equations (3.18) and (3.19a, b) imply that

$$\sigma_{p_t(v)} = \frac{(\sigma_x^2 + \sigma_w^2)^{1/2}}{1+\gamma\theta}$$

From Equations (3.17)–(3.19),

$$
\begin{aligned}
\rho_{Q_t p_t(v)} &= \frac{E(Q_t - EQ_t)[p_t(v) - Ep_t(v)]}{\{E(Q_t - EQ_t)^2 E[p_t(v) - Ep_t(v)]^2\}^{1/2}} \\
&= \frac{E\{\epsilon_t[\epsilon_t + w_t(v)]/(1 + \gamma\theta)^2\}}{\sigma_x(\sigma_x^2 + \sigma_w^2)^{1/2}/(1 + \gamma\theta)^2} \\
&= \frac{\sigma_x}{(\sigma_x^2 + \sigma_w^2)^{1/2}}
\end{aligned}
$$

Substituting these expressions in Equation (3.20), we get

$$
\begin{aligned}
E[Q_t/\bar{Q}_t, p_t(v)] &= \frac{\sigma_x^2}{\sigma_x^2 + \sigma_w^2}[p_t(v) - \bar{Q}_t] + \bar{Q}_t \\
&= \frac{\sigma_x^2}{\sigma_x^2 + \sigma_w^2}p_t(v) + \frac{\sigma_w^2}{\sigma_x^2 + \sigma_w^2}\bar{Q}_t
\end{aligned}
$$

# Aggregate–relative confusion: implications for the distribution of inflationary expectations and for inflation uncertainty

## 1    Introduction

Economic models involving inflationary expectations usually treat them as being uniform across all individuals in the economy at a given time [e.g., Sargent (1973), Cukierman (1977), Turnovsky (1977)]. This is dictated more by analytical convenience than by reality. The little directly observed data that exist on inflationary expectations suggest that at the same time different people may have widely differing views about the future rate of inflation. This observation is based on data from two surveys of inflationary expectations in the United States: the Livingston survey of forecasters and the University of Michigan Survey Research Center (SRC) consumer survey.

The Livingston survey of forecasters and business economists was begun in 1947 by Joseph A. Livingston, a newspaper columnist. (The survey is currently maintained and updated by the Federal Reserve Bank of Philadelphia.) The number of survey respondents is usually between 30 and 75. A consistent time series for the expected rate of inflation in the consumer price index (CPI) has been constructed from this semi-annual survey by John Carlson (1977).

The SRC at the University of Michigan includes a question about inflationary expectations in its quarterly consumer survey. Until 1966 the survey obtained only qualitative information about the expected direction of price change. Starting in 1966, respondents who expected price increases were also asked how much of an increase they anticipated. In recent years the question has been improved to allow an open-ended response. The question refers to consumer prices generally and inflation over one year. The number of respondents varies from survey to survey but is always at least several hundred and often more than 1,000. Finally, unlike the Livingston survey, the respondents are representative of the entire population (Juster and Comment 1978).

Casual observation of the data from both surveys suggests that expectations are not uniform. Furthermore, the cross-sectional distribution of inflationary expectations in both surveys undergoes substantial changes over time. In particular, the cross-sectional variance of inflationary expectations seems to increase in times of unstable prices. This chapter is devoted to an investigation of the relationship between the cross-sectional variance of price and inflationary expectations on one hand, and the variance in both the rate of monetary growth and the general rate of inflation on the other.

The multimarket rational expectations equilibrium model from Chapter 3 is a natural framework within which to investigate this relationship. It will be recalled that an essential feature of this model is that the flow of information among markets is not instantaneous. Although suppliers have full information about the current price in their own market, their information about prices in other markets and consequently about the general price level is incomplete. In forming their perceptions about the current general price level and the rate of inflation, individuals in a given market (say, market $v$) also use information about the current equilibrium price in their own market. Because this price is subject to economy-wide forces as well as to a market-specific demand shock, individuals in different markets come up with different forecasts of both current and future price levels. As a result they also come up with different views about the future rate of inflation.

Basically, individuals in different markets have different views about the future rate of inflation because each market has a different current information set $I_t(v)$. More simply, individuals infer different things about the aggregate state of the economy because they see different parts of the total picture. The implications for the distribution of perceptions about the general price level are seen from Equation (3.12*), which is reproduced here for convenience:

$$Q_t^*(w_t) = (1-\theta)p_t(w_t) + \theta \bar{Q}_t \tag{4.1a}$$

where, from (3.19c) [p. 44],

$$\theta \equiv \frac{\tau^2}{\tau^2 + \sigma^2} = \frac{\sigma_w^2}{\sigma_x^2 + \sigma_w^2} \tag{4.1b}$$

It will be remembered that $\bar{Q}_t$ is information common to all markets, whereas $p_t(w_t)$ is shared by only individuals who happen to participate in a market that has currently sustained the relative demand shock $w_t$. As we saw in Section 3 of Chapter 3, knowledge of $\bar{Q}_t$ is equivalent to knowledge of the last period's price level, which participants in all markets know from the periodic publication of price indexes. On the other hand, $p_t(w_t)$ reflects partly unanticipated shocks to current monetary growth and is therefore also used in forming perceptions about the current general level of prices.

Equation (4.1a) states that given the information currently available in market $w$, the optimal forecast of the current general price level is a weighted average of the common (lagged) information on $\bar{Q}_t$ and of the market-specific (current) information on $p_t(w_t)$. Therefore the perceived current general price level $Q_t^*(w_t)$ varies over markets as a function of the distribution of the realizations of the relative demand shocks $w$ in those markets.

The real-life element modeled here is that individuals have better, cheaper, and more timely access to information on the prices of goods in markets in which they participate regularly. The costs of gathering information from diverse markets may cause information gaps even when the markets are physically close. Some general price information is available to everyone at very little cost (through the newspaper publication of price indexes, for example). Given the substantial delays between data collection and publication, however, that information becomes available more slowly than the information about the price in one's own market.

It should be noted that "markets" here can be interpreted as referring either to markets for the same good in different locations or to markets for different goods, or both. The crucial feature defining a market is that all individuals in it have the same current information.

## 2      Effect of monetary variability on the distribution of price level perceptions over markets[1]

It will be recalled from Equation (3.18) that

$$p_t(w_t) = Q_t + w_t/(1+\gamma\theta) \tag{4.2}$$

It follows that the variance of individual prices over the distribution of relative demand shocks is given by

$$\sigma_w^2/(1+\gamma\theta)^2 \tag{4.3}$$

This also happens to be the variance of relative prices [see Equation (3.19b)]. Because $\theta$ is a decreasing function of the variance of the rate of monetary growth $\sigma_x^2$, Equation (4.3) implies that the variance of $p_t(w_t)$ over the distribution of $w_t$ is an increasing function of $\sigma_x^2$. Furthermore, because the realizations of the $w_t$ values in the various markets are all from the same distribution, for a large number of markets it is possible to approximate the distribution of a given set of realizations of $w$ by the theoretical distribution of $w$. Hence the expression in (4.3) also represents the cross-sectional variance of individual relative prices over markets. It follows that this variance is also an increasing function of $\sigma_x^2$.

We shall now use this result to derive the effect of an increase in the variance of the rate of monetary expansion $\sigma_x^2$ on the distribution of perceptions about the current general price level. From Equation (4.1a), the perception of the general price level is a weighted average of the common information $\bar{Q}_t$ and of the market-specific information contained in the individual market price $p_t(w_t)$. When $\sigma_x^2$ increases, the spread of these prices across markets increases, too. Hence, ceteris paribus, the distribution of perceptions across markets widens as well. In addition, when $\sigma_x^2$ increases, the weight $(1-\theta)$ that is given to the individual price in Equation (4.1a) increases as well. This reinforces the positive influence of an increase in $\sigma_x^2$ on the variance of perceptions about the current general price level across markets. These considerations lead to the following proposition.

**Proposition 1:** *Ceteris paribus, an increase in the variance of monetary expansion increases the variance of the perceived current general price level across markets.*

The fact that individuals in different markets or information centers partially use different bits of information also makes their forecasts of the price level for the *next* period different. An expression for the price level expected for the next period in market $w_t$ can be derived by appealing again to the notion of rational expectations: Individuals know the structure of the economy. They use it in conjunction with the currently available information to form an optimal forecast of the next period's general price level. In particular, they know that Equations (3.16) and (3.17) describe the behavior of the general price level not only in period $t$ but in period $t+1$ as well. Substituting the first of these two equations into the second and leading by one period, we get

$$Q_{t+1}=x_t+\delta-\alpha-\beta(t+1)+\frac{\epsilon_{t+1}}{1+\gamma\theta}$$

The expected value of this expression conditional on the information $I_t(w_t)$ that is available in market $w_t$ in period $t$ can be written, using Equations (3.15) and (3.16), as

$$Q_{t+1}^*(w_t)\equiv E[Q_{t+1}/I_t(w_t)]$$

$$=E\left[\left(\bar{Q}_t+\delta-\beta+\epsilon_t+\frac{\epsilon_{t+1}}{1+\gamma\theta}\right)\Big/I_t(w_t)\right] \qquad (4.4)$$

The term $Q_{t+1}^*(w_t)$, which is defined formally by the expected value that follows it in Equation (4.4), is the general price level in period $t+1$ as forecasted by individuals in market $w$ in period $t$. The first three terms inside the braces in the right-hand-side expression are known with certainty in period $t$. Their conditional expected value is therefore equal to those terms. The expected value of $\epsilon_{t+1}$ as of period $t$ is equal to the unconditional expected value of $\epsilon_{t+1}$, which is zero. Hence Equation (4.4) may be written as

$$Q^*_{t+1}(w_t) = \bar{Q}_t + \delta - \beta + E[\epsilon_t / I_t(w_t)] \tag{4.5}$$

Given $I_t(w_t)$, the last term of this expression is not zero because an observation of $p_t(w_t)$, which partially reflects movements in $\epsilon_t$, can be used to sharpen the forecast of $\epsilon_t$. Intuitively, because it is known that the next period's price level depends on the current rate of monetary expansion, it is useful to make an accurate forecast of this rate. The current rate of monetary expansion decomposes into a certain component $\delta$ and an uncertain component $\epsilon_t$. There is no problem in forecasting $\delta$, but $\epsilon_t$ is still unknown in period $t$. The observation on $p_t(w_t)$ conveys information about $\epsilon_t$, however. As shown in Section A1 of the Appendix to this chapter, given $p_t(w_t)$, the optimal forecast of $\epsilon_t$ is

$$E[\epsilon_t / I_t(w_t)] = (1 - \theta)(\epsilon_t + w_t) \tag{4.6}$$

Substituting Equation (4.6) into (4.5), we get

$$Q^*_{t+1}(w_t) = \bar{Q}_t + \delta - \beta + (1 - \theta)(\epsilon_t + w_t) \tag{4.7}$$

So the forecast of the next period's price level differs across markets again because the realizations of the market-specific demand shocks $w_t$ differ across markets. Individuals in different markets come up with different forecasts of the current rate of growth in nominal aggregate demand and therefore with different forecasts of the future price level. The current forecasts of $\epsilon_t$ are contaminated by differing realizations of the specific demand shocks across markets because suppliers temporarily confuse between relative and aggregate shocks to demand in their own market.

Suppose now that $\sigma_x^2$, the variance in the rate of change of nominal income, increases. Because in this fixed-velocity world nominal income and money are directly proportional to each other, $\sigma_x^2$ is also the variance of the rate of change in the money supply. As a result the weight $(1 - \theta)$ assigned to the stochastic term $(\epsilon_t + w_t)$ in Equation (4.7) increases, and the theoretical variance of $Q^*_{t+1}(w_t)$ over the distribution of $w_t$ increases as well. The measured cross-sectional variance of perceptions about the future price level and this theoretical variance can be identified when there is a large number of different markets or information centers. This leads to the following proposition.

**Proposition 2:** *A ceteris paribus increase in the variance of the rate of change of nominal income increases the cross-sectional (over-markets) variance in the price level expected for the next period.*

### 3     Monetary variability, the cross-sectional variance of inflationary expectations, and inflation variance

That individuals in different markets have different expectations about the future price level creates a whole range of inflationary expectations across markets. The cross-sectional distribution of inflationary expectations is related to that of $Q_{t+1}^*(w_t)$ from the previous section, but it is not always equal to it. Whether those two distributions are equal or not depends on the base price level used to define the expected rate of inflation. Two alternative definitions are possible: In one, the base price level used in the definition is the last available figure on the general price level in period $t$, which is $Q_{t-1}$. This leads to the following definition of the expected rate of inflation in market $w_t$:

$$\pi_L^*(w_t) \equiv Q_{t+1}^*(w_t) - Q_{t-1} \tag{4.8a}$$

The other uses as the base price level the perception of the current price level in market $w_t$, $Q_t^*(w_t)$. This leads to another definition of the expected rate of inflation in market $w_t$:

$$\pi^*(w_t) = Q_{t+1}^*(w_t) - Q_t^*(w_t) \tag{4.8b}$$

Some surveys of inflationary expectations are implicitly based on one definition, whereas some are based on the other. In particular, the data on inflationary expectations from the Livingston survey as published in Carlson (1977) and Wachtel (1977) are based on Equation (4.8a). [This is the reason for the subscript L attached to $\pi$ in (4.8a).] There is no indication on Livingston's questionnaire as to where the respondent thinks the price level stands at the time the forecast is made. Usually when the survey is taken, the actual consumer price index (CPI) for two months earlier is the last available figure on the general price level. Therefore Carlson (1977) and Wachtel (1977) construct inflation rate forecasts by computing the annual inflation rate implied by the growth of the CPI from its actual value two months prior to the survey to its predicted level on the forecast horizon. Therefore, $\pi_L^*(w_t)$ is the appropriate definition in this case.

By contrast, the SRC at the University of Michigan asks directly about expected inflation rather than about the expected price level. For this case it seems reasonable that the span covered by the inflation forecast is from the time the survey question is asked to the forecast horizon specified in the questionnaire. Because individuals do not know the current price level at the time of the survey with certainty, they use the optimal forecast $Q_t^*(w_t)$ instead. Thus in this case, $\pi^*(w_t)$ from Equation (4.8b) is more appropriate.

3a      *Cross-sectional variance of the inflationary expectation*[2] $\pi_L(w_t)$

In period $t$, $Q_{t-1}$ is known with certainty in all markets, so $\pi_L^*(w_t)$ differs across markets only to the extent that $Q_{t+1}^*(w_t)$ differs across markets. Hence the variance of $\pi_L^*(w_t)$ is the same as the variance of $Q_{t+1}^*(w_t)$. It follows therefore from Proposition 2 that the variance of $\pi_L^*(w_t)$ is an increasing function of the variability of the rate of monetary expansion $\sigma_x^2$. The formal expression for this variance (derived in Section A2 of the Appendix) is

$$V(\pi_L^*) = V(Q_{t+1}^*) = (1-\theta)^2 \sigma_w^2 \qquad (4.9a)$$

from which it can be seen that this variance is an increasing function of $\sigma_x^2$.


3b      *Cross-sectional variance of the inflationary expectation* $\pi^*(w_t)$

The expression for the variance of $\pi^*(w_t)$ across markets is more complicated than that for $V(\pi_L^*)$. This is because $\pi^*(w_t)$ varies across markets not only because of the variation in $Q_{t+1}^*(w_t)$ but also because of the variation in $Q_t^*(w_t)$. Subtracting Equation (4.1a) from (4.7) and using Equations (3.17) and (3.10*) to substitute $p_t(w_t)$ and $Q_t$ out, we get, after rearranging,

$$\pi^*(w_t) = \delta - \beta + \frac{\gamma\theta(1-\theta)}{1+\gamma\theta}(\epsilon_t + w_t) \qquad (4.10)$$

As shown in Section A3 of the Appendix, the variance of this expression over the distribution of $w_t$ is

$$V(\pi^*) = \gamma^2 \sigma_w^2 \left[\frac{\theta(1-\theta)}{1+\gamma\theta}\right]^2 \qquad (4.9b)$$

For a large number of markets or information centers the cross-sectional variance of $\pi^*(w_t)$ is equal to $V(\pi^*)$ in Equation (4.9b). It turns out that this variance is an increasing function of $\sigma_x^2$ only when certain restrictions are satisfied by the parameters of the economy. This is more precisely expressed in the following proposition.

     **Proposition 3:** *Other things being equal, an increase in the variance of the rate of change in nominal income $\sigma_x^2$ increases the variance of inflationary expectations across markets $V(\pi^*)$ if and only if*

$$r \equiv \sigma^2/\tau^2 < \sqrt{1+\gamma} \qquad (4.11)$$

*where $r$ is the ratio of the variance of the (log of) the general price level* *to the variance of relative prices, and γ is the elasticity of supply with respect to the* perceived *relative price in any given market.*[3]

## 3c    *Distribution of the actual rate of inflation*[4]

The actual rate of inflation in the general price level is, by definition,

$$\pi_t = Q_t - Q_{t-1} \tag{4.12}$$

Because $Q_t$ and $Q_{t-1}$ depend, respectively, on the realizations of the random aggregate demand shocks $\epsilon_t$ and $\epsilon_{t-1}$, the actual rate of inflation is also a random variable. Using Equation (3.17) in (4.13), we get

$$\pi_t = \bar{Q}_t - \bar{Q}_{t-1} + \frac{\epsilon_t - \epsilon_{t-1}}{1+\gamma\theta} = \delta - \beta + \frac{\epsilon_t + \gamma\theta\epsilon_{t-1}}{1+\gamma\theta} \tag{4.13}$$

where the second equality follows by using Equation (3.16) to calculate $\bar{Q}_t - \bar{Q}_{t-1}$ and rearranging. The expected value of the rate of inflation in (4.13) over the distribution of $\epsilon$ is $\delta - \beta$. The variance of $\pi_t$ over the distribution of $\epsilon$ is therefore

$$V(\pi) \equiv \underset{\epsilon}{E}(\pi_t - \underset{\epsilon}{E}\pi_t)^2 = \underset{\epsilon}{E}\left(\frac{\epsilon_t + \gamma\theta\epsilon_{t-1}}{1+\gamma\theta}\right)^2 = \frac{1+(\gamma\theta)^2}{(1+\gamma\theta)^2}\sigma_x^2 \tag{4.14}$$

Section A4 of the Appendix shows that this variance too is an increasing function of the variance $\sigma_x^2$.

## 3d    *Relationship between the cross-sectional variance of inflationary expectations and the variance of inflation*

The previous two sections suggest that the variance of inflation and the cross-sectional variance of inflationary expectations increase with the variance of the rate of change in nominal income $\sigma_x^2$. The following proposition states this basic result more rigorously.

**Proposition 4:** *If the variance of relative demand shocks $\sigma_w^2$ is constant and the variance of the rate of change in nominal income $\sigma_x^2$ changes over time, then:*

(a) *there will be a positive relation between the cross-sectional variance of inflationary expectations $V(\pi_L^*)$ and the variance of the rate of inflation over time; and*

(b) *if, in addition, $r < \sqrt{1+\gamma}$, there will also be a positive relationship between the cross-sectional variance of inflationary expectations $V(\pi^*)$ and the variance of the rate of inflation.*

Thus, if changes in the variance of relative demand shocks $\sigma_w^2$ are small in comparison to the policy-induced changes that alter the variance $\sigma_x^2$, a positive relationship should be expected between the variance of inflationary expectations and the variance of the rate of inflation. This is a basic result of this chapter. More intuitively, it means that when the behavior of inflation becomes more erratic, there is more disagreement about the future course of inflation.

## 4    Inflation uncertainty, inflation variance, and the variance of inflationary expectations[5]

There is a general feeling among economists that substantial social costs of inflation are caused by its unpredictability. In his Nobel lecture, Milton Friedman (1977) conjectured that more monetary variability is harmful for employment and production. Papers by Mullineaux (1980) and Blejer and Leiderman (1980) present empirical evidence to support this conjecture. In addition, unpredictability creates undesirable and unjust redistributive effects. Thus any serious investigation, whether theoretical or empirical, of the social costs created by uncertainty about inflation must develop an appropriate measure of inflation uncertainty. This section is devoted to the development of such a measure within the context of the model discussed here. The conceptual framework appears in this section, and an empirical implementation is discussed in the next section.

It would seem that the variance of inflation is an obvious measure of inflation uncertainty; however, variability does not necessarily mean unpredictability (Ibrahim and Williams 1978, Engle 1980, Fischer 1981). To clarify the difference between these two concepts, consider the case in which the rates of inflation for the next three periods are known in advance to be 1 percent, 10 percent, and 20 percent, respectively. This example suggests that the uncertainty of inflation is related to the stochastic (and therefore unpredictable) variability of actual inflation around some current point estimate of its future magnitude.

For the case in which individuals report their expected rate of inflation over a time span starting from the time for which the last CPI figure is available, the appropriate measure of expected inflation [from Equation (4.8a)] is $\pi_L^*(w_t)$. More precisely, $\pi_L^*(w_t)$ is the prediction at time $t$ by an individual in market $w_t$ of the rate of inflation that is to take place between period $t-1$ and period $t+1$. The actual rate of inflation over the same period is given by

$$_{t-1}\pi_{t+1} \equiv Q_{t+1} - Q_{t-1} \tag{4.15}$$

A natural measure of inflation uncertainty is the variance of the deviation of the actual rate of inflation in Equation (4.15) from the prediction made using (4.8a). We refer to this deviation as the *forecast error* and to its variance as *inflation uncertainty*. This variance focuses directly on the possible deviation between actual and predicted inflation. It measures the extent to which actual inflation may deviate on average from predicted inflation because of factors that are still random in period $t$. Hence it is a natural measure of inflation uncertainty.

Subtracting Equation (4.8a) from (4.15), we get the forecast error

$$FE_t \equiv {}_{t-1}\pi_{t+1} - \pi_L^*(w_t) = Q_{t+1} - Q_{t+1}^*(w_t) \tag{4.16}$$

It is shown in Section A5 of the Appendix that

$$FE_t = \theta\epsilon_t + \frac{\epsilon_{t+1}}{1+\gamma\theta} - (1-\theta)w_t \tag{4.17}$$

Thus the uncertainty of inflation is caused by the fact that in period $t$ individuals know neither the current nor the future value of the aggregate demand shock; they also do not know the current value of the relative demand shock that has occurred in their market.

Part of the uncertainty about inflation is created simply by uncertainty about the future. This is why $\epsilon_{t+1}$ appears in Equation (4.17). The other part is caused by the current confusion between aggregate and relative shocks to demand. This is the reason for the appearance of $\epsilon_t$ and $w_t$ in (4.17). The expected value of the forecast error is zero, and its variance is

$$V(FE) = \left[\theta^2 + \frac{1}{(1+\gamma\theta)^2}\right]\sigma_x^2 + (1-\theta)^2\sigma_w^2 \tag{4.18}$$

This variance increases when $\sigma_x^2$ increases (for details, see Section A5 of the Appendix). We saw earlier that an increase in $\sigma_x^2$ also increases the variance of inflation and the cross-sectional variance of inflationary expectations $V(\pi_L^*)$. We thus arrive at the following proposition.

**Proposition 5:** *If $\sigma_w^2$ is constant and $\sigma_x^2$ changes over time, then:*

(a)  *inflation variance $V(\pi)$ and inflation uncertainty $V(FE)$ are positively related;*
(b)  *the variance of inflationary expectations $V(\pi_L^*)$ and inflation uncertainty $V(FE)$ are positively related; and*
(c)  *inflation uncertainty $V(FE)$ is positively related to the variance of the rate of change of nominal income $\sigma_x^2$.*

Thus, although inflation variance and inflation uncertainty are not identical, they are positively related when most of the changes in the two variances are caused by changes in the variability of monetary policy. Under such circumstances, inflation uncertainty is also positively related to the cross-sectional variance of inflationary expectations $V(\pi_L^*)$.

The relationship between inflation uncertainty and the cross-sectional variance of inflationary expectations $V(\pi_L^*)$ can be developed further by defining the mean expected inflation over the distribution of $w_t$:

$$E\pi_{Lt}^* \equiv \underset{w}{E}\pi_L^*(w_t) = \bar{Q}_t + \delta - \beta - Q_{t-1} + (1-\theta)\epsilon_t \qquad (4.19)$$

where the last equality follows by substituting Equation (4.7) into (4.8a) and taking the expected value over the distribution of $w_t$. Subtracting (4.19) from (4.15), we get

$$B_t \equiv _{t-1}\pi_{t+1} - E\pi_{Lt}^* = Q_{t+1} - Q_{t-1} - [\bar{Q}_t + \delta - \beta - Q_{t-1} + (1-\theta)\epsilon_t]$$

$$= \theta\epsilon_t + \frac{\epsilon_{t+1}}{1+\gamma\theta} \qquad (4.20)$$

where the last equality follows by using Equations (3.16) and (3.17). The left-hand side of (4.20) is the difference between the ultimate realization of the inflation rate and the mean prediction of this rate over all markets as of period $t$. This is a mean forecast error that persists even when expectations are averaged over all markets in the economy so that the market-specific errors have averaged out. We shall therefore refer to it as the *mean bias in expectations in period t*. Not surprisingly, this bias depends on the (yet unknown) realizations of the random components of money growth in periods $t$ and $t+1$ (respectively, $\epsilon_t$ and $\epsilon_{t+1}$). In period $t$ the mean bias in expectations is therefore a stochastic variable with zero expected value and a variance

$$V(B) = \left[\theta^2 + \frac{1}{(1+\gamma\theta)^2}\right]\sigma_x^2 \qquad (4.21)$$

By comparing the right-hand side of Equation (4.18) with the sums of the right-hand sides of (4.9a) and (4.21), we can see that

$$V(FE) = V(\pi_L^*) + V(B) \qquad (4.22)$$

Equation (4.22) expresses a basic result concerning the relationship between inflation uncertainty and the (cross-sectional) variance of inflationary expectations $V(\pi_L^*)$: Inflation uncertainty is equal to the variance of inflationary expectations plus the variance of the mean bias of expected inflation. An immediate implication of (4.22) is that inflation uncertainty is larger than either the variance of inflationary expectations or the variance of the mean bias.


# 5    Some empirical evidence

For the United States, Propositions 2–4 have been tested empirically in Cukierman and Wachtel (1979) by using the cross-sectional variance of inflationary expectations from the Livingston survey and the University of Michigan SRC survey. Because, as suggested by Equation (4.9a), the Livingston variance of inflationary expectations is identical to the Livingston variance of the price level expected for the next period, Proposition 2 was tested by checking whether the first variance is positively related over time to the variance of the rate of change in nominal income. Proposition 3 was tested by first checking whether the condition in Equation (4.11) is satisfied and then checking whether there is a positive relationship between the cross-sectional variance of inflationary expectations from the SRC surveys and the variance of the rate of change in nominal income. Proposition 4 was tested by checking whether there is a positive relationship between both the Livingston variance and the SRC variance of inflationary expectations on one hand and the variance of inflation on the other.

The observations on the variance of inflation and the variance of the rate of change in nominal income needed to perform these tests were obtained by computing moving variances – that is, the variance in the appropriate rate of change over a two-year span centered on the current period. Two alternative measures were used for the moving variance of the rate of change in nominal income: one based on total nominal gross national product (GNP), which is available quarterly, and the other on personal income, which is available monthly. Similarly, two alternative measures were used for the moving variance of inflation: one based on the GNP deflator (available quarterly) and the other on the CPI (available monthly). For the data available monthly the moving variance was based on 25 (monthly) observations of the rate of change, whereas for the quarterly data only 9 (quarterly) observations were included. In each case, a centered two-year span was used and the monthly or quarterly percentage rates of change were expressed on an annual basis. The simple coefficients of correlation between the cross-sectional variances of inflationary expectations and the various moving variances are summarized in Table 2.

Except for the last correlation in Table 2 (which is negative and not significant), all coefficients of correlation are positive and significant. In addition, independent evidence suggests that the condition in Equation (4.11) is likely to have been satisfied in the postwar U.S. economy, which is the period covered in Table 1.[6] Thus the empirical evidence supports the implications developed in Propositions 2-4.

The implications of Proposition 5 can be tested in a similar manner. The basic message of this proposition is that inflation uncertainty is positively related to inflation variance, to the Livingston variance of inflationary expectations, and to the variance of the rate of change in nominal income. To test these implications, data on all those variances are needed.

Table 2. *Coefficients of correlation between the cross-sectional variances of inflationary expectations and the moving variances of nominal income change and inflation rate*

|  | Time period | Coefficient of correlation |
|---|---|---|
| Inflationary expectations from Livingston data: | | |
| Consumer price index | 6/48–12/75 | 0.77 |
| GNP deflator | 6/48–12/75 | 0.22 |
| GNP | 6/47–12/75 | 0.29 |
| Personal income | 6/47–12/75 | 0.91 |
| Inflationary expectations from SRC data: | | |
| Consumer price index | 1966II–76I | 0.64 |
| GNP deflator | 1966II–76I | 0.69 |
| GNP | 1966II–76I | 0.163 |
| Personal income | 1966II–76I | −0.08 |

*Note:* Roman numerals designate quarters.
*Source.* Cukierman and Wachtel (1979: Table 2).

Except for the variance of inflation uncertainty $V(FE)$, these data have been developed for the experiments described in Table 2. An empirical proxy for $V(FE)$ for each time period can be obtained by noting that for a given sample of individuals, an unbiased estimate of $V(FE)$ is the mean square error of forecast in this sample. In particular, if we use the individual inflation forecasts from the Livingston survey, this measure becomes

$$\tilde{V}_t(FE) = \frac{\sum_{i=1}^{m_t} [_{t-1}\pi_{t+1} - \pi_{L_t}^*(i)]^2}{m_t} \tag{4.23}$$

where $\pi_{L_t}^*(i)$ is the inflation forecast of individual $i$ in the survey made at time $t$, $m_t$ is the total number of individuals answering the survey in period $t$, and the tilde (~) in $\tilde{V}_t(FE)$ means that it is an estimate. Let $\bar{\pi}_{L_t}^*$ be the mean inflation forecast from the survey taken in period $t$. Adding and subtracting $\bar{\pi}_{L_t}^*$ inside the brackets on the right-hand side of Equation (4.23), we get

$$\tilde{V}_t(FE) = \frac{\sum_{i=1}^{m_t} [(\pi_{L_t}^*(i) - \bar{\pi}_{L_t}^*) + (\bar{\pi}_{L_t}^* - {}_{t-1}\pi_{t+1})]^2}{m_t}$$

$$= \frac{\sum_{i=1}^{m_t} [\pi_{L_t}^*(i) - \bar{\pi}_{L_t}^*]^2}{m_t} + (\bar{\pi}_{L_t}^* - {}_{t-1}\pi_{t+1})^2 \tag{4.24}$$

which is the empirical counterpart of Equation (4.22).

Table 3. *Coefficients of correlation between inflation uncertainty, $V(FE)$, and other variances of the model*

| | |
|---|---|
| Moving variance of nominal income change | |
| GNP | 0.55 |
| Personal income | 0.51 |
| Moving variance of the rate of inflation | |
| GNP deflator | 0.63 |
| CPI | 0.63 |
| Livingston variance of inflationary expectations | 0.29 |

*Note:* All correlations cover the period June 1948 to December 1975.
*Source:* Cukierman and Wachtel (1982b: Table 2).

The first term in the numerator on the right-hand side of (4.24) is the Livingston variance of inflationary expectations in period $t$, and the second is the square of the difference between the mean inflation forecast and actual inflation. The last term is therefore an estimate of the variance of the mean bias in expected inflation $V(B)$ in period $t$. It follows from Equation (4.24) that a measure of inflation uncertainty can be obtained by taking the Livingston variance of inflationary expectations for each period and adding to it the mean square bias of expected inflation for the period. Simple coefficients of correlations between this measure of inflation uncertainty and the other variances mentioned in Proposition 5 appear in Table 3. All the correlations are positive, which supports the various implications of Proposition 5. Thus, although neither the cross-sectional variance of inflationary expectations nor the variance of inflation can be identified with inflation uncertainty, both are positively related to this uncertainty.

## 6    Concluding comments

Various proxies for the measurement of inflation uncertainty have been used in the recent literature. For example, Klein (1975) has used the variance of inflation $V(\pi)$. Levi and Makin (1980) and Mullineaux (1980) have used the Livingston variance of inflationary expectations $V(\pi_L^*)$. As should be clear from the preceding discussion, neither of these can be identified with inflation uncertainty at the conceptual level. Because both $V(\pi)$ and $V(\pi_L^*)$ are positively associated with inflation uncertainty, however, the results presented here may be taken as a partial justification for using them as proxies. At the same time it seems that the variance of the forecast error of inflation is a first-best measure of inflation uncertainty. In particular, because inflation uncertainty is equal to the Livingston variance of inflationary expectations plus the mean square bias of those expectations, it is clear that the Livingston variance is a downward-biased measure of inflation uncertainty. Furthermore this bias varies over time as both the variance $\sigma_x^2$ and the unanticipated shocks to monetary growth vary over time.[7]

## Appendix

A1     *Derivation of the optimal predictor $E[\epsilon_t/I_t(w_t)]$ in Equation (4.6)*

It can be seen from Equations (3.17) and (3.10*) [p. 44] that an observation on $p_t(w_t)$ amounts to an observation on the sum $\epsilon_t + w_t$. Using (3.20), we can therefore write

$$E[\epsilon_t/I_t(w_t)] = E[\epsilon_t/s_t] = \rho_{\epsilon_t s_t} \frac{s_t - Es_t}{\sigma_{s_t}} \sigma_{\epsilon_t} + E\epsilon_t \qquad (A4.1)$$

where $s_t \equiv \epsilon_t + w_t$, but $E\epsilon_t = Es_t = 0$, $\sigma_{\epsilon_t} = \sigma_x$, and $\sigma_{s_t} = \sigma_x^2 + \sigma_w^2$. Also,

$$\rho_{\epsilon_t s_t} = \frac{E(\epsilon_t - E\epsilon_t)(s_t - Es_t)}{\sigma_{\epsilon_t} \cdot \sigma_{s_t}} = \frac{\sigma_x^2}{\sigma_x(\sigma_x^2 + \sigma_w^2)^{1/2}}$$

Substituting those results into Equation (A4.1), we obtain

$$E[\epsilon_t/I_t(w_t)] = (1 - \theta)(\epsilon_t + w_t)$$

which is Equation (4.6) in the text.

A2     *Derivation of $V(\pi_L^*)$ in Equation (4.9a)*

From Equation (4.7),

$$E_w Q_{t+1}^*(w_t) = \bar{Q}_t + \delta - \beta + (1 - \theta)\epsilon_t$$

The variance of $Q_{t+1}^*(w_t)$ over the distribution of $w_t$ is, by definition,

$$V(\pi_L^*) = V(Q_{t+1}^*) \equiv E_w[Q_{t+1}^*(w_t) - E_w Q_{t+1}^*(w_t)]^2$$
$$= E_w[(1 - \theta)w_t]^2 = (1 - \theta)^2 \sigma_w^2$$

A3     *Derivation of $V(\pi^*)$ in Equation (4.9b)*

The expected value of $\pi_t^*(w_t)$ over the distribution of $w_t$, from Equation (4.10), is

$$\underset{w}{E}\pi_t^*(w_t)=\delta-\beta+\frac{\gamma\theta(1-\theta)}{1+\gamma\theta}\epsilon_t$$

The variance of $\pi_t^*(w_t)$ over the distribution of $w_t$ is

$$V(\pi^*)\equiv\underset{w}{E}[\pi_t^*(w_t)-\underset{w}{E}\pi_t^*(w_t)]^2=\underset{w}{E}\left[\frac{\gamma\theta(1-\theta)}{1+\gamma\theta}w_t\right]^2=\gamma^2\theta^2\left[\frac{\theta(1-\theta)}{1+\gamma\theta}\right]^2$$

A4    *Demonstrating that the variance of inflation $V(\pi)$ is an increasing function of $\sigma_x^2$*

Partially differentiating Equation (4.14) with respect to $\sigma_x^2$ and rearranging, we get

$$\frac{\partial V(\pi)}{\partial\sigma_x^2}=\frac{1}{(1+\gamma\theta)^3}\{\gamma\theta[1+(\gamma\theta)^2-2\gamma\theta(1-\theta)+2(1-\theta)+\gamma\theta]+1\}$$

$$\geq\frac{1}{(1+\gamma\theta)^3}\{\gamma\theta[(1-\gamma\theta)^2+2(1-\theta)+\gamma\theta]+1\}>0$$

A5    *Derivation of Equation (4.17) and demonstration that $V(FE)$ increases in $\sigma_x^2$*

**A5a:** Substituting Equations (3.17) and (4.7) into (4.16), we obtain

$$FE_t=\bar{Q}_{t+1}+\frac{\epsilon_{t+1}}{1+\gamma\theta}-[\bar{Q}_t+\delta-\beta+(1-\theta)(\epsilon_t+w_t)]$$

Using Equations (3.15) and (3.16) to calculate the difference $\bar{Q}_{t+1}-\bar{Q}_t$, substituting the result in the preceding equation, and canceling terms, we obtain

$$FE_t=\theta\epsilon_t+\frac{\epsilon_{t+1}}{1+\gamma\theta}-(1-\theta)w_t$$

which is Equation (4.17) in the text.

**A5b:** Partially differentiating Equation (4.18) with respect to $\sigma_x^2$ and rearranging, we get

$$\frac{\partial V(FE)}{\partial\sigma_x^2}=\theta^2+\frac{1}{(1+\gamma\theta)^2}\left[1+\frac{2\gamma\theta(1-\theta)}{1+\gamma\theta}\right]$$

which is unambiguously positive.

# Implications of inflation uncertainty and differential inflationary expectations for the bond market and its allocative efficiency

## 1    Introduction[1]

Discussions of bond market equilibrium in an inflationary environment traditionally rely on a version of Fisher's (1896) theory of interest, in which the inflationary expectation, whether correct or not, is the same for all participants in the bond market at a given time.[2] As a consequence, given the equilibrium nominal rate of interest, there is only one real rate of interest, which is equal to the nominal rate minus the uniformly expected rate of inflation. As should be clear from Chapter 4, however, inflationary expectations are far from uniform, and their cross-sectional distribution tends to vary over time. This chapter develops the implications of varying degrees of inflation uncertainty and a divergence of views about future inflation for the bond market.

Chapter 4 showed how monetary uncertainty affects inflationary expectations. This chapter will investigate the effects of inflation uncertainty and differential inflationary expectations on the allocative efficiency of the bond market, the volume of trade in bonds, the size of windfall gains and losses, and Fisher's theory of interest.

The implications of differential expectations for the equilibrium of the bond market are presented in Section 2. A generalization of Fisher's theory of interest for the case of heterogeneous expectations appears in Section 3. Section 4 investigates how inflation uncertainty and the variability of inflationary expectations over time and individuals affect the allocative efficiency of the bond market. Section 5 focuses on the relationship between the nonuniformity of expectations and the volume of trade in the bond market. The effect of inflation uncertainty on the amount of unexpected redistribution throughout the bond market is the focus of the discussion in Section 6.

## 2    Bond market equilibrium with heterogeneous expectations

Consider a loan market composed of many borrowers and lenders whose real stock demands and supplies of funds depend on the real rate of interest each of them perceives. The real rate perceived by an individual is equal to the market nominal rate of interest minus the rate of inflation expected by that individual for the period of the loan. Assuming that the loan market clears instantaneously, the equilibrium nominal interest rate is determined by the condition that the excess demand for loans is zero. Formally, let

$$I_B = \{a_B - [n - \pi^*(B)]\}/b_B \tag{5.1a}$$

and let

$$I_L = \{-a_L + [n - \pi^*(L)]\}/b_L \tag{5.1b}$$

These are, respectively, borrower $B$'s real stock demand function for funds and lender $L$'s real stock supply function. Here, $n$, $\pi^*(L)$, and $\pi^*(B)$ are the nominal interest rate and the rates of inflation expected by lender $L$ and borrower $B$, respectively. All other symbols are positive parameters. No time indexes are attached to the variables in Equations (5.1) because the analysis that follows refers to only one point of time.

Equation (5.1a) states that the demand for funds by borrower $B$ is inversely related to the real rate perceived at the time the loan is contracted. This real rate is given in turn by the market nominal rate $n$ minus the rate of inflation $\pi^*(B)$ expected at that time by borrower $B$ for the period of the loan. Similarly, (5.1b) states that the supply of funds by lender $L$ is positively related to the real rate perceived at the time the decision is made to grant a loan. This real rate is equal to the nominal rate $n$ minus the rate of inflation expected by the lender for the period of the loan $\pi^*(L)$. Obviously, $\pi^*(L)$ and $\pi^*(B)$ usually differ from each other as well as across different lenders and borrowers. (It is implicitly assumed, without loss of generality, that in the relevant range $I_B$ and $I_L$ are always nonnegative.)

It is intuitively clear from this setup that the equilibrium nominal rate of interest depends on the expectations of the participants in the bond market. Equating total demands for funds with total supplies of funds and solving for the equilibrium nominal rate of interest, we obtain:

$$n = \sum_s v_s a_s + \sum_s v_s \pi^*(s) \tag{5.2}$$

where $v_s \equiv (1/b_s)/[\sum_s (1/b_s)]$ and measures the sensitivity of the demand for or supply of funds of trader $s$ with respect to the real interest rate relative to the sum of that same parameter over all market participants. The index $s$ runs over all participants in the bond market, be they lenders or borrowers.

When expectations are uniform, $\pi^*(s) = \pi^*$ for all $s$, and Equation (5.2) specializes to

$$n = \sum_s v_s a_s + \pi^* \tag{5.3}$$

In this particular case the real rate is perceived to be identical by all individuals and is equal, as in Fisher's theory of interest, to the nominal rate minus the uniformly expected rate of inflation; that is,

$$R = n - \pi^* = \sum_s v_s a_s \tag{5.4}$$

where $R$ is the uniformly perceived real rate of interest. Note that when expectations are uniform, this real rate is independent of the expected rate of inflation.[3] With heterogeneous expectations, however, different individuals act on the basis of different perceptions about the real rate of interest, since they all face the same nominal rate $n$ but have differing views about the future course of inflation. Using Equations (5.3) and (5.4), we find the real rate of interest faced by individual $i$ is

$$r_i = n - \pi^*(i) = R + \sum_s v_s \pi^*(s) - \pi^*(i) \equiv R + \bar{\pi}^* - \pi^*(i) \tag{5.5}$$

where $\bar{\pi}^*$ is defined by the last equality in (5.5), and $\pi^*$ is a weighted average of the expectations of individual traders with weights $v_s$. The weight $v_s$ measures the sensitivity of the demand for or supply of funds of trader $s$ with respect to the real interest rate relative to the sum of that same parameter over all participants in the bond market. Thus, the inflationary expectation of a trader whose demand (or supply) is relatively sensitive to the real rate will affect the mean expected inflation $\bar{\pi}^*$ more than the expectation of a trader whose demand (or supply) is not very sensitive to the real rate of interest.

Equation (5.5) suggests that individual $i$ will perceive a higher (lower) than average real interest rate than in the case of uniform expectations if his or her expectation is lower (higher) than $\bar{\pi}^*$.


## 3    Generalization of Fisher's theory of interest to the case of differential inflationary expectations

The simple version of Fisher's theory of interest, which says that the nominal rate equals the real rate plus the expected rate of inflation, does not hold for heterogeneous expectations. The relationship can, however, be generalized to the heterogeneous case provided $\bar{\pi}^*$ is used as the expected rate of inflation. In this case it follows directly by substitution of Equation (5.4) into (5.2) and from the definition of $\bar{\pi}^*$ that

$$R = n - \bar{\pi}^* \tag{5.6}$$

Equation (5.6) means that the real rate from the identical expectations case satisfies the Fisher relation even in the heterogeneous expectations case provided the mean inflationary expectation $\bar{\pi}^*$ is used to represent the central tendency of those expectations. It should also be noted that

$$R = \sum_i v_i r_i \tag{5.7}$$

where $r_i$ is defined as in (5.5). Equation (5.7) follows from (5.5) by multiplying both sides of (5.5) by $v_i$ and summing over all individuals. It says that the weighted average of real rates perceived by different individuals that is formed by using the weights $v_i$ equals the (unique) real rate that holds when expectations are identical.

## 4     Effect of inflation uncertainty and heterogeneous expectations on the allocative efficiency of the bond market

When the real rate of interest perceived by different traders varies, some basic conditions of welfare economics are violated. First, the marginal return to capital investment is not equalized across different borrowers because each invests to the point at which the return on the least profitable project is equal to the real cost of borrowing as perceived (Leijonhufvud 1977). Second, the marginal return to lenders is not equalized across lenders. Finally, the marginal rates of return on investment are not equalized with savers' subjective marginal rates of discount. Thus a heterogeneity of expectations seriously affects the ability of the bond market to allocate funds in an efficient manner.

Differences in expected inflation and differences between the perceived and realized real rates distort the allocation of funds in comparison to a situation in which no such differences exist. These welfare losses are illustrated graphically in Figure 1, which represents the real stock demand and supply curves of the loans of two loan demanders (firms $a$ and $b$) and two loan suppliers (individuals $c$ and $d$). The demand for funds schedules of different traders represent their (nontransferable) physical investment opportunities, and the supply of funds schedules represent the alternative portfolio investment possibilities as well as the tastes of lenders.

Every point on a given supply curve shows the real rate of return at which the lender is willing to transfer a given amount of funds from other assets to loan assets. Hence, the area between the rate of return that a

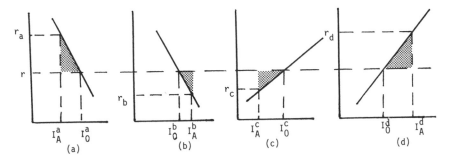

Figure 1 [Reprinted by permission of *Economic Letters* from Cukierman (1978).]

lender gets and the supply curve up to the amount of loans given measures the consumer surplus. Similarly, the area between the demand curve for funds and the real interest rate in the market up to the amount of loans measures the producer's surplus of a typical loan demander. If traders knew in advance the actual rate of inflation $\pi$, they would also know the ex post actually *realized* value of the real rate of interest $r$, because

$$r = n - \pi \tag{5.8}$$

Under these ideal circumstances, traders would have chosen the quantities labeled $I_O^i$, where $i = a, b, c, d$, in Figure 1. Firm $a$ borrows and invests only $I_A^a$, though. It therefore forgoes a producer's surplus measured by the shaded area between $I_O^a$ and $I_A^a$.[4] Firm $b$, on the other hand, invests too much. It therefore also forgoes a producer's surplus measured by the shaded area above the curve between $I_O^b$ and $I_A^b$ in Figure 1(b). Similarly, trader $c$, who is a supplier of funds, lends too little because he or she overestimates the inflation rate and forgoes the surplus measured by the shaded area in Figure 1(c). Lender $d$ underestimates the inflation rate and lends too much. The lender forgoes the surplus measured by the shaded area below the curve in Figure 1(d). It is clear that the larger the divergence between the ex ante real rate $r_i$ and the ex post real rate $r$, the larger the welfare losses of trader $i$ will be in comparison to a full certainty situation in which $r = r_i$. However,

$$r_i - r = n - \pi^*(i) - (n - \pi) = \pi - \pi^*(i) \tag{5.9}$$

so the difference between the ex ante (perceived) real rate and the ex post (actually realized) real rate for trader $i$ depends on the error in the forecast of inflation. As a matter of fact, as shown in Section A1 of the Appendix to this chapter, for a given forecast error $\pi^*(i) - \pi$, the consumer or producer surplus lost by trader $i$ is given by

$$L_i \equiv [\pi^*(i) - \pi]^2 / 2b_i \tag{5.10}$$

In general, given the currently available information, the inflation forecast error is a stochastic variable. In consequence the loss $L_i$ is a stochastic variable, too. A deterministic measure of the total welfare losses in the bond market is the expected value of the sum of the losses in Equation (5.10) over all traders:

$$EL \equiv E \sum_i L_i = \tfrac{1}{2} \sum_i \frac{E[\pi^*(i) - \pi]^2}{b_i} \tag{5.11}$$

If there is no uncertainty about inflation, $EL = 0$. When uncertainty exists, the larger the mean square forecast error is, the larger the loss is. We saw in Section 4 of Chapter 4 that $E[\pi^*(i) - \pi]^2$ is a measure of inflation uncertainty. So the basic message of Equation (5.11) is that the bond market functions less efficiently, the greater the uncertainty associated with future inflation.

Equation (5.10) also suggests that for a given level of inflation uncertainty, welfare losses are larger for traders whose demand for or supply of funds is more sensitive to the real rate of interest ($b_i$ small).

The expected value inside the sum on the right-hand side of Equation (5.11) can be further rewritten as

$$E[\pi^*(i) - \pi]^2 = E[\pi^*(i) - E\pi^* + (E\pi^* - \pi)]^2$$
$$= V_0(\pi^*) + E(\pi - E\pi^*)^2 - 2E[\pi^*(i) - E\pi^*](\pi - E\pi^*) \tag{5.12}$$

where $E\pi^*$ is the overall mean expected inflation across time and across individuals, and

$$V_0(\pi^*) \equiv E[\pi^*(i) - E\pi^*]^2 \tag{5.13}$$

is the *overall* variance of inflationary expectations. This variance differs somewhat from the variance of inflationary expectations investigated in Chapter 4 because it includes the variability of expectations over time as well as over individuals. By contrast, the variances of inflationary expectations from Chapter 4, $V(\pi^*)$ and $V(\pi_L^*)$, measure only the cross-sectional variability of inflationary expectations [cf. Equations (4.9a) and (4.9b)]. The subscript o in $V_0(\pi^*)$ in Equation (5.13) designates it as the combined variance of inflationary expectations over time and over individuals. For the model presented in Chapter 4, $V_0(\pi^*)$ is always larger than $V(\pi^*)$ because in this model the over-time variability of inflationary expectations is not correlated with their cross-sectional variability. As a matter of fact, for the model of Chapter 4,

$$V_0(\pi^*) = V(\pi^*) + V_\epsilon(\pi^*) \tag{5.14}$$

where $V_\epsilon(\pi^*)$ is the over-time variability of inflationary expectations. To see this, note from Equation (4.10) that the overall expected value of $\pi^*$ over the distributions of both $\epsilon$ and $w$ (which correspond, respectively, to the distributions over time and over individuals) is $\delta - \beta$. The overall variance of inflationary expectations is therefore

$$V_0(\pi^*) = E\left[\frac{\gamma\theta(1-\theta)}{1+\gamma\theta}(\epsilon_t + w_t)\right]^2$$

$$= \gamma^2\left[\frac{\theta(1-\theta)}{1+\gamma\theta}\right]^2\sigma_w^2 + \gamma^2\left[\frac{\theta(1-\theta)}{1+\theta\gamma}\right]^2\sigma_x^2 \equiv V(\pi^*) + V_\epsilon(\pi^*)$$

A similar relationship holds for the respective variances of $\pi_L^*$.

Equation (5.14) says that the overall variability of inflationary expectations can be broken down into two components: the over-time variability $V_\epsilon(\pi^*)$ and the cross-sectional variability $V(\pi^*)$, which was the focus of much of the discussion in Chapter 4.

It is instructive to interpret the results of Equations (5.11) and (5.12) in terms of the multimarkets model presented in Chapter 4.[5] Proposition 5(c) of that chapter showed that inflation uncertainty increases when the variance of monetary growth increases. It follows from (5.11) that as the variance of monetary growth increases, welfare losses in the bond market increase as well.

For the model of Chapter 4, $E\pi^* = E\pi = \delta - \beta$. Therefore, the second term on the right-hand side of Equation (5.12) is the variance of the rate of inflation and the third term is the overall covariance between actual and expected rates of inflation. As can be seen by comparing the right-hand sides of Equations (4.10) and (4.13), this covariance is positive because the deviations of $\pi^*(i)$ and $\pi$ from their common mean are both positively related to $\epsilon_t$. It follows from Equations (5.12) and (5.11) that, ceteris paribus, the larger the covariance between actual and expected inflation rates is, the smaller the welfare losses in (5.11) are. These implications are summarized in the following proposition.

**Proposition 1:** *Ceteris paribus and provided $E\pi^* = E\pi$, the total amount of welfare losses (EL) caused by uncertain inflation in the bond market increases in direct proportion to the inflation uncertainty facing traders, the overall variance of inflationary expectations, the variance of actual inflation, and the sensitivity of demands for and supplies of funds to changes in perceived real rates of interest, and is inversely related to the covariance between actual and expected inflation.*

This proposition applies, in particular, to the model of Chapter 4.

In general, the inflation uncertainty that faces individual $i$ is not necessarily equal to the inflation uncertainty that faces other individuals; nor is the variance of the individual inflation forecast around the mean necessarily identical for all individuals. For the model of Chapter 4, these variances are the same for all individuals. Even when these variances differ across individuals, however, an increase in any one of them increases the welfare losses in Equation (5.11).

A ceteris paribus increase in $V(\pi^*)$ increases through Equation (5.14) the overall variance of inflationary expectations $V_o(\pi^*)$, which through (5.12) and (5.11) causes an increase in $EL$. We saw in Chapter 4 that the cross-sectional Livingston variance of inflationary expectations can be used as an estimator of $V(\pi^*)$. This leads to the conclusion that a ceteris paribus increase in the cross-sectional Livingston variance of inflationary expectations increases welfare losses in the bond market. Furthermore, the measure of inflation uncertainty derived in Chapter 4 by combining the Livingston variance and the square of the mean forecast error in (4.24) can be taken to be positively associated with the size of the welfare losses caused by inflation uncertainty in the bond market.

## 5     Effect of differential expectations on the volume of trade in bonds

In a world of uniformly changing expectations, any change in the uniformly held expectation would change only the nominal rate of interest and not the real rate confronted by different individuals. Consequently, there would be no change in positions as a result of the change in inflationary expectations. When expectations are not uniform, however, any change in either their general level or their distribution across individuals will induce a change not only in the nominal rate of interest but in the position of each individual in the capital market as well.

Consider the case in which the current inflationary expectations of two individuals, $a$ and $b$, are 5 percent and 10 percent, respectively. In the following period, $a$'s estimate of future inflation increases to 10 percent and $b$'s decreases to 5 percent. Assuming for simplicity that these offsetting changes do not change the nominal rate of interest, the real rate perceived by $a$ is now lower than before, whereas that perceived by $b$ is higher than before. As a result, $a$ wants to sell some bonds (or issue more if he was a borrower to start with), and $b$ wants to buy more (or borrow less if she was originally a borrower). There is an incentive for $a$ to decrease his portfolio and for $b$ to increase hers. Thus a reallocation of inflationary expectations across individuals generates a positive trading volume in the bond market. It therefore seems intuitively plausible, ceteris paribus, that there will be less trade in loans when expectations change uniformly than when they change in a diffused manner.

An important question in this context is whether this relationship is monotonic. More precisely, what happens to the volume of trade in loan obligations when the overall variability of inflationary expectations increases? To answer this question, we shall focus on the relationship between the desired holdings of bonds of a typical borrower or lender and the variance of inflationary expectations. Substituting Equation (5.6) into (5.1a) and (5.1b) and using the definition of $\bar{\pi}^*$, we get

$$I_B = (1/b_B)\{a_B - R + [\pi^*(B) - \bar{\pi}^*]\} \tag{5.15a}$$

$$I_L = -(1/b_L)\{a_L - R + [\pi^*(L) - \bar{\pi}^*]\} \tag{5.15b}$$

Equations (5.15a) and (5.15b) describe, respectively, the desired level of borrowing of $B$ and the desired level of lending of $L$, each as a function of the deviation of the individual's expected inflation from the average inflation expected by participants in the bond market. These equations make it clear that the variability of lending and borrowing of individual traders depends on the variability of their expectations relative to the average inflation expected in the bond market. Section A2 of the Appendix to this chapter shows that the variance in the position of an individual borrower or lender in the bond market is

$$\text{Var } I_i = \frac{V_0(\pi^*)}{b_i^2}\left\{\left[(1-v_i)^2 + \sum_{s \neq i} v_s^2\right] + \left[\sum_{k \neq j}\sum v_k v_j - 2(1-v_i)\right]\rho\right\}$$

$$\equiv \frac{V_0(\pi^*)}{b_i^2}K(\rho) \tag{5.16}$$

where $\rho$ is the coefficient of correlation between the expectations of different traders.

Section A2 of the Appendix also shows that when $\rho = 1$, the term in braces in the middle of Equation (5.16) is zero, making Var $I_i$ zero as well. This means that when the expectations of different traders are perfectly and positively correlated, the volume of trade shrinks to zero because there is no reason for individuals to change their positions in the bond market. In this case, expectations are uniform across traders and any change in this uniform expectation affects only the Fisher premium and the nominal rate of interest. When $\rho < 1$, the term in braces in the middle of (5.16) is positive (see Section A2 of the Appendix), so that any increase in the overall variance of inflationary expectations $V_0(\pi^*)$ causes an increase in Var $I_i$ and in the volume of trade of the typical trader. The following conclusions may be drawn:

1. The volume of trade in the bond market is positively related to the overall variance of inflationary expectations.
2. For a given variance, the volume of trade is negatively related to the correlation between the inflationary expectations of different traders.
3. Individuals whose demands for (or supplies of) bonds are more sensitive to the perceived real rate will, on average, adjust their portfolios by larger amounts than individuals who are less sensitive to changes in the perceived real rate.

## 6        Effect of differential expectations on unexpected redistribution through the bond market

The accepted wisdom is that perfectly anticipated inflation does not create any unexpected redistribution in the bond market.[6] The nominal rate adjusts so that the real rate obtained by lenders and paid by borrowers is not affected by inflation. When the rate of inflation is not perfectly anticipated, however, there is some unexpected redistribution between borrowers and lenders.

It is customary to measure inflation-induced redistribution in the bond market as the decrease in the real value of debt caused by *total* inflation. This measure clearly overestimates the extent of unexpected redistribution because at least part of it has been compensated for in advance through a higher nominal rate of interest. Thus, conventionally measured redistribution includes two distinct components: expected and unexpected redistributions. Because the first component was anticipated when the loan agreement was made, it represents a voluntary exchange between two parties. The unanticipated component was not part of the deal, and it creates windfall profits or unexpected losses. The second effect is considered socially undesirable because it does not represent a remuneration to productive activity. In a society dominated by risk-averse individuals, total welfare could be increased by reducing the average size of unanticipated redistribution.

When economists talk about the harmful effects of inflation-induced redistributions, they usually have unanticipated redistribution in mind. However, the literature on the redistributive effects of inflation has consistently focused on measuring total rather than unexpected redistribution (e.g., Bach and Ando 1957, Burger 1969, Bach and Stephenson 1974, Wolff 1979). This approach is probably dictated by the paucity of data on price expectations. Because it focuses on an inappropriate concept of redistribution, however, it may give a grossly misleading picture of unexpected redistribution.

In this section we consider the effects of the distributions of inflation and of inflationary expectations on the amount of unexpected redistribution through the bond market. The windfall gains of borrower $B$ are equal to the difference between the real rate he had expected to pay $r_B$ and the realized real rate $r$ multiplied by the total borrowing of this borrower $I_B$. Similarly, the unexpected redistributional gains of lender $L$ are equal to the difference $r - r_L$ multiplied by the total amount of bonds she holds. Hence, the inflation-induced real unexpected gains of borrower $B$ and lender $L$ (real because $I_B$ and $I_L$ are measured in real terms) are given, respectively, by

$$UG_B \equiv (r_B - r)I_B = [\pi - \pi^*(B)]I_B \qquad (5.17a)$$

$$UG_L \equiv (r - r_L)I_L = -[\pi - \pi^*(L)]I_L \qquad (5.17b)$$

where the equalities follow by using the expressions for $r_i$ and $r$ from Equations (5.5) and (5.8), respectively.

Because both actual and expected inflation rates are stochastic, the unanticipated gains of borrowers and lenders are stochastic as well. We can characterize the "size" of these gains by computing the expected value of unexpected redistribution. There are two possible alternative measures. One is the expected value, given that individuals have already chosen their positions in the bond market. The other is the expected value before individuals know their positions in the bond market – that is, before inflationary expectations have been "allocated" to participants in the bond market. The first measure is relevant from the point of view of each individual trader after he or she has taken a position. The second may be relevant from the point of view of an economic planner who is considering whether it is socially desirable to establish a bond market. If the social planner considers any unanticipated redistribution as undesirable but does not know the positions taken by various traders, the second measure should be used.

Assuming that expectations are not systematically biased [that is, $E\pi = E\pi^*(i)$ for all $i$], the expected value of unanticipated gains, *given* the traders' positions, is zero. As can be seen by comparing Equation (5.17a) with (5.17b), this is true for both borrowers and lenders. Given traders' positions, the variance of the unexpected redistribution is a measure of the amount of risk that a trader has to bear from a position in the bond market. This variance is proportional to the variance of $\pi - \pi^*(i)$, which as we saw in Section 4 is a prime determinant of welfare losses in the bond market. [An explicit expression for this variance appears in Equation (5.12).] Hence the same factors that determine the size of welfare losses also determine the variance of unexpected redistribution, given traders' positions. In particular, this variance will change in direct proportion to the overall variance of inflationary expectations and the variance of inflation, and in inverse proportion to the covariance between actual and expected inflation rates.

We turn now to the calculation of the expected value of unexpected redistribution before positions are known. Substituting Equation (5.6) into (5.1a) and (5.1b) and substituting the resulting equations, respectively, into (5.17a) and (5.17b), we obtain

$$UG_B = [\pi - \pi^*(B)]\frac{a_B - R + \pi^*(B) - \sum_s v_s \pi^*(s)}{b_B} \tag{5.18a}$$

$$UG_L = [\pi - \pi^*(L)]\frac{a_L - R + \pi^*(L) - \sum_s v_s \pi^*(s)}{b_L} \tag{5.18b}$$

Because expectations are not systematically biased, the expected value of unanticipated gains for *either* the borrower or the lender before positions are known is

$$EUG = (1/b_i)E\left\{[\pi - \pi^*(i)]\left[\pi^*(i) - \sum_s v_s \pi^*(s)\right]\right\} \tag{5.19}$$

where $i = B, L$.

Part A3 of the Appendix shows that the expected value of the right-hand side of Equation (5.19) is equal to

$$-(1 - v_i)(1 - \rho)V_0(\pi^*) \tag{5.20}$$

Substituting (5.20) into (5.19), we get

$$EUG_i = -(1/b_i)(1 - v_i)(1 - \rho)V_0(\pi^*) \tag{5.21}$$

which is always nonpositive because $v_i < 1$ and $\rho \leqslant 1$.

Equation (5.21) suggests three interesting conclusions:

1. As long as the overall variance of inflationary expectations is positive [i.e., $V_0(\pi^*) > 0$] and there is some degree of nonuniformity in those expectations (i.e., $\rho < 1$), the expected value of windfall gains for the typical trader in the bond market before positions are known is negative.
2. The expected value of windfall losses is an increasing function of the overall variance of inflationary expectations.
3. When expectations are uniform ($\rho = 1$), the expected value of windfall losses is zero. *Actual* losses and gains could be nonzero, but with full uniformity of expectations the *expected value* is zero.

Hence for the bond market as a whole, the expected value of the unanticipated losses of the typical trader before positions are known increases as the overall variance of inflationary expectations increases, whether this increase is caused by cross-sectional or over-time variability.

**Appendix**

A1    *Derivation of Equation (5.10)*

For borrower $i$, it follows from Equation (5.1a) and the definitions of $I_A^i$ and $I_O^i$ implied by Figure 1 that

$$I_A^i = \frac{a_i - r_i}{b_i} = \frac{a_i - [n - \pi^*(i)]}{b_i} \qquad (A5.1)$$

$$I_O^i = \frac{a_i - r}{b_i} = \frac{a_i - (n - \pi)}{b_i} \qquad (A5.2)$$

Each of the shaded areas in Figure 1 is equal analytically to half the rectangle whose sides are $r_i r$ and $I_A^i I_O^i$, where $i = a, b, c, d$. Hence,

$$L_i = \tfrac{1}{2}(r_i - r)(I_A^i - I_O^i) \qquad (A5.3)$$

Subtracting Equation (A5.2) from (A5.1) and canceling terms, we get

$$I_A^i - I_O^i = \frac{\pi^*(i) - \pi}{b_i} \qquad (A5.4)$$

Substituting Equations (5.9) and (A5.4) into (A5.3) yields

$$L_i = \frac{[\pi^*(i) - \pi]^2}{2b_i}$$

which is Equation (5.10) in the text.

A2    *Derivation of Equation (5.16) and proof that* Var $I_i$ *increases in $V_0(\pi^*)$ and decreases in $\rho$*

**A2a**    *Derivation of Equation (5.16):* The variance of either $I_B$ or $I_L$ is, from (5.15),

$$\text{Var } I_i = (1/b_1)^2 \, \text{Var}[\pi^*(i) - \bar{\pi}^*]; \qquad i = B, L \qquad (A5.5)$$

Because by assumption $E\pi^*(i) = E\pi^*$ for all $i$, the variance on the right-hand side of (A5.5) is

$$E[\pi_i^* - E\pi^* - (\bar{\pi}^* - E\pi^*)]^2 = E\left[\pi_i^* - E\pi^* - \sum_s v_s(\pi_s^* - E\pi^*)\right]^2 \qquad (A5.6)$$

where the equality follows by using the definition of $\bar{\pi}^*$ in Equation (5.5). For notational simplicity we let $\pi^*(i) \equiv \pi_i^*$. Rearranging the square in the term on the right-hand side of (A5.6), we get

$$V_0(\pi^*)(1-2v_i) - 2\sum_{s\neq i} v_s \, \mathrm{Cov}(\pi^*) + E\left[\sum_s v_s(\pi_s^* - E\pi^*)\right]^2 \qquad \text{(A5.7)}$$

where

$$V_0(\pi^*) \equiv E(\pi_i^* - E\pi^*)^2 \qquad \text{(A5.8)}$$

and

$$\mathrm{Cov}(\pi^*) \equiv E[(\pi_i^* - E\pi^*)(\pi_j^* - E\pi^*)]; \qquad i\neq j \qquad \text{(A5.9)}$$

Opening the square in the extreme right-hand-side term of (A5.7), passing the expectations operator through, using the fact that $\sum_s v_s = 1$, and rearranging terms, we get

$$\mathrm{Var}[\pi^*(i) - \bar{\pi}^*] = \left[(1-v_i) + \sum_{s\neq i} v_s^2\right] V_0(\pi^*)$$

$$+ \left[\sum_{k\neq j}\sum v_k v_j - 2(1-v_i)\right] \mathrm{Cov}(\pi^*) \qquad \text{(A5.10)}$$

Equation (5.16) follows by factoring out $V_0(\pi^*)$ from the right-hand side of (A5.10), noting that $\rho = \mathrm{Cov}(\pi^*)/V_0(\pi^*)$, and substituting the resulting expression into (A5.5).

**A2b**   *Proof that* $\mathrm{Var}\, I_i$ *increases in* $V_0(\pi^*)$ *and decreases in* $\rho$: For $\rho = 0$, the term in brackets on the right-hand side of Equation (5.16) reduces to

$$K(\rho = 0) \equiv (1-v_i)^2 + \sum_{s\neq i} v_s^2 > 0 \qquad \text{(A5.11)}$$

For $\rho = 1$, this term becomes

$$K(\rho = 1) \equiv (1-v_i)^2 - 2(1-v_i) + \sum_{s\neq i} v_s^2 + \sum_{k\neq j}\sum v_k v_j$$

$$= -(1-v_i)(1+v_i) - v_i^2 + \sum_s v_s^2 + \sum_{k\neq j}\sum v_k v_j$$

$$= -1 + v_i^2 - v_i^2 + \left(\sum_s v_s\right)^2 = 0 \qquad \text{(A5.12)}$$

So as $\rho$ increases from 0 to 1, $K(\rho)$ decreases from a positive number to zero. This can happen only if the coefficient of $\rho$ in $K(\rho)$ is negative, which implies in turn that the minimal value of $K(\rho)$ is achieved when $\rho = 1$. By Equation (A5.12), this minimal value is zero. It follows that for any $\rho < 1$, the term in brackets on the right-hand side of (5.16) is positive, which implies that Var $I_i$ is an increasing function of $V_0(\pi^*)$. Because the coefficient of $\rho$ in Equation (5.16) is negative, an increase in $\rho$ decreases Var $I_i$.

## A3  Derivation of Equation (5.20)

$$E[\pi - \pi^*(i)]\left[\pi^*(i) - \sum_s v_s \pi^*(s)\right]$$

$$= E\{\pi - E\pi - [\pi^*(i) - E\pi^*]\}\left\{\pi^*(i) - E\pi^* - \sum_s v_s[\pi^*(s) - E\pi^*]\right\}$$

$$= \text{Cov}(\pi, \pi^*) - V_0(\pi^*) - E(\pi - E\pi)\left\{\sum_s v_s[\pi^*(s) - E\pi^*]\right\}$$

$$+ E[\pi^*(i) - E\pi^*]\left\{\sum_s v_s[\pi^*(s) - E\pi^*]\right\} \tag{A5.13}$$

where $\text{Cov}(\pi, \pi^*)$ is the (uniform) covariance between actual and expected inflation rates. The last term on the right-hand side of Equation (A5.13) is equal to

$$v_i V_0(\pi^*) + (1 - v_i) \text{Cov}(\pi^*) \tag{A5.14}$$

The penultimate term on the right-hand side of (A5.13) is equal to

$$-\text{Cov}(\pi, \pi^*) \tag{A5.15}$$

Substituting Equations (A5.14) and (A5.15) into (A5.13) and rearranging, we obtain

$$-(1 - v_i)[V_0(\pi^*) - \text{Cov}(\pi^*)] = -(1 - v_i)(1 - \rho)V_0(\pi^*)$$

where $\rho \equiv \text{Cov}(\pi^*)/V_0(\pi^*)$. It follows that

$$E[\pi - \pi^*(i)]\left[\pi^*(i) - \sum_s v_s \pi^*(s)\right] = -(1 - v_i)(1 - \rho)V_0(\pi^*)$$

which is Equation (5.20) in the text.

# CHAPTER 6

# Aggregate–relative confusion: implications for relative price variability

## 1    Introduction and some evidence

A basic postulate of neoclassical economics is that relative prices are determined only by real factors, whereas the general price level depends on the quantity of money. A doubling of the quantity of money will, in this view, double all prices without affecting relative prices. This dichotomy between the determinants of relative prices and those of the general price level is a useful device to organize our thinking about the economy. It should be viewed as a first approximation, however, rather than a full account of the possible relationships between relative prices and the general price level. Recent evidence brought by Glejser (1965) for the Organization for Economic Cooperation and Development (OEDC) countries, Vining and Elwertowski (1976) and Parks (1978) for the United States, Blejer (1981) for Argentina, Hercowitz (1981) for Germany, Blejer and Leiderman (1982) for Mexico, and Fischer (1981a, 1982) for the United States and Germany suggests that changes in the general level of prices are not really independent of changes in relative prices.[1]

This evidence raises two basic questions. One concerns the direction of causality between relative price changes and changes in the general price level. The other can be stated as follows: Is it necessary to totally abandon the idea that there is a dichotomy between the determinants of general and relative prices to explain their observed relationship, or is there hope of explaining it by an appropriate modification of the dichotomy paradigm? The answer to the first question has not yet been definitely determined [although Fischer (1981a, 1982) presents evidence that there is two-way causality] and is not discussed here. As to the second question, this chapter advances the view that incomplete information caused by the aggregate–relative confusion can explain interrelationships between general and relative price changes even within an economy that is basically dichotomized.

Vining and Elwertowski (1976) suggest a measure of relative price variability that is based on the cross-sectional variance of rates of change of individual prices around the general rate of inflation. They use data on the individual components of the consumer price index (CPI) and the wholesale price index (WPI) in the United States to construct time series for the variance of relative price change in the postwar period. They then compare this measure of relative price variability with the instability of the general rate of inflation in each period. Their basic finding is that the instability in the general rate of inflation tends to be positively related to the variance of the relative price change. A similar result is obtained by Padoa-Schioppa (1979) for Italy during the period 1954–76. Section 2 explains this relationship in terms of the aggregate–relative confusion.

Section 3 focuses on the relationship between the relative price variability and the cross-sectional variance of inflationary expectations. The relationship of the relative price variability to inflation uncertainty is discussed briefly in Section 4. Sections 5 and 6 focus on the effects of the aggregate–relative confusion on relative price variability when supply elasticities differ across markets. A brief survey of other approaches appears in Section 7.

## 2    Relative price variability and the variability of inflation[2]

Within the framework of the model of Chapters 3 and 4, the relative price in market $w$ at time $t$ is, from Equation (4.2),

$$p_t(w_t) = Q_t + w_t/(1+\gamma\theta) \tag{6.1}$$

where $w_t$ is the realization of the relative demand shock in that market in period $t$. From Equation (4.3), the variance of this expression is

$$\tau^2 = \sigma_w^2/(1+\gamma\theta)^2 \tag{6.2}$$

Because $\theta$ is a decreasing function of $\sigma_x^2$, it follows that the variance of relative prices $\tau^2$ is an increasing function of the variance of the rate of change in nominal income $\sigma_x^2$. Because $\sigma_x^2$ also represents the variance of the rate of monetary expansion, it follows that the variability of relative prices increases with the variability of monetary expansion. The origin of the positive relationship between the variance of relative prices and $\sigma_x^2$ can be understood intuitively by expressing the cyclical component of output from Equation (3.3b) as

$$y_{ct}(w_t) = \gamma\theta[p_t(w_t) - Q_t] + a\epsilon_t \tag{6.3}$$

This equation relates the cyclical component of output in market $w_t$ to the relative price in that market. It is obtained by adding and subtracting the term $a\epsilon_t$ to Equation (3.3b) and by using (3.17) and (3.23b). Because it reflects the behavior of producers, it is a supply curve. The coefficient $\gamma\theta$ measures the elasticity of the response of output to the actual relative price in the market. This elasticity depends on $\theta$, which is inversely related

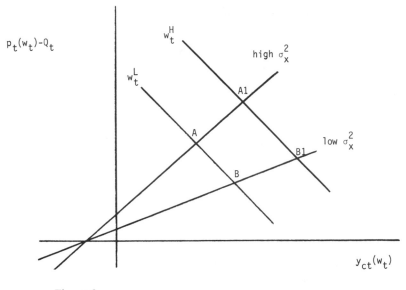

Figure 2

to the variance of the aggregate monetary shock $\sigma_x^2$. The higher this variance, the smaller the portion of any actual relative price that individuals interpret as a change in the relative price of the good they sell. This phenomenon arises because of the aggregate–relative confusion: Suppliers in market $w_t$ do not know the current actual general price level $Q_t$. They therefore guess it, using all the information currently available to them. When $\sigma_x^2$ is high, they tend to attribute most of the movement in $p_t(w_t)$ to general monetary shocks, and $\theta$ is therefore low. When $\sigma_x^2$ is low, they attribute most of the changes they observe in $p_t(w_t)$ to specific relative demand factors, and $\theta$ tends to be be high.

The typical supply curve from Equation (6.3) is depicted in the $y_{ct}$; $[p_t(w_t) - Q_t]$ plane in Figure 2. The figure shows two supply curves corresponding to two alternative values of $\sigma_x^2$. The steeper curve corresponds to a higher variance of monetary expansion $\sigma_x^2$, reflecting the Lucas hypothesis on the slope of the Phillips curve. The equilibrium levels of the relative price and the cyclical component of output in market $w_t$ can be located in the figure by adding a demand schedule. Subtracting $y_{nt}$ from both sides of Equation (3.4) and adding and subtracting $Q_t$ from the right-hand side, we obtain

$$y_{ct}^d(w_t) = y_t^d(w_t) - y_{nt} = x_t - Q_t - y_{nt} - [p_t(w_t) - Q_t] + w_t$$

Using Equations (3.15), (3.16), (3.17), and (3.23b) and rearranging, we can rewrite this as

$$y_{ct}^d(w_t) + p_t(w_t) - Q_t = a\epsilon_t + w_t \qquad (6.4)$$

which is a demand curve in the $y_{ct}(w_t)$; $p_t(w_t) - Q_t$ plane. Two such demand curves for two different realizations of $w_t$ in two different markets are drawn in Figure 2. When $\sigma_x^2$ is low, the market with a relatively low realization of the relative demand shock $w_t^L$ is in equilibrium at point $B$, whereas the market with a high relative demand $w_t^H$ is in equilibrium at point $B1$. For the high value of $\sigma_x^2$, the corresponding equilibrium points for the *same* realizations of $\epsilon_t$ and of the two relative demand shocks are $A$ and $A1$, respectively. It is easily seen that for the low value of $\sigma_x^2$, the difference between the relative prices in the two markets is small in comparison to their difference when $\sigma_x^2$ is high. As $\sigma_x^2$ increases, the typical supply curve becomes steeper. As a result a given vector of relative demand shock realizations causes more dispersion in relative prices and less dispersion in the cyclical components of output across markets. Basically, by influencing the slope of the supply curve in Figure 2, the magnitude of $\sigma_x^2$ determines whether a given distribution of relative demand shocks across markets causes much dispersion in relative prices with little dispersion in the cyclical components of output, or little relative price variability with a lot of dispersion in the cyclical components of output across markets.

Suppose now that $\sigma_w^2$ is constant, whereas $\sigma_x^2$ changes over time. As a result both $\theta$ and $\tau^2$ become time-dependent. To stress this dependence, we rewrite Equations (6.1) and (6.2) as

$$p_t(w_t) - Q_t = w_t/(1 + \gamma\theta_t) \qquad (6.1a)$$

$$\tau_t^2 = \sigma_w^2/(1 + \gamma\theta_t)^2 \qquad (6.2a)$$

Lagging Equation (6.1a) by one period and subtracting it from (6.1a), we obtain

$$p_t(w_t) - Q_t - [p_{t-1}(w_{t-1}) - Q_{t-1}] = \frac{w_t}{1 + \gamma\theta_t} - \frac{w_{t-1}}{1 + \gamma\theta_{t-1}} \qquad (6.5)$$

This equation represents the change in relative prices between periods $t-1$ and $t$ in a market that sustains relative demand shocks $w_t$ and $w_{t-1}$ in periods $t$ and $t-1$, respectively. Because $w_t$ and $w_{t-1}$ are statistically independent, the variance of the relative price change $V_t(\pi^R)$ is

$$V_t(\pi^R) = \sigma_w^2[(1 + \gamma\theta_t)^{-2} + (1 + \gamma\theta_{t-1})^{-2}] = \tau_t^2 + \tau_{t-1}^2 \qquad (6.6)$$

In other words, the variance of the relative price change in period $t$ is equal to the sum of the variances of relative price levels in periods $t-1$ and $t$. Because $\tau_t^2$ is positively related to $\sigma_{xt}^2$ and $\tau_{t-1}^2$ is positively related to $\sigma_{x,t-1}^2$, it follows that the variance of the relative price change in Equation (6.6) is positively related to both $\sigma_{xt}^2$ and $\sigma_{x,t-1}^2$. For a large number of markets the cross-sectional variance of the relative price change computed by Vining and Elwertowski (1976) is an empirical measure of $V_t(\pi^R)$.

We saw in Chapter 4 that the variance of inflation is positively related to $\sigma_x^2$ as well. Taken together with the argument developed here, this leads to the following proposition.

**Proposition 1:** *If the variance of relative demand shocks $\sigma_w^2$ is constant and the variance of the rate of change in nominal income $\sigma_x^2$ changes over time, then over time there will be*

(a)   *a positive association between the variance of the relative price change $V(\pi^R)$ and the variance of the rate of inflation $V(\pi)$;*

(b)   *a positive association between the variance of relative prices $\tau^2$ and the variance of inflation $V(\pi)$; and*

(c)   *a positive association between $\tau^2$ and $V(\pi^R)$ on the one hand and the variance of monetary growth $\sigma_x^2$ on the other.*

Part (a) of this proposition is the association discovered empirically by Vining and Elwertowski (1976). Thus, the aggregate–relative confusion explains the positive association between general and relative price variability even within an economy that is otherwise dichotomized.

To demonstrate this point more sharply, it is instructive to compare the results of Proposition 1 with the result that holds when there is no aggregate–relative confusion. In this case, individuals in all markets have perfect information about the current price level. As explained in Section 2 of Chapter 3, the relative price in market $w_t$ is then

$$p_t(w_t) - Q_t = w_t/(1+\gamma) \qquad (6.7)$$

Equation (6.7) is (3.9) with the market index $v$ replaced by the realization of the relative demand shock in that market $w_t$. Because $Q_t$ is known in period $t$, (6.7) also represents the perceived relative price, so that the cyclical component of output is

$$y_{ct}(w_t) = \gamma[p_t(w_t) - Q_t] \qquad (6.8)$$

as in (3.3), and is independent of $\sigma_x^2$. Thus, when there is no aggregate–relative confusion, the slope of the supply curve in Figure 2 is independent of monetary variability. As a result, relative price variability is also independent of monetary variability. This can be seen formally too by noting from Equation (6.7) that in this case the variance of relative prices is $\sigma_x^2/(1+\gamma)^2$, which does not depend on $\sigma_x^2$.

This amplifies the fact that the crucial element responsible for the positive relationship between relative price variability and $\sigma_x^2$ is the aggregate–relative confusion. Without this confusion, individuals in all markets know the current value of the general price level exactly, and the distribution of relative prices is independent of monetary variability. This is not surprising, since the deterministic part of the model of Chapters 3 and 4 is dichotomized. Within this dichotomized framework the relationship between relative price variability and monetary variability is obtained by appealing to incomplete information about the general price level in local markets. Although the economy is basically dichotomized, incomplete information creates a link between monetary variability and relative price variability. The theory presented here takes the view that most of the changes in relative price variability are induced by policy: Shifts in the variability of monetary policy cause changes in the distribution of relative prices. The implication of this theory is that causality runs from monetary variability to relative price variability.

## 3      Relative price variability and the cross-sectional variance of inflationary expectations

We saw in Section 3 of Chapter 4 that the variance of inflationary expectations $V(\pi_L^*)$ is an increasing function of $\sigma_x^2$. We also saw that, subject to the condition in Proposition 3 of Chapter 4, the variance of inflationary expectations $V(\pi^*)$ is also an increasing function of $\sigma_x^2$. These results, together with Proposition 1(c) of this chapter, lead to the following proposition.

**Proposition 2:** *If the variance of relative demand shocks $\sigma_w^2$ is constant and the variance of the rate of change in nominal income $\sigma_x^2$ changes over time, then:*

(a) *the Livingston variance of inflationary expectations $V(\pi_L^*)$ is positively related to both the variance of relative prices $\tau^2$ and the variance of relative price change $V(\pi^R)$; and*

(b) *if in addition $\sigma^2/\tau^2 < \sqrt{1+\gamma}$, the variance of inflationary expectations $V(\pi^*)$ is also positively related to both $\tau^2$ and $V(\pi^R)$.*

Cukierman and Wachtel (1982a) have shown that Proposition 2 remains true even when the model is generalized to include an aggregate supply shock and an interaction term between the aggregate supply and demand shocks in addition to the aggregate demand shock $\Delta x$. Examining the evidence for the United States, they use two proxies for the variability of relative prices and two for the variance of inflationary expectations. The two proxies for relative price variance are from Parks (1978) and Vining and Elwertowski (1976). Both calculate the cross-sectional variance of the annual rates of change in the prices of individual com-

Table 4. *Coefficients of correlation between the variance of a relative price change and the variance of inflationary expectations*

| Relative price change | Inflationary expectations | Time period | Correlation |
|---|---|---|---|
| Vining–Elwertowski | Livingston | 1948–74 | 0.518[a] |
| Parks | Livingston | 1947–75 | 0.263 |
| Vining–Elwertowski | SRC | 1966–74 | 0.963[a] |
| Parks | SRC | 1966–75 | 0.863[a] |

[a] Statistically significant at the 0.01 level.
*Source:* Cukierman and Wachtel (1982a: Table 1).

modities around some measure of the general rate of inflation. Parks's Table 3 shows the variance in the annual rate of change in relative prices among the 12 components of the implicit price deflator for personal consumption expenditures for the period 1930–75. Vining and Elwertowski's Table 2 provides a broader-based measure, showing the variance of the relative price change across individual items in the CPI. The number of items used in the computation of each variance varies from 110 to 311 over their sample period (1948–74). The two proxies for the variance of inflationary expectations are the Livingston variance and the SRC variance of inflationary expectations, both of which were discussed at the beginning of Chapter 4. Note that all the variances just described are measured cross-sectionally, so an observation on each variance is available for each time period. Each proxy for the variance of inflationary expectations can therefore be matched with each proxy for the variance of the relative price change.

Coefficients of correlation between the measure of variance of the relative price change $V_t(\pi^R)$ and of the dispersion of inflationary expectations $V_t(\pi^*)$ and $V_t(\pi_L^*)$ are shown in Table 4. The results confirm the hypothesis that there is a positive and significant correlation between the variance of the relative price change and the variance of inflationary expectations across households. The only exception is for the correlation between the Parks measure of $V_t(\pi^R)$ and the Livingston measure of $V_t(\pi_L^*)$, which is positive but not significant.

The relationship is strongest with the Vining and Elwertowski measure for $V_t(\pi^R)$ and the SRC measure of $V_t(\pi^*)$. This may be because the Vining and Elwertowski measure is the variance among a much larger number of items in the price index than the Parks measure is. (The Parks

variances are weighted variances, however, whereas the Vining and Elwertowski variances are not.) Moreover, it measures the variability of
consumer prices, and the surveys of expected inflation also pertain to
consumer prices. In addition the SRC measure of inflationary expectations, which is based on a wider sample, is more representative of the
general population, whereas Livingston surveys a relatively small number
of professional forecasters and economists. This could explain why the
coefficients of correlation with the Livingston measure of $V_t(\pi_L^*)$ are generally smaller and less significant.

Cukierman and Wachtel (1982a) show that for the extended model that
includes an aggregate supply shock as well as an aggregate demand shock
the expressions for the variance of relative prices (4.3) and the Livingston
variance of inflationary expectations (4.9a) become, respectively,

$$\tau^2 = \frac{(\sigma_a^2 + \sigma_w^2)^2 \sigma_w^2}{[\sigma_a^2 + (1+\gamma)\sigma_w^2]^2} \tag{6.9}$$

$$V(\pi_L^*) = \frac{\sigma_a^4 \sigma_w^2}{(\sigma_a^2 + \sigma_w^2)^2} \tag{6.10}$$

where

$$\sigma_a^2 \equiv \sigma_x^2 + \sigma_u^2 - 2\rho\sigma_x\sigma_u \tag{6.11}$$

In this expression, $\sigma_u^2$ is the variance of the stochastic rate of change of
productivity and $\rho$ is the coefficient of correlation between the shock to
the rate of change of aggregate demand and the shock to the rate of
change of aggregate productivity. Note that Equations (6.9) and (6.10)
are identical to (4.3) and (4.9a) with $\sigma_x^2$ replaced by $\sigma_a^2$ from (6.11). Hence
all the statements of Proposition 2 still hold with $\sigma_x^2$ replaced by $\sigma_a^2$. In
particular, if $\sigma_w^2$ is constant and both $\sigma_x^2$ and $\sigma_u^2$ change over time, we
should expect to find a positive association between $\tau^2$ and $V(\pi_L^*)$ over
time.

Examination of Equations (6.9) and (6.10) reveals that $\tau^2$ and $V(\pi_L^*)$
are nonlinear functions of the exogenous variance $\sigma_x^2$ and $\sigma_u^2$. A sharper
test of the association between $\tau^2$ and $V(\pi_L^*)$ due to their common dependence on the exogenous variance $\sigma_x^2$ and $\sigma_u^2$ can be obtained by estimating
(6.9) and (6.10) and finding how much of this association is explainable
in terms of changes in $\sigma_x^2$ and $\sigma_u^2$.

To answer this question, Cukierman and Wachtel (1982a) estimated
Equations (6.9) and (6.10) as a system of two nonlinear equations consid-
ering $\tau^2$, $V(\pi_L^*)$, $\sigma_x^2$, and $\sigma_u^2$ as variables and $\sigma_w^2$, $\gamma$, and $\rho$ as parameters
to be estimated. The variable $\tau^2$ was derived from the Parks variance of
relative price change, $V(\pi_L^*)$ was proxied by the Livingston variance of

inflationary expectations, $\sigma_x^2$ by the moving variance of the rate of change in the gross national product (GNP), and $\sigma_u^2$ by an eight-quarter moving variance of the rate of change in real output per worker-hour in the private business sector.

Three alternative nested versions of the model of Equations (6.9) and (6.10) were estimated and the proportion of the correlation between $\tau^2$ and $V(\pi_L^*)$ explainable in terms of the variation in $\sigma_x^2$ and $\sigma_u^2$ was computed for each. The three versions were (1) the full model, (2) the full model with $\rho$ constrained to be zero, and (3) the full model with $\rho$ and $\sigma_u^2$ constrained to be zero. For the last case, the model reduces to the model of Chapters 3 and 4 that does not feature an aggregate supply shock. The proportion of correlation between $\tau^2$ and $V(\pi_L^*)$ explainable in terms of the variation in $\sigma_x^2$ and $\sigma_u^2$ was 36 percent for model 1, 29 percent for model 2, and 53 percent for (the simpler) model 3.

Similar results were obtained when linear approximations of Equations (6.9) and (6.10) were taken prior to estimation. In general these results suggest that up to half the correlation between the variance of relative prices and the Livingston variance of expected inflation can be attributed to changes over time in the variance of aggregate supply and demand shocks.

## 4      Relative price variability and inflation uncertainty

We saw in Proposition 5(c) of Chapter 4 that inflation uncertainty is positively related to the variance of monetary growth $\sigma_x^2$. In conjunction with Proposition 1(c), this leads to the following proposition.

**Proposition 3:** *If $\sigma_w^2$ is constant and $\sigma_x^2$ changes over time, the variance of relative prices and the variance of the relative price change are both positively associated with inflation uncertainty.*

Stated slightly differently, Proposition 3 says that an increase in monetary variability increases both the dispersion of relative prices and inflation uncertainty.

## 5      Effect of different supply elasticities on relative price variability

So far we have implicitly assumed that all supply elasticities are the same. When this assumption is relaxed and differing supply elasticities are allowed in different markets, the absolute size of the random aggregate shock $\epsilon_t$ becomes one determinant of relative price variability. With unanticipated money growth or unanticipated inflation in conjunction with different supply elasticities across markets, relative price variability becomes directly dependent on the absolute size of these unanticipated shocks.

This hypothesis is developed and tested by Parks (1978) and Hercowitz (1981, 1982) within similar but not identical frameworks. Both use multi-market equilibrium models; however, Parks uses a nonstochastic model and a measure of unanticipated price inflation for the surprise variable, whereas Hercowitz uses a stochastic model of the Barro (1976) type and a measure of unanticipated *money* growth as the surprise variable. The prediction of both models is that the variance of the relative price change should be positively related to the unanticipated nominal shock, taken by Parks as unanticipated inflation and by Hercowitz as unanticipated monetary growth. Parks finds that for the United States there is a significant positive association between the variance of the relative price change and unanticipated price inflation squared. Hercowitz (1981) finds that during the period of hyperinflation in Germany there was a significant positive association between the variance of the relative price change and the second power of unanticipated monetary growth. Application of the same model to the postwar U.S. economy (Hercowitz 1982), however, failed to be substantiated.

In this section a mechanism that explains the effect of nominal shocks on relative price dispersion is presented. This is done within the framework of the basic model of Chapter 3, which differs from the Parks model in that it is stochastic and it incorporates the aggregate–relative confusion explicitly. In those respects it is similar in spirit, though not in structural detail, to the model used by Hercowitz.

To incorporate differing supply elasticities across markets, the cyclical component of output from Equation (3.3) is respecified as

$$y_{ct}(v, w_t) = \gamma(v)[p_t(v, w_t) - Q_t^*(v, w_t)]; \qquad \gamma(v) > 0 \qquad (6.12)$$

where $w_t$ is implicitly understood to be the relative demand shock realized in market $v$ at time $t$. The basic difference between this specification and that of Chapter 3 is that the elasticity of supply $\gamma$ depends on the market index $v$. As a result, the equilibrium values of the cyclical component of output, the local price, and the general price level as perceived in the market all become dependent on the market index $v$ as well as on $w_t$. The dependence on $w_t$ will now be subsumed in the notation so that $y_{ct}(v, w_t)$ will be written as $y_{ct}(v)$, and similarly for the other variables. The demand function remains as in Equation (3.4).

Because expectations are rational, the actual and perceived structures of the economy have to be the same. Technically this means that the expected value of the current general price level has to be determined simultaneously with the equilibrium values of the other variables. This could be done in two ways. One way would be to guess a solution for the perceptions of individuals about the economy and show that, given these perceptions, people act in a way that actually makes those perceptions correct up to a random shock. This is the route followed in Section 3a of Chapter 3. Another way would be to use the method of undetermined coefficients as in Lucas (1973), which is more systematic. The solutions obtained for the equilibrium values of individual prices and the general price level using this latter method are derived in Section A1 of the Appendix to this chapter. They are, respectively,

$$p_t(v) = \bar{Q}_t + \lambda(\theta)[1 + \theta F(v)](\epsilon_t + w_t) \tag{6.13}$$

$$Q_t = \bar{Q}_t + \lambda(\theta)\epsilon_t \tag{6.14}$$

where $\bar{Q}_t = x_{t-1} + \delta - \alpha - \beta t$, as in Equation (3.16); and

$$\lambda(\theta) \equiv \frac{1}{1 + \bar{\gamma}\theta}; \qquad \bar{\gamma} \equiv \sum_v \frac{u(v)/[1 + \gamma(v)]}{\sum_v u(v)/[1 + \gamma(v)]} \tag{6.15a}$$

$$F(v) \equiv \frac{\bar{\gamma} - \gamma(v)}{1 + \gamma(v)} \tag{6.15b}$$

for all $v$. Note that $\bar{\gamma}$ is a weighted average of the supply elasticities in the different markets of the economy. As shown in Section A2 of the Appendix, the general price level as currently perceived in market $v$ becomes

$$Q_t^*(v) = [1 - \theta(v)]p_t(v) + \theta(v)\bar{Q}_t \tag{6.16}$$

where

$$\theta(v) \equiv \frac{1 + F(v)}{1 + \theta F(v)}\theta; \qquad 0 \leqslant \theta(v) \leqslant 1 \tag{6.16a}$$

It can be seen from Equation (6.16) that as in the case of uniform supply elasticities, $Q_t^*(v)$ is a weighted average of the individual market price $p_t(v)$ and of the common information summarized in $\bar{Q}_t$. However, the weights assigned to $p_t(v)$ and $\bar{Q}_t$ depend on the market index $v$. This dependence is a direct consequence of the fact that supply elasticities differ across markets. To see this, note from (6.15b) that when supply elasticities are identical, $F(v) = 0$, and Equations (6.16) and (6.16a) reduce respectively to (3.12) and (3.12a) because in this case $\theta = \theta(v)$ for all $v$.

To understand the new element introduced into the weighting of Equation (6.16) by different supply elasticities, note that by substituting (6.15b) into (6.16a) and rearranging, we have

$$\theta(v) = \frac{1+\bar{\gamma}}{1+\theta\bar{\gamma}+(1-\theta)\gamma(v)} \theta \qquad (6.16b)$$

from which it follows that the weight given to the current price in market $v$, $1-\theta(v)$, is an increasing function of the elasticity of supply in the market. This can be understood intuitively as follows: The more elastic the supply in a market, the less a given perceived relative demand shock affects the price in this market. Because of the aggregate–relative confusion, unanticipated monetary growth is partly interpreted as a relative demand shock. In a market with a large supply elasticity, a given monetary surprise has a large output response and a small price response. Individuals in such a market, knowing that even small fluctuations in the local price may be associated with a sizable change in the money supply and the general price level, therefore give a relatively large weight to their observations of the local price.

By contrast, in a market with a low elasticity of supply, the same aggregate monetary surprise causes a large movement in the local price. Individuals therefore give less weight to the price in this market as an indicator of the currently unknown general price level. In markets where the supply elasticity is equal to the mean elasticity $\bar{\gamma}$, the term $\theta(v)=\theta$. This implies that the weighting of local and aggregate information used for expectation formation in markets with the mean supply elasticity $\bar{\gamma}$ in an economy with divergent elasticities is the same as the uniform weighting of those two pieces of information in an economy with identical elasticities [compare Equations (6.16) and (6.16a) for $\theta(v)=\theta$ with (4.1a)].

The relative price in market $v$ can be obtained by subtracting Equation (6.14) from (6.13):

$$p_t(v) - Q_t = \lambda(\theta)\theta F(v)\epsilon_t + \lambda(\theta)[1+\theta F(v)]w_t \qquad (6.17)$$

Note that when supply elasticities are equal,

$$F(v) = 0; \qquad \lambda(\theta) = \frac{1}{1+\gamma\theta} \qquad (6.18)$$

for all $v$, and Equation (6.17) reduces to (6.1). So when there are no differences in supply elasticities, relative prices are unaffected by the *level* of the shock to the rate of monetary expansion $\epsilon_t$. When supply elasticities differ, however, $F(v) \neq 0$. In this case, $\epsilon_t$ affects relative prices in direct proportion to the size of $F(v)$.

As can be seen from Equation (6.15b), $F(v)$ depends on the deviation of the elasticity of supply in market $v$ from the mean elasticity $\bar{\gamma}$. Hence $F(v)$ is a measure of the extent to which the supply elasticity in market $v$

deviates from some economy-wide average. The effect of $\epsilon_t$ on relative prices is thus directly related to divergences in supply elasticities across markets. Furthermore, the effect of a given aggregate shock $\epsilon_t$ on the relative price in market $v$ will be positively correlated with the divergence between the supply elasticity in market $v$ and the mean economy-wide elasticity.

When the number of markets is large, the cross-sectional realizations of $w_t$ in the various markets constitute a good approximation for the theoretical distribution of $w$. The variance of relative prices can therefore be defined as the expected value, over the distribution of $w$, of the weighted mean square percentage deviation of prices in individual markets from the general price level:

$$\tau_t^2 \equiv E_w \sum_v u(v)[p_t(v) - Q_t]^2 \tag{6.19}$$

Because all prices are measured in logarithms, $p(v) - Q_t$ is a percentage deviation. Substituting Equation (6.17) into (6.19), opening the square, and noting that the expected value of $w$ is zero, we find that the variance of relative prices becomes

$$\tau_t^2 = \sum_v u(v)[\lambda(\theta)]^2 [1 + \theta F(v)]^2 \sigma_w^2 + \sum_v u(v)[\lambda(\theta)\theta F(v)]^2 \epsilon_t^2 \tag{6.20}$$

Note first that when all elasticities are equal [i.e., $F(v) = 0$], the second term in (6.20) vanishes and the first, using (6.18), reduces to (6.2), which is the variance of relative prices when all supply elasticities are equal. Thus the new element here is the second term, which says that the larger $\epsilon_t^2$ is, the larger the relative price dispersion is. Note also that the larger the dispersion of supply elasticities across markets (as measured by the coefficient of $\epsilon_t^2$), the larger is the relative price dispersion induced by a given realization of $\epsilon_t^2$.

The effect of unanticipated nominal growth on relative price dispersion can be understood intuitively when the cyclical component of output in Equation (6.12) is rewritten as

$$y_{ct}(v) = \gamma(v)\theta(v)[p_t(v) - Q_t] + \gamma(v)\theta(v)\lambda(\theta)\epsilon_t \tag{6.21}$$

[Equation (6.21) is obtained by substituting (6.16) into (6.12), canceling terms, adding and subtracting $\gamma(v)\lambda(\theta)\theta\epsilon_t$ to the right-hand side of the resulting expression, and using (6.14).] It relates the cyclical component of output supplied in market $v$ to the actual relative price in that market. It can therefore be plotted in the relative price–cyclical output plane as was done in Figure 2. Section A3 of the Appendix shows that the demand curve for the cyclical component of output in market $v$ can be written, analogously to (6.4), as

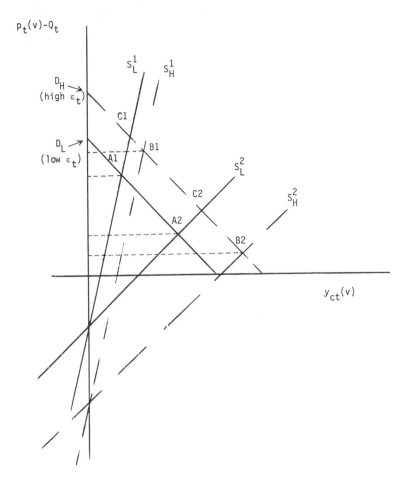

Figure 3

$$y_{ct}^{d}(v) + p_t(v) - Q_t = [1 - \lambda(\theta)]\epsilon_t + w_t \qquad (6.22)$$

This is a 45-degree negatively sloped demand curve in the $[p_t(v) - Q_t]$, $y_{ct}(v)$ plane whose position is determined by the realization of the aggregate shock $\epsilon_t$ and the relative shock $w_t$.

The demand and supply curves of Equations (6.21) and (6.22) are drawn in Figure 3. The basic distinction between Figures 3 and 2 is that in Figure 3 the supply curves of different markets have different elasticities even for a given $\sigma_x^2$. Because we are going to investigate the effects of a change in $\epsilon_t$, we have to take into consideration that a change in $\epsilon_t$ affects supply schedules as well as demand schedules. The two upward-sloping solid lines are supply curves in two different markets for a relatively low value of $\epsilon_t$. The two upward-sloping broken lines represent the supply curves of the same two markets for a high value of $\epsilon_t$. In general the curve labeled $S_j^i$, where $j =$ L, H and $i = 1, 2$, represents the supply curve of market $i$ when $\epsilon_t$ is in state of nature $j$. Because the supply curves of the two markets have different elasticities, they appear in Figure 3 as two straight lines with different slopes. They must thus intersect once. Section A4 of the Appendix shows that this intersection always lies at the point $y_{ct}(1) = y_{ct}(2) = 0$, and $p_t(1) - Q_t = p_t(2) - Q_t = -\lambda(\theta)\epsilon_t$ for any given value of the aggregate demand shock $\epsilon_t$. This means that the two supply curves always intersect along the ordinate. Furthermore, for positive values of $\epsilon_t$ the intersection occurs at negative values of the relative price, and the higher $\epsilon_t$ is, the lower the point of intersection is. To focus on the dispersion element introduced by different supply elasticities, it is assumed that the realizations of the relative demand shocks $w$ in both markets are equal to zero. The demand curves in both markets are thus identical and equal to

$$y_{ct}^d(v) + p_t(v) - Q_t = [1 - \lambda(\theta)]\epsilon_t \qquad (6.22a)$$

Two such demand curves for alternative positive values of $\epsilon_t$ are shown in Figure 3. The curve $D_L$ is the demand facing both markets when $\epsilon_t$ is low. The curve labeled $D_H$ is the demand facing both markets when $\epsilon_t$ is high.

The stage is now set to consider the effect of an increase in the unanticipated nominal shock on the relative price variability. When $\epsilon_t$ is positive but relatively low, market 1 is in equilibrium at point $A1$ and market 2 at point $A2$. The vertical distance between these two points along the relative price axis measures the degree of price dispersion between the two markets. Now $\epsilon_t$ goes up to a higher value. As a result, demand in both markets goes up to $D_H$, and the supply curves in markets 1 and 2 become $S_H^1$ and $S_H^2$, respectively. The new equilibrium points are $B1$ in market 1 and $B2$ in market 2. Again the distance between these two points along the relative price axis measures the degree of price dispersion between the two markets for the higher value of $\epsilon_t$. This vertical distance clearly increases with $\epsilon_t$.

To gain a further understanding of the mechanism behind this result, it is convenient to perform the shift from points $A1$ and $A2$ to points $B1$ and $B2$ in two stages. In the first stage, the change in $\epsilon_t$ is allowed to shift the demand curve but not the supply curves. In the second the change in $\epsilon_t$ is allowed to shift the supply curves as well. After the first stage, the two markets are in equilibrium at points $C1$ and $C2$, respectively. The relative prices of both markets have increased, but the increase is greater in the market where the price was originally higher because this market has a steeper supply curve, and the demand curve shifts parallel to its original position. So without the shift in the supply curves, relative price dispersion increases. In stage two, the *uniform* downward shifts of the supply curves are recognized. The relative prices in both markets go down, but the relative price of market 1 (which is higher) goes down by less because the supply curve of this market is steeper. Both supply curves shift parallel to their original positions. As can be seen by comparing the vertical distance between $C1$ and $C2$ with the vertical distance between $B1$ and $B2$ in Figure 3, the result is a further increase in the relative price dispersion. Thus the relative price dispersion increases both because of the shift that an increase in $\epsilon_t$ induces in the demand curves and because of the shift that it induces in the supply curves.

Both these shifts, however, are caused by the aggregate–relative confusion: An increase in $\epsilon_t$ (even without any change in $w_t$, which is held at zero) is partially interpreted as an increase in the relative price in both markets. Because in both markets $w_t$ is held to zero, the perceived relative price increases by the same amount in both. In market 2, which has a high supply elasticity, this change in perception causes a large increase in output and therefore a relatively small increase in relative price. In market 1, with the low supply elasticity, the same change causes a small increase in output and therefore a relatively high increase in relative price. Thus an increase in the unanticipated nominal shock $\epsilon_t$ increases relative prices more in markets with low elasticities of supply. It is intuitively obvious that the greater the disparity between the elasticities of supply in the different markets, the larger will be the relative price dispersion induced through this mechanism for a given $\epsilon_t$. This provides an intuitive explanation for the variance-like form of the coefficient of $\epsilon_t^2$ in Equation (6.20).

We may sum up by saying that when supply elasticities differ across markets, relative price variance is caused by two elements: One corresponds to the first term on the right-hand side of (6.20) and is caused by different realizations of the relative demand shocks across markets. The other corresponds to the second term on the right-hand side of (6.20) and is caused by the interaction of different supply elasticities across markets with the aggregate–relative confusion.

## 6    Effects of monetary variability on relative price variability when supply elasticities differ

Section 2 of this chapter showed that when supply elasticities are uniform, an increase in monetary variability $\sigma_x^2$ increases the relative price variability. We shall now try to determine whether the same result carries over to the case of nonuniform elasticities.

This analysis is a bit more complicated because $\sigma_x^2$ now affects relative price variability through two terms, as can be seen from the right-hand side of (6.20). The first term on the right-hand side of this equation, corresponding to the variance of relative prices with uniform elasticities in (6.2), is still an increasing function of $\sigma_x^2$. To see this, note that by using the definitions in Equations (6.15a) and (6.15b), the first term on the right-hand side of (6.20) may be written as

$$\sum_v \frac{u(v)}{[1+\gamma(v)]^2}\left[1+\gamma(v)\frac{1-\theta}{1+\bar\gamma\theta}\right]^2\sigma_w^2$$

which is obviously a decreasing function of $\theta$. Because $\theta\equiv\sigma_w^2/(\sigma_w^2+\sigma_x^2)$ is a decreasing function of $\sigma_x^2$, it follows that the first component of the variance of relative prices on the right-hand side of (6.20) increases when the monetary variance $\sigma_x^2$ increases. Also with a higher $\sigma_x^2$, the average realizations of $\epsilon_t^2$ are higher; this makes the second term on the right-hand side of (6.20) higher as well, provided the coefficient of $\epsilon_t^2$ does not decrease. As shown in Section A3 of the Appendix, however, when $\sigma_x^2$ increases, the coefficient of $\epsilon_t^2$ decreases. Intuitively, when $\sigma_x^2$ increases, individuals in all markets tend to interpret movement in their own prices as being caused more by changes in the general price level. As a result, output in *all* markets becomes less responsive to unanticipated monetary shocks. This effect blurs the differences in output response and therefore in the response of relative prices between markets with low and high values of $\gamma(v)$. [Hercowitz (1981) mentions a similar effect.]

Up to now, the discussion has centered on the variance of relative price *levels*. Because the empirical tests by Parks (1978) and Hercowitz (1981, 1982) focus on the relationship between the variance of the relative price *change* and unanticipated nominal shocks, it is useful to derive an expression for this variance as well. The change in the relative price in market $v$ can be obtained by lagging Equation (6.17) by one period and subtracting the result from (6.17):

$$\pi_t^R(v)\equiv p_t(v)-Q_t-[p_{t-1}(v)-Q_{t-1}]$$
$$=\lambda(\theta)\theta F(v)(\epsilon_t-\epsilon_{t-1})+\lambda(\theta)[1+\theta F(v)](w_t-w_{t-1}) \tag{6.23}$$

Analogous to Equation (6.19), the variance of the relative price change for the case of different supply elasticities is defined as

$$V_t(\pi^R)=E\sum_w\sum_v u(v)[\pi_t^R(v)]^2 \tag{6.24}$$

Substituting (6.23) into (6.24), opening the square, and noting that $w_t$ is serially uncorrelated and has an expected value of zero, we obtain

$$V_t(\pi^R)=2\sum_v u(v)[\lambda(\theta)]^2[1+\theta F(v)]^2\sigma_w^2$$
$$+\sum_v u(v)[\lambda(\theta)\theta F(v)]^2(\epsilon_t-\epsilon_{t-1})^2 \tag{6.25}$$

Except for the fact that it is multiplied by 2, the first term on the right-hand side of (6.25) is the same as the first term in the expression for the variance of relative price levels in (6.20). The second term in (6.25) differs from the second term of (6.20) only in that $\epsilon_t^2$ has been replaced by $(\epsilon_t - \epsilon_{t-1})^2$.

Comparison of Equations (6.25) and (6.20) suggests that the variance of the relative price *change* bears the same relationship to $(\epsilon_t - \epsilon_{t-1})^2$ as the variance of relative price *levels* does to $\epsilon_t^2$. If $\sigma_x^2$ is constant over time, it follows from (6.25) that the variance of the relative price change is equal to a positive constant plus another positive constant multiplied by the change in the monetary growth shock squared. This is the type of equation that Hercowitz (1981) estimated relatively successfully for Germany during the hyperinflation. When estimated for the postwar United States (Hercowitz 1982), the same equation did not support the theory. A modified version of this equation, however, which uses the change in unanticipated inflation as a measure of $\epsilon_t - \epsilon_{t-1}$, supports the theory even for the postwar U.S. economy (Parks 1978). Because Hercowitz uses a measure of unanticipated monetary growth for $\epsilon_t$, whereas Parks uses a measure of unanticipated inflation, the difference in results is probably due to the different proxies used for unanticipated nominal shocks.

## 7    Concluding comments and a review of other approaches

At the risk of repetition, it should be stressed that all the theories presented above assume a direction of causality that runs from aggregate nominal shocks to relative price variability.

Work by Fischer (1981a, 1982) on Germany and the United States using the notion of Granger causality suggests that there is two-way causality between the distribution of inflation and the distribution of relative prices. The reason relative price variability causes inflation can be explained by the response of aggregate policy to changes in relative prices (Schultze 1959). Fischer (1981a) also finds that in general there is no single direction of causality. In some time periods the dominant direction of causality is from relative prices to inflation, and in other periods the dominant direction is reversed. Cukierman (1983) proposes a criterion for discerning between periods in which the relationship between inflation variance and the variability of relative prices is caused mostly by changes in exogenous aggregate variability and periods in which this relationship is caused mostly by changes in exogenous relative variability. This criterion is based on the sign of the correlation between the variance of the relative price change and the variance of the relative output change. A positive correlation indicates that the dominant effect is a change in relative variances. A negative correlation indicates that the underlying change is in aggregate variances. Cukierman applies this criterion to the postwar U.S. economy and finds rather frequent shifts in the direction of causality.

In a different direction, Bordo (1980) estimates the speed of the response of prices to monetary expansion and finds substantial differences in the speeds of adjustment across different industries. He attributes these differences to differing tendencies to use long-term contracts in different industries. Taylor (1981) proposes a theory of relative price variability that is based on multiperiod staggered contracts. Because only the contracts that are currently signed incorporate recent information, this information causes relative price and wage dispersion. Amihud and Mendelson (1982) explain relative price variability in terms of different responses of inventories and prices to a given demand shock. Sheshinski and Weiss (1977) consider a model of perfectly anticipated inflation in which there are real costs of changing nominal prices. Because of those costs, price adjustments occur at discrete intervals. An implication of their model is that if the timing of firms' price adjustments is independent, the variance of relative price changes should increase with the *level* of inflation. Padoa-Schioppa (1981) considers a certainty model in which differentiated monopolists set prices for two periods in a staggered manner. She shows that when the (exogenous) rate of increase in wages increases, both the rate of inflation and relative price variability increase.

The literature on indexed bonds customarily assumes that the real return on such bonds is certain (e.g., Liviatan and Levhari 1977). Once relative price uncertainty is explicitly acknowledged, however, even indexed bonds yield an uncertain return. The implications of this for the tendency to index bonds and wages are investigated by Cukierman (1981b, 1982b).

## Appendix

### A1     Derivation of the rational expectations equilibrium of Equations (6.13) and (6.14) when supply elasticities differ

Equating supply (6.12) and demand (3.4) in market $s$ and solving for the equilibrium price in that market, we obtain

$$p_t(s) = \frac{1}{1+\gamma(v)} [x_{t-1} + \delta - (\alpha + \beta t) + \gamma(s)Q_t^*(s) + \epsilon_t + w_t(s)] \qquad (A6.1)$$

This equation is not a complete solution, since $Q_t^*(s)$ depends on $p_t(s)$, which conveys information about the general price level, so $p_t(s)$ and $Q_t^*(s)$ have to be solved simultaneously. This is done here by using the method of undetermined coefficients. Because the model is log linear, the solutions are log linear functions of the exogenous variables. A general form of the solution for $p_t(s)$ is

$$p_t(s) = \pi_0(s) + \pi_1(s)x_{t-1} + \pi_2(s)t + \pi_3(s)\epsilon_t + \pi_4(s)w_t(s) \tag{A6.2}$$

where $\pi_i(s)$, $i = 0, 1, \ldots, 4$, are unknown coefficients that have to be determined. Substituting (A6.2) into the definition of the general price level (3.6), we obtain

$$Q_t = \sum_v u(v)p_t(v) = \sum_v u(v)\pi_0(v) + \sum_v u(v)\pi_1(v)x_{t-1} + \sum_v u(v)\pi_2(v)t$$
$$+ \sum_v u(v)\pi_3(v)\epsilon_t + \sum_v u(v)\pi_4(v)w_t(v) \tag{A6.3}$$

By using an argument similar to that presented in Appendix A of Cukierman and Wachtel (1979), it can be shown that when there is a large number of relatively small markets, the last term in Equation (A6.3) tends toward zero. Because people know the structure of the model, they know the coefficients $\pi_i(s)$. They therefore use (A6.3) and the information currently available in their own market to produce an optimal guess of the current general price level. Thus,

$$Q_t^*(s) = \sum_v u(v)\pi_0(v) + \sum_v u(v)\pi_1(v)x_{t-1} + \sum_v u(v)\pi_2(v)t$$
$$+ \sum_v u(v)\pi_3(v)E[\epsilon_t/I_t(s)] \tag{A6.4}$$

The observation of the local price $p_t(v)$ amounts, from (A6.1), to an observation on the sum $\epsilon_t + w_t(s)$. So

$$E[\epsilon_t/I_t(s)] = E\{\epsilon_t/[\epsilon_t + w_t(s)]\} = (1-\theta)[\epsilon_t + w_t(s)] \tag{A6.5}$$

where the last equality follows from Equation (4.6). Substituting (A6.5) into (A6.4), we get

$$Q_t^*(s) = \sum_v u(v)\pi_0(v) + \sum_v u(v)\pi_1(v)x_{t-1} + \sum_v u(v)\pi_2(v)t$$
$$+ \sum_v u(v)\pi_3(v)(1-\theta)[\epsilon_t + w_t(s)] \tag{A6.6}$$

Substituting (A6.6) into (A6.1), we get

$$p_t(s) = \frac{1}{1+\gamma(s)}\left\{ x_{t-1} + \delta - (\alpha + \beta t) + \gamma(s)\sum_v u(v)\pi_0(v) \right.$$
$$+ \gamma(s)\sum_v u(v)\pi_1(v)x_{t-1} + \gamma(s)\sum_v u(v)\pi_2(v)t$$
$$\left. + \gamma(s)\sum_v u(v)\pi_3(v)(1-\theta)[\epsilon_t + w_t(s)] + \epsilon_t + w_t(s) \right\}$$
$$\tag{A6.7}$$

Both Equations (A6.2) and (A6.7) express $p_t(s)$ in terms of the exogenous variables. Because both these equations are representations of $p_t(s)$ for *any* values of the exogenous variables, it follows that the coefficients of identical variables in (A6.2) and (A6.7) should be equal. Equating these coefficients across the right-hand sides of (A6.2) and (A6.7), we obtain the following set of equations:

$$\pi_0(s) = k(s)\left[\delta - \alpha + \gamma(s) \sum_v u(v)\,\pi_0(v)\right] \tag{A6.8a}$$

$$\pi_1(s) = k(s)\left[1 + \gamma(s) \sum_v u(v)\,\pi_1(v)\right] \tag{A6.8b}$$

$$\pi_2(s) = k(s)\left[\gamma(s) \sum_v u(v)\,\pi_2(v) - \beta\right] \tag{A6.8c}$$

$$\pi_3(s) = k(s)\left[1 + \gamma(s)(1-\theta) \sum_v u(v)\,\pi_3(v)\right] \tag{A6.8d}$$

$$\pi_4(s) = k(s)\left[1 + \gamma(s)(1-\theta) \sum_v u(v)\,\pi_3(v)\right] \tag{A6.8e}$$

for all $s$, where

$$k(s) \equiv 1/[1 + \gamma(s)] \tag{A6.9}$$

Note that the right-hand sides of Equations (A6.8d, e) are equal. Hence $\pi_3(s) = \pi_4(s)$ for all $s$, and Equation (A6.8e) and the unknowns $\pi_4(s)$ can be dropped.

Multiplying each of equations (A6.8a–d) by $u(s)$, summing over all markets, noting that $\sum_v u(v) = 1$, and rearranging, we obtain, respectively,

$$\sum_v u(v)\,\pi_0(v) = \delta - \alpha \tag{A6.10a}$$

$$\sum_v u(v)\,\pi_1(v) = 1 \tag{A6.10b}$$

$$\sum_v u(v)\,\pi_2(v) = -\beta \tag{A6.10c}$$

$$\sum_v u(v)\,\pi_3(v) = 1/(1 + \bar{\gamma}\theta) \tag{A6.10d}$$

where

$$\bar{\gamma} \equiv \frac{u(v)\,k(v)}{\sum_v u(v)\,k(v)}\,\gamma(v) \tag{A6.11}$$

Substituting each of the equations in (A6.10) into the correspondingly numbered equation in (A6.8), we obtain

$$\pi_0(s) = \delta - \alpha; \qquad \pi_1(s) = 1; \qquad \pi_2(s) = -\beta \tag{A6.12a}$$

$$\pi_3(s) = \pi_4(s) = \frac{1}{1 + \bar{\gamma}\theta}\left[1 + \theta\,\frac{\bar{\gamma} - \gamma(s)}{1 + \gamma(s)}\right] \tag{A6.12b}$$

for all $s$. Substituting (A6.12) into (A6.2), we get

$$p_t(s) = \delta - \alpha + x_{t-1} - \beta t + \frac{1}{1+\bar{\gamma}\theta}\left[1 + \theta\,\frac{\bar{\gamma}-\gamma(s)}{1+\gamma(s)}\right][\epsilon_t + w_t(s)]$$

$$= \bar{Q}_t + \lambda(\theta)[1 + \theta F(s)][\epsilon_t + w_t(s)] \qquad (A6.13)$$

which is Equation (6.13) in the text.

Substituting Equations (A6.10) into (A6.3), we obtain the solution for the general price level:

$$Q_t = \delta - \alpha + x_{t-1} - \beta t + \frac{1}{1+\bar{\gamma}\theta}\,\epsilon_t \equiv \bar{Q}_t + \lambda(\theta)\epsilon_t \qquad (A6.14)$$

where the last term on the right-hand side of (A6.3), which is

$$\sum_v u(v)\lambda(\theta)[1 + \theta F(v)]w_t(v)$$

has been dropped because when the number of markets is large, it converges in probability to zero. Equation (A6.14) is identical to (6.14) in the text.

## A2   *Derivation of Equation (6.16)*

Substituting Equations (A6.10) into (A6.6), we get

$$Q_t^*(s) = \delta - \alpha + x_{t-1} - \beta t + \frac{1-\theta}{1+\bar{\gamma}\theta}[\epsilon_t + w_t(s)]$$

$$= \bar{Q}_t + \frac{1-\theta}{1+\bar{\gamma}\theta}[\epsilon_t + w_t(s)] \qquad (A6.15)$$

Rearranging (6.13) in the text, we get

$$\epsilon_t + w_t(s) = \frac{p_t(s) - \bar{Q}_t}{\lambda(\theta)[1 + \theta F(s)]} \qquad (A6.16)$$

Equation (6.16) in the text follows by substituting (A6.16) into (A6.15) and rearranging.

## A3   *Derivation of Equation (6.22)*

By subtracting $\alpha + \beta t$ from both sides of the equation that describes the typical demand curve (3.4), we obtain the demand for the cyclical component of output as

$$y_{ct}^d(s) \equiv y_t^d(s) - (\alpha + \beta t) = x_t + w_t(s) - (\alpha + \beta t) - p_t(s)$$

$$= \bar{Q}_t + \lambda(\theta)\epsilon_t + [1 - \lambda(\theta)]\epsilon_t + w_t(s) - p_t(s) \qquad (A6.17)$$

Rearranging (A6.17), we obtain

$$y_{ct}^d(s) + p_t(s) - Q_t = [1 - \lambda(\theta)]\epsilon_t + w_t(s)$$

which is Equation (6.22) in the text.

A4　　*Proof that for any given $\epsilon_t$ the supply curves of Figure 3 intersect at $y_{ct}(v) = 0$ and $p_t(v) - Q_t = -\lambda(\theta)\epsilon_t$*

For any two markets indexed by 1 and 2, the supply equations are, respectively, from (6.21),

$$y_{ct}(1) = \theta(1)\gamma(1)[p_t(1) - Q_t + \lambda(\theta)\epsilon_t] \qquad (A6.18)$$

$$y_{ct}(2) = \theta(2)\gamma(2)[p_t(2) - Q_t + \lambda(\theta)\epsilon_t] \qquad (A6.19)$$

Letting $y_{ct}(1) = y_{ct}(2) = y_{ct}$ and letting $p_t(1) = p_t(2) = p_t$ in Equations (A6.18) and (A6.19), we obtain, after rearranging,

$$[\theta(1)\gamma(1) - \theta(2)\gamma(2)][p_t - Q_t + \lambda(\theta)\epsilon_t] = 0 \qquad (A6.20)$$

For $\gamma(1) \neq \gamma(2)$, $\theta(1)\gamma(1) \neq \theta(2)\gamma(2)$, so that (A6.20) implies

$$p_t - Q_t = -\lambda(\theta)\epsilon_t \qquad (A6.21)$$

After we substitute (A6.21) into either (A6.18) or (A6.19), it follows that $y_{ct} = 0$; so for any $\epsilon_t$, the supply curves in (A6.18) and (A6.19) intersect at the point $y_{ct}(v) = 0$, and $p_t(v) - Q_t = -\lambda(\theta)\epsilon_t$.

A5　　*Proof that the coefficient of $\epsilon_t^2$ in Equation (6.20) is a decreasing function of $\sigma_x^2$*

Using the definitions in Equations (6.15a) and (6.15b), we can write this coefficient as

$$C_2 \equiv \sum_v u(v)\left[\frac{\bar{\gamma} - \gamma(v)}{1 + \gamma(v)} \cdot \frac{\theta}{1 + \bar{\gamma}\theta}\right]^2 \qquad (A6.22)$$

Differentiating (A6.22) partially with respect to $\theta$ gives

$$\frac{\partial C_2}{\partial \theta} = 2\frac{\theta}{(1 + \bar{\gamma}\theta)^3}\sum_v u(v)\left[\frac{\bar{\gamma} - \gamma(v)}{1 + \gamma(v)}\right]^2 > 0 \qquad (A6.23)$$

Because $\theta$ is a decreasing function of $\sigma_x^2$, it follows from (A6.23) that $C_2$ is a decreasing function of $\sigma_x^2$.

# Place of the aggregate–relative confusion within the economics of asymmetric information: some concluding reflections

## 1    Introduction

This chapter is devoted to a comparison of the macroeconomic literature on rational expectations with the finance literature on the information content of prices and to a discussion of the effects of an economy-wide capital market on the aggregate–relative confusion.

The similarities and differences between the multimarkets rational expectations models used in macroeconomic analysis and the finance models in which prices aggregate information are discussed in Section 2. Section 3 focuses on the modifications that occur in the basic multimarkets model of Chapters 3, 4, and 6 in the presence of an economy-wide capital market.

## 2    Aggregation of information by prices and the aggregate–relative confusion

The multimarkets model used in Chapters 3–6 to illustrate the implications of the aggregate–relative confusion bears more than a token resemblance to the finance models discussed in Sections 3–5 of Chapter 2 in which prices aggregate private information. In both cases individuals learn some relevant information from market prices; however, in the macroeconomic framework individuals typically obtain only partial information from prices so that some confusion between aggregate and relative shocks persists. In the finance literature there are, by contrast, some cases in which market prices are fully revealing. This section discusses the methodological similarities and differences between the two classes of models.

In both the macroeconomic and the finance literature the basic premise is that individuals come to the market with initially different information sets, and that the equilibriums that arise have to be self-fulfilling.[1] In the finance literature individuals always observe all current market prices. These observations transmit at least some information from the private to the public domain, and in some important cases all the relevant information is transferred to the public domain. By contrast, in the macro-economic rational expectations literature, individuals never observe all current prices; if they were to do so, the aggregate–relative confusion would vanish because the current general price level would have been perfectly revealed.[2] Thus, information is never fully aggregated within the macroeconomic framework because individuals are prevented from observing all current prices.

In the finance literature, whenever full aggregation does not occur, it is because the number of markets is small relative to the amount of noise in the system. In some sense this is also true of the aggregate–relative confusion; the general price level is not fully revealed as long as there is enough noise in comparison to the number of prices that individuals are *allowed to observe*. Viewed in this way, the difference between the typical finance and macroeconomic models is that in the finance literature the number of prices observed by individuals is identical to the number of market prices. In the macroeconomic literature the number of prices currently observed is smaller than the number of currently existing market prices.

Another methodological difference is that most microeconomic and finance models start from explicit maximization of expected utility for particular utility functions, whereas most of the macroeconomic literature starts with exogenously given demand and supply functions.

## 3    Aggregate–relative confusion in the presence of a centralized bond market

In the presence of a centralized bond market, in which obligations that originate in various markets are traded, the interest rate can under certain circumstances fully reveal the current general price level to individuals in all markets, thus annihilating the aggregate–relative confusion.[3] This effect is illustrated within the context of the multimarket equilibrium model of Chapter 3 by the addition of a centralized bond market whose clearing determines a nominal interest rate $n$ that is observed currently by individuals in all markets. More specifically $n_t$ is the interest rate on a one-period loan that starts in period $t$ and is repaid in period $t+1$. Let

$$B_t^d[w_t(v)] = \eta_0 + \eta\left(n_t - \{Q_{t+1}^*[w_t(v)] - Q_t^*[w_t(v)]\}\right); \quad \infty > \eta > 0 \quad (7.1)$$

be the demand for bonds by all individuals in market $v$, and let $w_t(v)$ be, as in Chapters 3, 4, and 6, the current realization of the relative demand shock in market $v$. The term in brackets on the right-hand side of (7.1) is the real rate of interest as perceived by individuals in this market. The effect of the real rate on the quantity that individuals in market $v$ desire to *lend* is assumed to be positive.[4] The terms $\eta_0$ and $\eta$ are constant coefficients and are, for simplicity, identical across markets. Thus, differences in the demand for bonds among markets arise only because of differences in the inflationary expectation $Q^*_{t+1}[w_t(v)] - Q^*_t[w_t(v)]$ across markets. Note that when $B^d_t[w_t(v)]$ is negative, individuals in market $v$ are net borrowers because their demand for bonds is negative.

Suppose that because of the way monetary policy operates, the government's demand for bonds depends on the quantity of money $x_t$. More precisely, let

$$fNx_t \tag{7.2}$$

be the government's excess demand for bonds in period $t$. Here $f$ is a constant coefficient and $N$ is the number of markets in the economy. Market clearing in the centralized bond market implies that

$$\sum_{v=1}^{N} B^d_t(v) + fNx_t = 0 \tag{7.3}$$

Equation (7.3) together with the equilibrium conditions in the individual markets determines the nominal rate of interest and individual prices in all markets. Because the government's excess demand for bonds depends on the current money supply, an observation on the current nominal rate of interest conveys information about the current money supply. As a matter of fact, the nominal rate of interest perfectly reveals $x_t$ and therefore the current monetary shock $\epsilon_t$. We shall demonstrate this by assuming that equilibrium is perfectly revealing and showing that the actual behavior that arises under this assumption permits the full revelation of information. This will establish the self-fulfilling nature of the model and demonstrate that a rational expectations, fully revealing equilibrium is possible in this case.

The model has already been solved under the assumption of full current information in Equations (3.8) and (3.9). The solutions for a representative individual market price and for the general price level are reproduced here for convenience:

$$p_t(v) = Q_t + w_t(v)/(1+\gamma) \tag{7.4}$$

$$Q_t = -\alpha - \beta t + x_t \tag{7.5}$$

Because individuals in all markets have full current information,

$$Q^*_t[w_t(v)] = Q_t \tag{7.6}$$

for all $v$. Leading (7.5) by one period, we get

$$Q_{t+1} = -\alpha - \beta(t+1) + x_{t+1} \tag{7.5a}$$

The best forecast of $x_{t+1}$ given full current information in period $t$ is $x_t + \delta$. Hence, from (7.5a),

$$Q_{t+1}^*[w_t(v)] = -\alpha - \beta(t+1) + x_t + \delta \qquad (7.7)$$

for all $v$. It follows from (7.6) and (7.7) that

$$Q_{t+1}^*[w_t(v)] - Q_t^*[w_t(v)] = \delta - \beta \qquad (7.8)$$

for all $v$. Substituting (7.8) into (7.1), using the resulting expression in (7.3), and rearranging, we get

$$n_t = \delta - \beta - \frac{\eta_0}{\eta} - \frac{f}{\eta} x_t \qquad (7.9)$$

which is the solution for the equilibrium nominal rate of interest in terms of known parameters and $x_t$. Because (7.9) is invertible, an observation of $n_t$ is equivalent to an observation on $x_t$, which can be used to calculate the actual general price level by using (7.5). Once the general price level is known, individuals in market $v$ can find the precise value of the relative shock to their market by using (7.4) and their observation of $p_t(v)$. Thus the existence of a centralized bond market in this case defuses the aggregate–relative confusion and with it all the accompanying real effects on output and relative prices.

This strong result depends, however, on the fact that there is only one aggregate shock; in this case, an observation on one economy-wide price ($n_t$) reveals the aggregate shock perfectly. If there are more aggregate shocks than centralized asset markets, however, observation of the current prices of these assets will not generally be sufficient to reveal the aggregate shocks perfectly, and the aggregate–relative confusion will survive. For example, if there is an additional exogenous stochastic component $\phi_t$ to excess demand for bonds, the equilibrium condition in the bond market in (7.3) is replaced by

$$\sum_{v=1}^{N} B_t^d(v) + fNx_t + \phi_t = 0 \qquad (7.3a)$$

The signal extraction problem facing the representative individual is, as before, to find the best estimate of $\epsilon_t$ given $p_t(v)$ and $n_t$. With two aggregate shocks and only one economy-wide price $n_t$, however, the equilibrium condition in (7.3a) does not enable individuals to identify $\epsilon_t$ perfectly. Hence the aggregate–relative confusion continues to exist.

Barro (1980) presents a model of this type in which individuals have, in addition to the current price in their own market, an observation of an economy-wide interest rate. They still confuse between aggregate and relative changes in prices because there are two unobserved aggregate shocks, one to money demand and one to money supply. Barro shows that the results of Chapter 3 carry over to the extended framework. In particular, unanticipated shocks to demand continue to have a positive effect on output, and the coefficient that relates output to these shocks is a decreasing function of the variance of monetary shocks.

Cukierman (1983) considers a model in which there is a dominant sector like energy whose effect on the general price level is nonnegligible. In this case the general price level is affected by both the monetary shock and the relative excess demand shock in the dominant market. As a result, to identify the current general price level exactly, individuals have to identify two "aggregate" shocks: the money supply shock and the specific shock to excess demand in the dominant sector. In this case, too, an observation on a single interest rate is not sufficient to produce a full revelation of the price level.

These examples suggest that in general the aggregate–relative confusion will survive the introduction of centralized trading in assets provided there are enough aggregate shocks in the economy. This criterion is analogous to the statement in the finance literature on the information content of prices (discussed in Chapter 2) to the effect that a full revelation of information by prices does not occur if there is enough noise in the system. Karni (1981) suggests that to maintain the aggregate–relative confusion in the presence of information emanating from economy-wide asset markets, the number of aggregate shocks must exceed the number of centralized markets. This condition is not sufficient because even when it is satisfied, there may be cases in which to identify the general price level individuals need to identify only a certain linear combination of the aggregate shocks, and this linear combination can be identified because of the specific structure of the economy.

# PART II

# Permanent–transitory confusion

# CHAPTER 8

# Permanent–transitory confusion and other reasons for persistence: overview

## 1    Introduction

The principal choices that people make in a market economy – choices between present and future consumption, between labor and leisure, between real and monetary assets – depend on their beliefs about the future. In forming their beliefs, individuals attempt to separate transitory and ephemeral changes from permanent and persistent changes. Even individuals who are fully informed about past and current variables cannot be certain about their future values. A basic inference problem that individuals face is to distinguish permanent values of variables like income, wages, and prices from current values.[1] Implicitly or explicitly, each of us makes judgments about the persistence of current developments before making major decisions.

For example, if the relative wage of a particular kind of labor goes up, the reactions of individual workers to this change will depend on whether they believe this change to be permanent or temporary. If the wage increase is perceived as permanent, there may be some increase in the supply of labor. (This will be the case if the substitution effect is larger than the income effect over the life cycle.) If the wage increase is perceived as temporary, however, the increase in the labor supply will be greater as individuals try to work more today because they believe the wage currently offered is unusually high.

Another example is an individual who tries to sell a house and finds that the current market price is substantially lower than the price for which the house was purchased. If the owner believes the drop in price to be temporary, he (or she) might decide to withhold the house from the market in the hope that he will be able to sell it later at a higher price. If the owner believes that the drop in price is permanent, he will sell immediately because waiting will not change the fact that he is permanently poorer.

Because of the basic uncertainty in which we live, individuals usually make errors about the persistence of economic and other developments. Sometimes they judge the persistence of current developments to be longer than it really is, and at other times they underestimate it. As the economy constantly changes its permanent position, individuals are constantly subject to confusion between permanent and transitory developments. Unlike the aggregate–relative confusion of Part I, this confusion does not disappear when the current values of all economic variables are known by everybody. The basic uncertainty concerning the permanence of the current state of the economy remains.[2]

The distinction between permanent and transitory changes is particularly appealing for an analysis of the labor market because it offers a potential way of reconciling a sluggish adjustment of real wages and the persistence of "unemployment" with market clearing and rational expectations. In Chapter 9 the phenomenon of stagflation is explained in terms of the permanent–transitory confusion concerning permanent productivity. Chapter 10 uses this confusion to analyze the effects of monetary shocks and the efficiency of the price system. An implication of the permanent–transitory confusion is that unexpected monetary shocks have persistent effects on the level and structure of output. Chapter 11 uses the framework presented in Chapter 10 to investigate the effects of this confusion for relative price variability and the variance of inflation.

All the effects of the permanent–transitory confusion to be discussed apply independently of whether individuals are subject to the aggregate–relative confusion or not. To focus on the effects of the first confusion, questions of differential information of the type analyzed in Part I are therefore abstracted from by endowing all individuals with the same information set.

Although the confusion between transitory monetary shocks and permanent demand and supply shifts dealt with in subsequent chapters transforms serially uncorrelated monetary disturbances into serially correlated movements in real variables, it is by no means the only mechanism that creates persistence. To maintain some perspective this chapter surveys briefly some of the alternative mechanisms responsible for sluggish movements in real variables.

## 2    Costs of adjusting capital stocks and gestation lags

As an empirical matter, capital formation normally is a process that takes time. The time lag between the moment a firm decides to increase its capital stock until this stock becomes fully productive varies among industries. In almost all cases, however, the lag is nonnegligible and in some cases may stretch over several years (Almon 1965, Jorgenson 1965).

Two approaches have been suggested to explain this lag. One relies on costs of adjustment and the other on technologically given gestation lags. The crucial element in the cost of adjustment approach is the postulate that, besides the cost of acquiring capital goods, there are installation costs that increase at an increasing rate with the amount of capital that is installed per period. This approach has been the subject of much investigation (Lucas 1967, Gould 1968, Treadway 1969). [See Sargent (1979: Chapter VI) for a summary view.] The individual firm is viewed as choosing its variable factor (taken to be labor) and investment in each period of time so as to maximize the discounted present value of profits. The firm produces a homogeneous output with two factors – labor and capital – and takes current and future values of prices, wages, and the interest rate as given. Profits in each period are equal to the price of the product multiplied by production minus the wage bill, the cost of acquiring new capital, and the costs associated with the adjustment of capital at a nonzero rate. Because these costs increase at an increasing rate, it does not pay the firm to adjust its capital stock in jumps. By spreading its capital formation activity over several periods, the firm decreases the costs of adjusting capital rapidly and increases the discounted value of its profits.

A consequence of this is that a change in external circumstances that increases the firm's demand for capital increases the actual capital stock gradually as the firm tries to avoid the range in which the costs of rapid investment become unprofitable. The increased demand for capital takes the form of higher investment activity over several periods rather than only in the period in which the information about the change in external circumstances arrives. By merging a model in which the capital stock adjusts gradually with the aggregate–relative confusion, Lucas (1975) obtains a propagation mechanism that transforms serially uncorrelated monetary shocks into serially correlated movements in capital and output.

The gestation lag approach takes the view that the lag between the start and the completion of capital projects is determined exogenously by technology. This approach is probably a reasonable approximation of reality for investment in structures for which the lag between starts and completions is reasonably stable. With gestation lags persistence is created directly by the structure of technology. A shock that pushes up current starts sets off a whole string of investments in subsequent periods until the completion of the projects that have been started. Models that incorporate gestation lags have been used by Kydland and Prescott (1982) to explain the comovements of economic variables over the cycle and by Taylor (1983) to derive optimal stabilization rules.

## 3 Consumption smoothing

Modern formulations of the life cycle–permanent income hypothesis start from the premise that the individual consumer chooses current and future planned consumption paths to maximize present discounted utility (using a subjective discount rate) subject to certain constraints. The constraints involve mainly the notion that, provided the consumer faces a perfect capital market, the present value (using the market interest rate) of the planned consumption path must equal the sum of current nonhuman wealth plus the discounted present value of present and future wage income (Hall 1978). Utility from consumption is separable over different time periods (i.e., utility from consumption in period $t$ is independent of consumption in period $t + j$ for all $j \neq 0$), and the marginal utility of consumption decreases within each period. Under these circumstances the consumer will usually spread any increase in current or future income over consumption expenditures in all periods. This strong result arises because, apart from a series of constants that depend on the ratio of the subjective discount rate to the market rate of interest, the consumer equates the marginal utility of consumption in all time periods. Any allocation of consumption over periods that does not fulfill this condition is suboptimal because the present value of utilities can be increased by reallocating consumption from periods of relatively low marginal utility to periods with high marginal utilities of consumption.

Thus, an increase in the wage rate will cause an increase in consumption expenditures that will be spread over many periods. More generally, any changes in exogenous parameters that affect the consumer will have persistent effects on consumption. Moreover, because additions to the individual's wealth are equal (by definition) to income minus consumption, the optimal spreading of consumption over time also implies that wealth will move sluggishly through time.

## 4    Disutility from intense and sustained periods of work

Beyond a certain level, individuals usually develop a strong aversion to marginal work units. Two formulations of this idea have appeared in recent literature. MaCurdy (1981) assumes that the disutility of work in any given period decreases at an increasing rate with the number of hours that the individual works. Sargent (1979: Chapter XVI) postulates that subsequent periods of high employment tire the worker and reduce utility by more than is reflected by the disutility from work in each period alone. The first formulation, by postulating a time-separable utility function, focuses on the persistence caused by increasing disutility from intense work *within* a given period. The second, by allowing nonseparability, also incorporates the increasing disutility from sustained periods of work.[3] Both formulations are incorporated in dynamic optimization problems in which the individual chooses paths for labor, leisure, and consumption subject to an intertemporal budget constraint, given present and future values (or expected values, in case of uncertainty) of the wage rate and of interest rates.

A basic result of both formulations is that, other things being equal, the individual has a preference for spreading work over time, at least past a certain point. In other words, the individual can be convinced to work more in a particular period only if offered an unusually high wage. If most workers share this characteristic, an increase in product demand that induces an increase in the demand for labor will be partially checked by the increase in wages necessary to induce individuals to work more. As a result, the response of production to an increase in demand will be spread over several periods, and real variables such as production and employment will move sluggishly over time.

## 5   Costs of adjusting labor inputs

Many kinds of labor should be viewed as quasi-fixed factors of production because in addition to the variable wage bill there are certain fixed employment costs (Oi 1962). Some are turnover costs associated with the process of hiring and firing. Others are training costs that make the worker more productive in future periods.

Both types of costs introduce an element of capital into the use of labor. Decisions on current labor input cannot be based on only the current wage and the current marginal productivity of the worker. In deciding whether to hire today, a firm must consider the future streams of product and wages that are associated with the worker as well as the current values of these variables. Here again, labor demand has to be derived from dynamic considerations.

Sargent (1978) formalizes these costs by considering a representative firm that chooses its current and future (contingent) labor inputs so as to maximize the expected present value of profits subject to a labor cost function that depends positively on the *change* in labor inputs from one period to the next. Sargent postulates that the costs of adjusting labor increase more than proportionally with the size of the change. His formulation is fully analogous to the increasing marginal costs of investment of Section 2 and, not surprisingly, yield a similar result: It pays to adjust the labor input gradually. As a consequence, whenever a change in external circumstances (such as changes in future prices or wages) changes the firm's demand for labor, the consequent adjustment occurs gradually, introducing sluggishness into the movement of employment over time.

Taken together with the discussion of the previous section, this suggests the existence of two built-in mechanisms that gradually adjust the labor market. One operates on the side of labor supply and is due to aversion to sustained employment periods. The other operates on the side of labor demand and is due to rising marginal costs of adjusting the labor pool. By merging these two persistence-creating mechanisms with the aggregate–relative confusion of Part I, it is possible to generate a framework in which serially uncorrelated monetary shocks are transformed into serially correlated movements in employment and output (Sargent 1979: Chapter XVI).

## 6    Persistence and inventories

In the presence of inventories, sales and production in any period need not be equal because inventories can be increased or run down depending on the relationship between production and sales. This gives a firm that tries to maximize the present value of its profits additional freedom in choosing the optimal paths of labor, output, and inventories. In the presence of decreasing marginal productivity and low enough storage costs, it will pay the firm to smooth its production, selling out of inventories in high-demand periods and building up inventories in low-demand periods.

When a firm with inventories and decreasing marginal productivity of labor is subjected to the aggregate–relative confusion, its optimal response transforms serially uncorrelated monetary shocks into serially correlated movements in employment and production. The mechanism inducing this transformation is described by Blinder and Fischer (1981) and is summarized in what follows: In the presence of the aggregate–relative confusion, a positive (serially uncorrelated) shock to monetary growth is partly interpreted by the firm as an increase in its relative price along the lines of Part I. The firm responds by selling out of inventories. In future periods the resulting depletion of inventories triggers a gradual inventory-rebuilding activity with consequent temporary but persistent increases in employment and output. The firm spreads the inventory-rebuilding activity over several periods because of the decreasing marginal productivity of labor. (Note that here costs of adjusting the labor input are abstracted from.) As a result, a one-time serially uncorrelated monetary shock triggers serially correlated movements in employment and output.

The presence of inventories can transform serially uncorrelated monetary impulses into serially correlated deviations of output and employment from trend even in the absence of a decreasing marginal productivity of labor if a higher than normal real wage is necessary to induce workers to work more. We saw in Section 4 that this will be the case when the typical worker dislikes sustained periods of work. Brunner et al. (1983) present an analysis in which this is the basic persistence-creating mechanism and the impact effect of unanticipated monetary shocks works through a negative "liquidity" effect on interest rates. In each period, prices and wages are fixed in advance but the money market clears instantaneously. As a result, an unanticipated monetary shock depresses the nominal and the real rates of interest in the short run and causes an unanticipated increase in demand. Firms supply part of the increased demand out of inventories. This causes inventories to drop below their normal level. In subsequent periods the demand for labor increases as firms strive to rebuild their depleted inventories. The increased demand for labor is satisfied only at a temporarily higher real wage rate, which discourages the instant rebuilding of inventories and causes firms to spread this activity over several periods. The result is that a serially uncorrelated monetary shock triggers serially correlated deviations of all real variables from their normal values.

## 7    Staggered contracts and persistence

Staggered contracts create sluggishness in the movements of both nominal and real variables. Taylor (1980) presents a macroeconomic analysis of the effects of staggered nominal contracts on the behavior of prices, employment, and output. A basic feature of his model is the existence of $N$-period nominal wage contracts. In each period a fraction $1/N$ of workers agree on a nominal wage rate that remains in effect for the next $N$ periods. In setting the contract, workers and employers aim at a wage rate that is equal to the average wage rate in the economy during the period of the contract. Because this average wage is affected by the overhang of past contracts as well as by current expectations regarding future wage settlements, the average wage rate becomes a distributed lag of past wages and a distributed lead of future expected wages. This interdependence among wage contracts introduces serial correlation into the movements of wage rates. The setting of the current contract is also influenced by the current and future expected levels of excess demand. Expectations regarding policy for future demand management affect the current contract through this term. Prices that are set at a fixed markup over wages also become serially correlated. Given the wage contract, employment and output are determined by demand. The model is closed through a simple quantity theory of money, which implies that aggregate demand and output are positively related to the level of real money balances. This positive dependence of demand on real money balances can be thought of as reflecting two effects: a real balance effect and a negative effect of real money balances on real rates of interest, which also stimulates aggregate demand.

Future monetary shocks that are anticipated at the time a wage contract is set are reflected in this contract. As a consequence, real money balances are not affected. Unanticipated monetary shocks change real money balances for a while, however, because wages and prices are temporarily fixed. For example, an unanticipated increase in the rate of monetary growth does not cause an immediate proportional increase in all wages and prices. Only after all contracts have been renegotiated (which will happen $N$ periods after the occurrence of the shock) will real balances return to their previous lower level. In the meantime real balances, aggregate demand, and therefore employment and output are higher than normal. Because of the slow movements in wages and prices, real balances move sluggishly over time. As a result aggregate demand, output, and employment all become serially correlated.

In view of the widespread existence of explicit or implicit wage contracts, this scenario seems reasonable. However, it leaves two unanswered microeconomic questions: First, what is the reason for nominal rather than indexed wage contracts? Second, what are the reasons for the excess capacity that enables production to adjust to satisfy aggregate demand?

# Permanent–transitory confusion: implications for stagflation and the persistence of unemployment

## 1    Introduction[1]

This chapter analyzes an economy in which decisions depend not just on the changes that occur but also on their persistence. The economy is subject to real shocks to the labor, commodity, and money markets and to nominal shocks to the money stock. Each shock has a permanent and a transitory component.

Individuals know both the deterministic structure and the stochastic structure of the economic model. They use all available information to form optimal forecasts of the permanent values of relevant variables, but this information does not permit them to distinguish permanent and transitory changes as soon as they occur.

All markets reach equilibrium and clear each period. The prices and quantities at which the markets clear depend, however, on the perceptions individuals in the aggregate hold about the persistence of the shocks that have occurred. Because people learn whether changes are permanent or transitory only by observing what has occurred, perceptions about permanent values change gradually, and differences between expected and actual permanent values can persist for a time. The resulting confusion explains the phenomenon known as *stagflation*.

This chapter shows that a large permanent reduction in productivity causes on impact both an increase in unemployment that persists for a time and an increase in prices. As information about the permanence of the shock accrues, real wages adjust toward their new equilibrium value, but during the transition, real wages are "sticky." These and other phenomena caused by the permanent reduction in productivity combine to generate many symptoms of stagflation. This pattern is qualitatively similar to what actually happened in the industrialized world following the 1973–4 quadrupling of oil prices.

The model of the economy presented in Section 2 is an augmented IS–LM model with an aggregate demand function, a money demand function, and demand and supply functions for labor. The demand for labor is derived from a neoclassical production function: the supply of labor depends on both the current and the perceived permanent wage rates. The various shocks to the economy and their (known) stochastic structure are also presented.

Section 3 explains the formation of beliefs or perceptions of permanent variables. First, an optimal forecast of the current permanent value of any given shock is derived. The forecasts of those permanent values are used to derive structural beliefs regarding permanent income, permanent wages, and the permanent values of other endogenous variables. Section 4 investigates the effects of the various shocks on the equilibrium levels of employment, prices, output, and the real wage rate, and discusses the working of the model. Section 5 shows that large permanent decreases in productivity are followed by periods of persistent underemployment of labor and by inflation. It is shown that inflation and unemployment can occur together – the pattern known as *stagflation*.[2]

## 2    Model

The model developed in this section has many of the features of an IS–LM model that includes markets for commodities, money, bonds, and labor. Equilibrium prevails on all markets. By Walras's law, when any three of the markets are in equilibrium, the fourth market is in equilibrium too. Because it is possible to conduct the analysis in terms of three markets, the bond market is excluded from explicit consideration. Current and permanent values differ, and the differences affect the equilibrium position of each market.

Productivity, aggregate demand, labor supply, money demand, and money supply are all subject to random shocks. Each shock has a permanent and a transitory component. The shocks to aggregate demand and money demand are related through the budget constraint. For simplicity they are therefore entered in those functions as the same shock but with a different coefficient in each function. Individuals in the economy have information on current and past values of the variables, but they are unable to observe the permanent and transitory components of shocks separately. (As we shall see, this informational limitation gradually disappears as new information becomes available.) Meanwhile they use the information on the current and past values of the variables to form optimal predictions of the components of each shock and to calculate permanent values of all variables. Expectations about the permanent values of the variables are rational.

## 2a     Demand for commodities

The demand for commodities is given by

$$e_t = k + \alpha y_t^p + \beta[r_t - ({}_tp_{t+1}^* - p_t)] + \epsilon_t; \quad 0 < \alpha < 1, \ \beta < 0 \quad (9.1)$$

where $e_t$, $y_t^p$, and $p_t$ are the logarithms of aggregate demand, real permanent income, and the general price level, respectively; $r_t$ is the nominal rate of interest; ${}_tp_{t+1}^*$ is the logarithm of the price level expected to prevail by the public in period $t+1$ as of period $t$; and $\epsilon_t$ is a random shock to aggregate demand. Equation (9.1) states that aggregate demand depends on permanent income [this is in line with Friedman's (1957) permanent income consumption function] and is inversely related to the real rate of interest. The real rate is the nominal rate $r_t$ (the yield to maturity on a one-period bond) minus the rate of inflation expected by the public ${}_tp_{t+1}^* - p_t$.

## 2b     Supply of commodities and labor market

Aggregate output $Y_t$ is produced with a Cobb–Douglas production function. Abstracting from the long-run effects of investment on capital accumulation, we assume the aggregate capital stock is fixed. Aggregate output can therefore be written as a function of the labor input $L_t$ and a random productivity factor $u_t$:

$$Y_t = \exp(u_t) L_t^\delta; \quad 0 < \delta < 1 \quad (9.2)$$

Note that wherever a nonrandom variable appears both by itself and in log form, a capital letter is used for the variable and a lowercase letter for the logarithm of the variable.

The marginal product of labor can be obtained from Equation (9.2) by differentiating partially with respect to labor:

$$\delta \exp(u_t) L_t^{\delta - 1}$$

If employers compete for labor, the marginal product of labor from this equation is equated to the real wage rate so that the demand for labor can be solved in terms of the real wage rate. Expressing the resulting solution in logarithmic form, we obtain

$$l_t^d = -\eta(w_t - u_t) + \eta \log \delta \quad (9.3)$$

where $\eta \equiv 1/(1-\delta) > 0$, $l_t^d$ is the logarithm of labor demanded, and $w_t$ is the logarithm of the real wage rate in period $t$.

The labor supply is

$$l_t^s = \omega(w_t - w_t^p) + \eta \log \delta \qquad\qquad (9.4)$$

where $w_t^p$ is the logarithm of the real wage perceived as permanent in period $t$, and $\omega$ is a positive constant. Workers compare the currently prevailing wage to the wage they currently perceive as permenent. Ceteris paribus, a decrease in $w_t$ or an increase in $w_t^p$ decreases the current supply of labor.[3]

An increase in $w_t$ relative to $w_t^p$ induces workers to work now and substitute future leisure for current leisure. When the current wage rate is less than $w_t^p$, some of those seeking work do not accept current employment. In the official statistics, this group is counted as unemployed. When the actual and the permanent real wage rates are equal, unemployment is zero. This suggests that within the model, unemployment may be defined as the difference between the labor supply when the two wage rates are equal ($w_t = w_t^p$) and the labor supply when the two wage rates are different. Hence the percentage of unemployment $n_t$ is given by

$$n_t = \omega(w_t^p - w_t) \qquad\qquad (9.5)$$

This formulation allows periods of overemployment as well as underemployment and implies that the actual rate of unemployment can be on either side of zero.

The stylized definition in Equation (9.5) does not imply that $n_t$ captures all the unemployment actually measured. Even when actual and perceived permanent real wage rates are equal, the actually measured rate of unemployment is nonzero because of labor market frictions associated with search and because of new entrants into the labor market. Nevertheless, $n_t$ probably captures an important part of the cyclical component of unemployment. It would be simple to assure the nonnegativity of $n_t$ by adding a positive constant frictional component of unemployment to the right-hand side of (9.5), but because we are focusing on the cyclical component, this constant is omitted.

The definition in Equation (9.5) could be made more realistic by interpreting the real wage rate as a proxy for *all* the benefits that a worker gets from a job, including location, type of occupation, and job satisfaction as well as salary. When interpreted in this broader fashion, Equation (9.5) says that when the weighted average of all those benefits currently offered on the market is perceived to be temporarily low, the number of individuals who choose to remain unemployed is higher. Job seekers who are offered work in a location or occupation other than what they prefer will choose to remain unemployed if they believe this state of affairs to be temporary, but they will be willing to accept the change if they believe that what the market currently offers reflects a permanent state. Thus the tendency to accept employment depends on workers' perceptions of the permanence of current labor market conditions. This is the basic idea of Equation (9.5).

## 2c  Money market

The real demand for money is positively related to permanent income (Friedman 1957, 1959; Laidler 1966) and inversely related to the nominal rate of interest. The specific form of the demand function in nominal terms is given by

$$m_t^d = B + p_t + y_t^p + br_t + g(y_t - y_t^p) - \theta\epsilon_t$$

$$1 > g > 0, \quad b < 0, \quad \theta \geqslant 0 \tag{9.6a}$$

where $m^d$ is the natural logarithm of nominal money demand and $b$ is a constant. The term $g(y_t - y_t^p)$ is the mirror image of the hypothesis that people relate their expenditures to permanent income even when permanent and actual incomes diverge. When permanent income is greater than actual income, the public reduces money balances to maintain spending. Conversely, when actual income exceeds permanent income, the public increases money balances.[4] The term $\theta\epsilon_t$ states that, through Walras's law, any shock to aggregate demand is partly reflected as a shock to money demand in the opposite direction. The parameter $\theta$ measures the portion of the shock to aggregate demand that individuals desire to finance by changing money balances.

The stock of money is given by

$$m_t^s = m + \psi_t \tag{9.6b}$$

where $m_t^s$ is the logarithm of the nominal stock in period $t$, $m$ is a constant, and $\psi_t$ is a random shock to the money supply.

## 2d  Equilibrium

Given the current realizations of the three shocks ($\epsilon_t$, $u_t$, and $\psi_t$), the permanent values of the wage rate $w_t^p$, the level of permanent income $y_t^p$, and the price level expected for the next period $_tp_{t+1}^*$, the market-clearing equations for the commodities, labor, and money markets and the production function can be used to determine the current values of output $y_t$, employment $l_t$, the price level $p_t$, the nominal rate of interest $r_t$, and the real wage $w_t$. Equations (9.7)–(9.9) equate the quantity of commodities demanded $e_t$ to $y_t$, and the quantities of money and labor demanded to the quantities supplied, as follows: For the commodities market,

$$y_t = k + \alpha y_t^P + \beta [r_t - (_t p_{t+1}^*) - p_t] + \epsilon_t \tag{9.7}$$

For the money market,

$$m + \psi_t = B + p_t + y_t^P + br_t + g(y_t - y_t^P) - \theta \epsilon_t \tag{9.8}$$

For the labor market,

$$l_t = -\eta(w_t - u_t) + \eta \log \delta = \omega w_t - \omega w_t^P + \eta \log \delta \tag{9.9}$$

Equation (9.10) restates the production function in logarithmic form:

$$y_t = u_t + \delta l_t \tag{9.10}$$

2e    *Permanent and transitory shocks: stochastic and information structures of the economy*

To capture the basic uncertainty concerning the permanence of shocks that affect the economy, each shock is assumed to have a permanent component and a transitory component. Individuals in the economy know the realizations of the actual shocks but never observe either component separately.

An extreme interpretation of a permanent shock cannot coexist with the notion that such a shock is subject to some nondegenerate probability distribution. If the shock is permanent in the strictest sense, it is expected to remain at its current level with probability 1 forever. Such a notion of permanence does not seem useful for analysis of the type of random shocks that affect economic systems, so we take the view that both component shocks are stochastic. What distinguishes them from each other is that the permanent component stays at its current value unless something else happens, whereas the transitory component vanishes unless another transitory shock hits the economy. The permanent component is therefore modeled as a random walk and the transitory component as a white noise process.[5] More precisely, following Muth (1960), it is assumed that each of the three stochastic shocks, $\epsilon_t$, $\phi_t$, and $u_t$, has a transitory component and a permanent component:

$$\epsilon_t = \epsilon_t^P + \epsilon_t^q, \qquad \psi_t = \psi_t^P + \psi_t^q, \qquad u_t = u_t^P + u_t^q \tag{9.11}$$

Let $x_t \equiv x_t^P + x_t^q$, where $x_t^i = \epsilon_t^i, \psi_t^i, u_t^i$, and $i = q, p$. We assume that

$$\Delta x_t^P \sim N(0, \sigma_{xp}^2); \qquad x_t^q \sim N(0, \sigma_{xq}^2) \tag{9.12}$$

where $\Delta x_t^P \equiv x_t^P - x_{t-1}^P$, $\sigma_{xp}^2$ is the variance of $\Delta x_t^P$, and $\sigma_{xq}^2$ is the variance of $x_t^q$. The permanent component of each shock $x_t^P$ is expected to remain at its previous value unless the change in this component deviates from its expected value. The expected value of a change in $x_t^P$ is zero; $x_t^P$ is a random walk. The transitory component $x_t^q$ is expected to vanish unless another transitory shock hits the system in the next period. The terms $\Delta\epsilon_t^p$, $\Delta\psi_t^p$, $\Delta u_t^p$, $\epsilon_t^q$, $\psi_t^q$, and $u_t^q$ are mutually and serially uncorrelated.

In each period, all individuals have full information about current and past values of all three shocks, but they cannot reliably separate the two components. This lack of information is not entirely dispelled by the passage of time. Even in period $t$, individuals do not know with certainty how much of the shock $x_{t-j}$, $j \geqslant 1$, they observed in the past is due to transitory changes and how much is due to permanent changes, and there is nothing in the aggregate statistics computed by the appropriate agencies to help them. Thus, there is always some uncertainty about the permanence of current levels of productivity, aggregate demand, and the money supply.[6]

## 3 Formation of beliefs about permanent variables

### 3a *Optimal forecasts of permanent values of exogenous shocks*

This section explains how individuals form optimal forecasts of the various shocks and modify their beliefs or perceptions about permanent income, permanent wages, and the permanent values of the other endogenous variables.

We focus on the optimal prediction of $x_t^p$, given the information on $x_t, x_{t-1}, x_{t-2}, \ldots$ available in period $t$. The information set of period $t$ includes the current value and all past values of $x$ and is denoted $I_t$. The problem of forming an optimal forecast about $x_t^p$ given $I_t$ can now be formulated as follows: Given

$$x_t = \Delta x_t^p + \Delta x_{t-1}^p + \cdots + \Delta x_{t-n}^p + \cdots + x_t^q$$
$$x_{t-1} = \qquad \Delta x_{t-1}^p + \cdots + \Delta x_{t-n}^p + \cdots + x_{t-1}^q$$
$$\vdots$$
$$x_{t-n} = \qquad\qquad\qquad \Delta x_{t-n}^p + \cdots + x_{t-n}^q \qquad (9.13)$$
$$\vdots$$

form an optimal forecast of

$$x_t^p = \Delta x_t^p + \Delta x_{t-1}^p + \cdots + \Delta x_{t-n}^p + \cdots \qquad (9.14)$$

Since $x_t^p$ has at least one stochastic component in common with each of $x_t, x_{t-1}, \ldots, x_{t-n}, \ldots$, it is correlated with each of these $x$ values. Hence the point estimate of the permanent component made in period $t$ for that period has a lower variance if the information about all past realizations of $x$ is used in computing the forecast. More formally, given $I_t$, the minimum-variance point estimate of $x_t^p$ is equal to the conditional expectations of $x_t^p$ where all the observations on $x$ up to and including period $t$ enter into the conditioning set $I_t$. Conditional expectations of variables from multinormal distributions are linear functions of the conditioning variables, however. [This is a direct consequence of Theorem 3.10 in Graybill (1961: 63).] Muth (1960: 302–4) has shown that the best (minimum-variance) linear estimator of $x_t^p$ given the information set $I_t$ is

$$Ex_t^p = \lambda \sum_{i=0}^{\infty} (1-\lambda)^i x_{t-i} \tag{9.15a}$$

where

$$\lambda \equiv \sqrt{h + \tfrac{1}{4}h} - \tfrac{1}{2}h; \qquad h \equiv \sigma_{xp}^2 / \sigma_{xq}^2 \tag{9.15b}$$

It follows that the prediction in Equation (9.15a) is the best estimate of the permanent component of period $t$ given information on $x$ up to and including that period and is therefore the rational expectation of the level of the permanent component in period $t$.[7]

Four features of $Ex_t^p$ should be noted.

1.  The optimal prediction of $Ex_t^p$ takes the form of a distributed lag on past values. All past values of the observed shocks $x_{t-i}$, where $i = 1, 2, \ldots$, are used to forecast the permanent component. The reason the rational expectation has the form of a distributed lag can be found in the structure of information. From Equation (9.14) we see that $x_t^p$ is influenced by each of the terms $\Delta x_{t-i}^p$, where $i = 0, 1, 2, \ldots$. All these terms are unknown in period $t$ and every past value of $x$ contains information about the permanent component, so it is rational to use this information to predict $x_t^p$. Stated less formally, Equation (9.14) emphasizes that even several periods after the realization of a permanent shock that changes $x_t$, people cannot be certain how much of the change is permanent and how much is transient. They therefore find it useful to use current and past values of $x$ to decide what is the permanent value of $x$.

2.  Each past value of $x$ enters the prediction formula with a positive weight. The higher the observed frequency of large $x$ values in the past, the more evidence there is that $x$ is permanently high, so that expectations regarding the permanent component are higher, too.

3.  The weights of the optimal forecast in Equation (9.15a) assume the form of a Koyck distributed lag and sum to unity.[8]

4.  The sum of the first $n$ coefficients, $S_n \equiv \lambda \sum_{i=0}^{n-1} (1-\lambda)^i$, is an increasing function of the ratio of the variance of permanent to the variance of temporary shocks $h$.[9] Because the weights sum to unity, the larger $h$ is, the faster people learn about a permanent change when such a change occurs. As $h \to 0$, $\lambda \to 0$ and the weights given to all past events are nearly equal. In this case, the transitory shocks cancel; the permanent com-

ponent is virtually constant over time, and people estimate $x_t^p$ by giving all past information equal weight. It is as if they estimate a constant mean using all the observations they have. At the other extreme, $h \to \infty$ and $\lambda \to 1$. Almost all the variation in $x$ is now caused by variations in the permanent component, so virtually all weight is concentrated on the most recent past, and no weight is given to earlier observations of $x$ (Muth 1960: end of Section 3).

### 3b    *Solutions for the permanent values*

By using Equation (9.15a) for each observation of the various shocks in (9.11), we can find the public's belief or perception about the permanent component of each shock in period $t$.

Let $E(\epsilon_t^p / I_t)$, $E(\psi_t^p / I_t)$, and $E(u_t^p / I_t)$ represent, respectively, the beliefs about the permanent values of the shocks to aggregate demand, money supply, and productivity in period $t$. For notational convenience, the conditioning information set $I_t$ will be deleted in future references to these beliefs. By assumption, the structure of the economic model is known to everyone. Knowledge of the structure is used with the beliefs about the shocks to form (rational) beliefs about the permanent values of the endogenous variables in period $t$.

Formally, the variables $y_t^p$, $l_t^p$, $p_t^p$, $w_t^p$, and $r_t^p$, which represent the beliefs of the public in period $t$ about permanent income, permanent labor input, permanent prices, permanent real wages, and the permanent value of the nominal interest rate, respectively, are solved from the system of Equations (9.7)–(9.10) after substituting the beliefs about the permanent values of the various shocks $E\epsilon_t^p$, $E\psi_t^p$, and $Eu_t^p$. Equations (9.7′) (9.10′) show the adjustments:

$$y_t^p = k + \alpha y_t^p + \beta r_t^p + E\epsilon_t^p \tag{9.7′}$$

$$m + E\psi_t^p = B + p_t^p + y_t^p + br_t^p - \theta E\epsilon_t^p \tag{9.8′}$$

$$l_t^p = -\eta(w_t^p - Eu_t^p) + \eta \log \delta = \eta \log \delta \tag{9.9′}$$

$$y_t^p = Eu_t^p + \delta l_t^p \tag{9.10′}$$

Only perceptions of the permanent values remain; $p_t^p$ has been substituted for $_t p_{t+1}^*$ because, given the information available in period $t$, the best forecast of the price level in period $t+1$ is the permanent level of prices that the public perceives in period $t$. [This is a consequence of the essentially stationary specification of the money supply process. The model can be easily extended to incorporate a (nonstochastic) positive rate of growth of the money supply.]

Table 5. *Solutions for permanent values*

$$w_t^p = Eu_t^p$$

$$l_t^p = \eta \log \delta$$

$$y_t^p = Eu_t^p + \delta\eta \log \delta$$

$$p_t^p = \left(\theta + \frac{b}{\beta}\right)E\epsilon_t^p - \left[1 + \frac{b}{\beta}(1-\alpha)\right]Eu_t^p + E\psi_t^p + K_p^p$$

$$r_t^p = -\frac{1}{\beta}E\epsilon_t^p + \frac{1-\alpha}{\beta}Eu_t^p + K_r^p$$

*Note:* $K_p^p$ and $K_r^p$ are combinations of the model's parameters that have no importance for the discussion.

Table 5 shows the solutions for the permanent values in terms of the perceived permanent shocks. (Hereafter, "permanent value" is used to refer to perceptions of the permanent values of shocks and endogenous variables. Behavior is always in terms of the perceived values, and the two sets – perceived and true – will almost always differ.) All permanent shocks shift the permanent values of the endogenous variables in the same direction as the initial shocks shown in Equations (9.7)–(9.10). The effects of the three shocks will be discussed in turn.

Permanent shocks to the stock of money $E\psi_t^p$ affect only the permanent price level. This is a reflection of the monetary neutrality of the model. Once the change in the money stock is perceived, it is reflected in $p_t^p$ and therefore in today's forecast of the next period's price $_tp_{t+1}^*$; all real variables are unaffected. Permanent real shocks to spending $E\epsilon_t^p$ include a permanent change in the preference for current relative to future consumption and a permanent change in the real value of government spending. An increase in $E\epsilon_t^p$ increases the permanent nominal rate of interest. Because there is no systematic monetary growth in the model, the permanent rate of inflation is zero. There is thus no difference between the real and the nominal rates of interest, and an increase in $E\epsilon_t^p$ also increases the permanent real rate of interest. The effect on the permanent price level is positive.

Permanent changes in productivity also induce nonneutral responses. Increased permanent productivity increases permanent output and the permanent real wage. Increased permanent output lowers the permanent price level and the real rate of interest. Permanent employment remains unchanged because we have assumed a vertical long-run supply curve of labor with respect to $w_t^p$. If we permit the elasticity of the labor supply with respect to $w_t$ to exceed the elasticity with respect to $w_t^p$ in Equation (9.4), the long-run supply of labor is positively sloped. Permanent increases in productivity increase $l_t^p$. The direction of all other permanent responses remains the same as in Table 5.

The oil shocks of 1974 and 1979 can be treated as permanent reductions in productivity. Once the public recognizes the permanent nature of the shocks, permanent output, permanent income, and permanent real wages fall. Prices and real interest rates are permanently higher, but the permanent price level does not continue to rise unless one of the permanent shocks changes from period to period.

Adjustments of beliefs about the permanent values of the endogenous variable in Table 5 take the form of distributed lags on past values of the shocks to spending, productivity, and money. This follows from the fact that optimal forecasts of the permanent components of the variables depend on only distributed lags on past observed values of the various shocks. This gradual adjustment is a result of the fundamental problem of separating permanent and transitory changes when these changes are not observed separately.

## 4      Working of the model

The perceived permanent values summarize all the available information about the present and future, but the available information can never be complete. New shocks can occur each period. Perceptions about the permanence of shocks change. The actual values of the endogenous variables depend both on the perceptions and on the shocks. In this section, we solve for the actual values of the endogenous variables and analyze the effects of the shocks on the principal variables of the model.

### 4a      *Solutions for actual values*

By substituting the permanent values from Table 5 into Equations (9.7)–(9.10) and solving for the equilibrium values of the endogenous variables, we can obtain $y_t$, $l_t$, $w_t$, $p_t$, and $r_t$ as functions of the actual shocks $x_t = \epsilon_t, u_t, \psi_t$, and perceived permanent values of the same shocks $Ex_t^p$. The solutions are shown in Table 6.

### 4b      *Responses to productivity changes*

If all shocks are permanent and fully perceived, $u_t = Eu_t^p$. Fully perceived permanent shocks to productivity change output and real wages in direct proportion to the size of the shock. Employment $l_t$ is unaffected.

Table 6. *Solutions for actual values*

$$w_t = \frac{\eta}{\eta+\omega}\left(u_t + \frac{\omega}{\eta}Eu_t^P\right)$$

$$l_t = \frac{\eta\omega}{\eta+\omega}(u_t - Eu_t^P) + \eta\log\delta$$

$$y_t = \frac{1}{\eta+\omega}\{[\eta+\omega(1+\delta\eta)]u_t - \delta\eta\omega Eu_t^P\} + \delta\eta\log\delta$$

$$p_t = \frac{1}{\beta(1-b)}\Bigg\{\beta\psi_t + (b+\theta\beta)\epsilon_t - (b+\beta g)\frac{\eta+\omega(1+\delta\eta)}{\eta+\omega}u_t$$

$$+ (b+\beta g)\frac{\delta\eta\omega}{\eta+\omega}w_t^P + [\alpha b - \beta(1-g)]y_t^P - b\beta p_t^P\Bigg\} + k_p$$

$$= \frac{1}{\beta(1-b)}\Bigg(\beta(\psi_t - bE\psi_t^P) - \frac{[\eta+\omega(1+\delta\eta)](b+\beta g)}{\eta+\omega}u_t + (\theta\beta + b)\epsilon_t$$

$$+ \left\{\frac{(b+\beta g)}{\eta+\omega}\delta\eta\omega - \beta(1-g) + b[\beta + \alpha + b(1-\alpha)]\right\}Eu_t^P - b(\theta\beta + b)E\epsilon_t^P\Bigg) + K_p$$

$$r_t = \frac{1}{\beta(1-b)}\Bigg\{-\beta\psi_t + \frac{1+\beta g}{\eta+\omega}[\eta+\omega(1+\delta\eta)]u_t - (1-\theta\beta)\epsilon_t$$

$$- \frac{1+\beta g}{\eta+\omega}\delta\eta\omega w_t^P - [\alpha - \beta(1-g)]y_t^P + \beta p_t^P\Bigg\} + K_r$$

*Note:* $K_p$ and $K_r$ are combinations of parameters that are of no interest to the discussion.

A transitory shock is at the opposite extreme. It is convenient to analyze the effects of a transitory shock by examining the effect of a change in $u_t$ when $Eu_t^P = u_t^P$. The increase in $u_t$ raises real wages, employment, and output and lowers the price level. Because a transitory shock is a one-time change, people expect the actual values to return to the permanent values.

The inability to separate permanent and transitory changes makes the adjustment to any shock a mixture of the responses to permanent and transitory changes. At first, the nature of the change in $u_t$ (or $\epsilon_t$ or $\psi_t$) is not correctly perceived. As its nature – permanent or transitory – becomes clearer, the responses of the endogenous variables change.

Suppose there is a permanent change in $u_t$. Initially $Eu_t^P$ changes very little. If the shock is positive, real wages, employment, and output rise and the price level falls. As the perception of permanence increases, $Eu_t^P$ starts to adjust, which reinforces the effect of $u_t$ on $w_t$ and wholly or partly offsets the effects of $u_t$ on employment and output.

The distinction between permanent and actual changes helps to explain why real wages appear to be "sticky." The initial response of the real wage to a permanent productivity shock is a fraction of the response to a fully perceived permanent shock [this fraction is $\eta/(\eta+\omega)$]. Once the permanence of the shock is recognized, the effect of $u_t$ on the real wage is reinforced by the response of $w_t$ to $Eu_t^p$. Equation (9.15) implies, however, that $Eu_t^p$ adjusts gradually, so the full adjustment of the real wage occurs gradually.

The stickiness of real wages means that the short-run elasticity of the real wage with respect to productivity is less than the long-run elasticity. For unemployment the opposite is true. The level of employment rises in response to a positive shock to productivity and falls in response to a negative shock. The response to the actual shock increases the demand for labor. As the permanence of the shock gradually becomes apparent and real wages adjust, the demand for labor is reduced and the level of employment declines.

The response of employment to a permanent productivity shock is reflected in output. Output initially overshoots and then gradually adjusts as the permanence of the shock is perceived and the increased or reduced productivity becomes fully reflected in the prevailing real wage. Permanent reductions in productivity permanently lower output. The unchanged labor force has lower productivity and produces less.

During the adjustment of perceived permanent changes to actual permanent changes in productivity, the price level may rise or fall. The direction of the adjustment will be determined by the speed with which the permanence of the shock is perceived and the relative effects of $w^p$, $y^p$, and $p^p$. The response of $p$ to $Eu_t^p$ is ambiguous because the positive effects of $Eu_t^p$ on $w_t^p$ and $y_t^p$ (for $\beta$ sufficiently small) combine with a negative effect of $Eu_t^p$ on $p_t^p$. The long-run adjustment once the permanence of the productivity shock is fully perceived is not in doubt: A permanent increase in productivity reduces the excess demand for output, and a permanent reduction increases it. The long-run elasticity of $p_t$ with respect to $u_t = Eu_t^p$ is $-[1+(b/\beta)(1-\alpha)]$, which is unambiguously negative.

## 4c    *Responses to monetary shocks*

Because the model is dichotomized, money does not affect output, employment, or wages. Actual and perceived monetary shocks affect only the price level and the rate of interest. A change in $\psi_t$ changes the price level by changing the excess supply of money and market interest rates. The change in interest rates changes spending. A change in $E\psi_t^p$ also affects spending by changing the perceived price level and the excess demand or supply in the commodity market.

The equation for $p_t$ in Table 6 shows that when all monetary shocks are permanent ($\psi_t = E\psi_t^p = \psi_t^p$), the price level changes equiproportionately.

Transitory shocks change the price level less than proportionally because the transitory shock temporarily changes interest rates and the demand for money is an offsetting direction. If a permanent change in money is less than fully perceived, the price level undershoots the stationary equilibrium value. The price level remains below the stationary equilibrium value following monetary expansion (and above it following monetary contraction) until the permanence of the shock is correctly perceived.

Substituting the expression for $p_t^p$ from Table 5 into the equation for $r_t$ in Table 6 and expressing $r_t$ in terms of $\psi_t - E\psi_t^p$ yields

$$r_t = \frac{1}{b-1}(\psi_t - E\psi_t^p) + \begin{bmatrix} \text{other terms that do not depend on} \\ \text{either actual or permanent money supply} \end{bmatrix}$$

which suggests that market interest rates fall in response to perceived transitory increases in the money supply. The reason is that when an increase in the money supply is perceived to be transitory, individuals expect the price level to be lower in the future. As a result the Fisher premium in interest rates becomes negative and pushes the nominal rate of interest down. Such a negative effect of increases in the money supply on nominal interest rates has been documented by Cagan (1972) for the United States and by Haberger (1963) for Chile. Note that movements in the nominal rate are completely dominated by the expected rate of change in the price level. The real rate of interest is therefore independent of either the actual or the perceived money supply, reflecting again the dichotomous nature of the model economy.

### 4d     *Responses to spending shocks*

Changes in actual and perceived aggregate demand affect neither employment, output, nor the real wage rate: The entire effect of spending shocks is borne by the price level and the rate of interest. Table 6 shows that prices and market rates of interest rise in response to positive shocks and fall in response to negative shocks. [For further details, see Brunner et al. (1980: 482).]

### 5     **Stagflation**

The sluggish adjustment of wages, prices, output, and employment that results from the confusion between permanent and transitory shocks can produce a rising level of unemployment and rising prices in response to a permanent decrease in productivity. This pattern, known as stagflation, is at times taken as evidence that prices are set without regard to market conditions. We show that this is not necessarily the case. Stagflation can occur even in a neoclassical framework when there is uncertainty about the permanence of shocks.

This section analyzes unemployment and inflation separately. Then we combine the responses and discuss the stagflation that followed the 1973–4 oil shock.

### 5a　Unemployment

Equation (9.5) makes unemployment dependent on the difference $w_t - w_t^p$. By substituting $w_t$ and $w_t^p$ from Tables 5 and 6 and leading unemployment $j$ periods, we obtain

$$n_{t+j} = \frac{\omega\eta}{\eta+\omega}(Eu_{t+j}^p - u_{t+j}) \tag{9.16a}$$

or

$$n_{t+j} = A(Eu_{t+j}^p - u_{t+j}) \tag{9.16b}$$

where $A \equiv \omega\eta/(\eta+\omega) > 0$. Unemployment is an increasing function of the difference between the perceived permanent level of productivity and its current value.

When the actual values of productivity and aggregate demand are equal to their respective perceived permanent components, the unemployment rate is zero. When people believe that the permanent level of productivity is higher than the actual level, they may refuse offers of employment in the belief that the actual situation is temporary. Unemployment in this case will be positive. Conversely, when it is generally believed that current productivity and (therefore) the real wage rate are temporarily high, individuals accept jobs more than usual and the rate of unemployment is negative (see also Section 2b). Note that in marked contrast to traditional Keynesian theory, unemployment is here conceived to be completely voluntary. That does not mean that those who choose to remain unemployed are necessarily happy about it; most probably they would prefer to be employed, but only at a wage higher than that currently offered by the market. Given the current relatively low real wage rate, they consider unemployment the better option.

The unemployment rate is not stationary. Each observation on unemployment, output, prices, wages, and interest rates leads to a revision of beliefs about permanent and transitory components, and each revision of beliefs changes perceived and actual values. Each period also brings additional shocks, however. The fundamental inference problem remains.

To illustrate the inference problem and its influence on unemployment, we start from a position in which the only reason for a difference between actual and perceived permanent productivity is that the actual shocks include a transitory component. Formally,

$$E_q u_{t-1} = u_{t-1}^p = E u_{t-1}^p \tag{9.17}$$

in which the index q on the expectation operator indicates that the expectation is over the distribution of the transitory component of the variable. The only reason that (positive or negative) unemployment occurs is that productivity is subject to transitory shocks. Unemployment is a white noise process with mean zero.

Suppose now that in period $t$ a large permanent shock to productivity reduces productivity by a large constant $Du^p$. People observe the effects of the shock but do not know whether the observed changes are permanent or transitory adjustments. For convenience we assume that without the shock, permanent productivity would have been constant at $u^p$. [10] The rates of unemployment before and after the shock are given by Equations (9.18) and (9.19), respectively: [11]

$$n_{t-j} = -A u_{t-j}^q; \qquad j < 0 \tag{9.18}$$

$$n_{t+j} = -A \left[ 1 - \lambda_u \sum_{i=0}^{j} (1-\lambda_u)^i \right] Du^p$$

$$+ A \left[ \lambda_u \sum_{i=1}^{j} (1-\lambda_u)^i u_{t+j-1}^q - (1-\lambda_u) u_{t+j}^q \right]; \qquad j \geqslant 0 \tag{9.19}$$

where, from (9.11), (9.12), and (9.15b),

$$\lambda_u = \left[ \frac{\sigma_{up}^2}{\sigma_{uq}^2} + \frac{1}{4} \left( \frac{\sigma_{up}^2}{\sigma_{uq}^2} \right)^2 \right]^{1/2} - \frac{1}{2} \frac{\sigma_{up}^2}{\sigma_{uq}^2}$$

By taking expected values (over $u_t^q$) of Equations (9.18) and (9.19) before and after the permanent reduction in productivity $Du^p$, we can compare the expected values of the rate of unemployment over the distribution of transitory shocks:

$$E_q n_{t-1} = 0 \tag{9.18'}$$

$$E_q n_{t+j} = -A \left[ 1 - \lambda_u \sum_{i=0}^{j} (1-\lambda_u)^i \right] Du^p; \qquad j \geqslant 0 \tag{9.19'}$$

Equation (9.18') shows that the expected value of the rate of unemployment before the change in permanent productivity is zero; unemployment deviates from its expected value only because of transitory shocks. [This can also be seen from (9.18).] After the reduction in permanent productivity, the expected value of unemployment becomes positive. This is because $1 - \lambda_u \sum_{i=0}^{j} (1-\lambda_u)^i > 0$ for all $i$ and $Du^p < 0$. The expected value of unemployment is largest immediately after the decrease in permanent productivity. It then falls monotonically to zero as information about the permanence of the shock accrues.

The persistence of unemployment depends on the relative variances of permanent and transitory shocks. The larger the variance of permanent productivity shocks $\sigma_{up}^2$ relative to the variance of transitory productivity shocks $\sigma_{uq}^2$, the shorter and the less severe is the period of unemployment following a shock of a given magnitude.

Inspection of Equation (9.19') also suggests that unemployment persists on the same side of zero for several periods. Persistent unemployment is a consequence of the more gradual adjustment of permanent productivity and permanent wages than of actual productivity and the actual wage rate. Initially, people interpret most of the decrease in the equilibrium real wage as transitory. If the shock persists, beliefs adjust gradually; the difference between perceived permanent wages and actual wages decreases, and the expected value of the rate of unemployment decreases. Formally, as $j$ increases from zero, the coefficient of $Du^p$ decreases in absolute value toward zero.

5b    *Persistent unemployment and business cycles*

Equation (9.16) implies that the rate of unemployment in period $t+j$ is a linear combination of the forecast errors of the productivity shocks. Given the information set $I_{t+j}$, these forecast errors are serially uncorrelated. The rate of unemployment conditioned on $I_{t+j}$ is therefore also serially uncorrelated; however, a sample of unemployment rates drawn from a period following a relatively large permanent shock will appear to be serially correlated. This serial correlation is a property of the sample; it provides no information about the underlying population, or about a larger sample drawn from the same population, or about a sample of equal size drawn for a different time period.

Evidence of ex post serial correlation in a particular sample is not evidence of the inefficient use of information. Rational agents who look back on the period find support for the hypothesis that a large permanent shock occurred but was misperceived at the time.

At the time that the seemingly serial correlation is generated, there is no way people can use this evidence to improve their forecast. The reason is that the covariance between the forecast errors in the population is zero. In retrospect, however, the same people realize that a large negative shock to permanent productivity did occur, causing perceptions about productivity to be higher than actual productivity for a while and inducing a finite period of seeming serial correlation in the rate of employment. By the time they realize this, though, the information can no longer be used to improve the decisions made in past periods. It is possible to show formally that the sample covariance between adjacent forecast errors following a large permanent shock will be nonzero for several periods after the shock.[12] Standard tests for serial correlation may then detect serially correlated forecast errors and serially correlated unemployment in finite samples, although there is no serial correlation in the population.

In retrospect, economists and statisticians can identify *finite* periods of serially correlated unemployment or, more generally, of serially correlated deviations of real variables from their trend. The amplitude and duration of unemployment in such periods depend on the relative variance of permanent and transitory components. The larger the relative variance of the permanent component, the faster is the speed of adjustment to the shock. For the same realization of a given large permanent shock, a relatively large variance of permanent shocks lowers the amplitude and decreases the duration of unemployment. Conversely, a relatively small variance of permanent shocks implies that a given permanent shock will induce a longer period of unemployment.

Throughout the discussion of unemployment, we have made the convenient assumption that the only permanent change that occurs is the permanent productivity shock $Du^p$. This permitted us to trace the effects of a permanent change in isolation. We can now remove the assumption of a single permanent shock and discuss the qualitative effects of a large permanent productivity change in a world in which $u_t^p$ changes continuously over time [in line with the assumptions in (9.12)] but usually by relatively small increments. If we now superimpose on this economy an unusually large negative permanent productivity shock in period $t$, it will dominate the scene for some time and all our preceding results will follow. In particular the lower the variance of permanent productivity shocks, the longer it takes people to learn about a permanent change of a given magnitude, and the longer the period of unemployment following the shock. By Equation (9.12), the probability that such a shock will occur is small but not zero. Hence, large shocks will not occur very often, but once they do, they will trigger the various effects described.

### 5c     *Expected inflation*

All the shocks in the model affect the level of the variables. Unless there are repeated shocks in the same direction, the measured rates of change decline toward zero. There is no permanent inflation.[13]

Individuals form expectations about the price level they expect to prevail in period $t+1$ on the basis of information available in period $t$. The perceived or anticipated price level is $_t p_{t+1}^* - p_t^p$. The anticipated rate of inflation, after substituting the equations in Tables 5 and 6 and canceling terms, is

$$_t p_{t+1}^* - p_t = -\frac{1}{1-b}(\psi_t - E\psi_t^{\mathrm{p}}) + \left(\frac{b}{\beta} + g\right)\frac{\eta + \omega(1+\delta\eta)}{(1-b)(\eta+\omega)}(u_t - Eu_t^{\mathrm{p}})$$

$$-\frac{(\eta+\omega)(\theta+b/\beta)}{(1-b)(\eta+\omega)}(\epsilon_t - E\epsilon_t^{\mathrm{p}}) \tag{9.20}$$

Equation (9.20) shows that when the actual shocks are equal to their perceived permanent values, the expected rate of inflation is zero. Elsewhere, the expected rate of inflation is directly or inversely related (depending on the shock under consideration) to the difference between the current realization of the shock and the perceived permanent value.

An increase in the money stock that is perceived as transitory induces a transitory increase in the price level, so $\psi - E\psi_t^{\mathrm{p}} > 0$ implies a negative expected rate of price change. A temporary positive shock to productivity has the opposite effect. The shock lowers the price level, but the lower price level is not expected to persist. The expected rate of change is positive.

In general, any shock that causes $x$ to deviate from $Ex_t^{\mathrm{p}}$ $(x_t = \psi_t, \epsilon_t, u_t)$ affects the expected rate of inflation in a direction opposite to the effect of $x_t$ on the current price level. This general rule leads to two propositions:

1.  A maintained increase in the permanent value of a shock that starts in period $t$ causes an initial change in the anticipated rate of price change (inflation) opposite to the initial effect of this shock on the price level. Expected inflation reverses its direction gradually. The reasoning is implicit in the gradual adjustment of permanent perceptions implied by (9.15), and in the fact that in (9.20) actual and permanent values have opposite effects on inflation.

2.  The expected rate of inflation and the duration of expected inflation following a permanent shock depend on the relative variances of the permanent and transitory components of the shock. This follows from the demonstration in footnote 9 that the sum $S_n$ of the first $n$ coefficients of the distributed lag increases as the relative size of the permanent variance increases.

## 5d    Stagflation

A permanent negative shock to productivity affects both unemployment and the rate of price change. This section brings some of our findings together to explain the combination of rising prices and unemployment that is known as stagflation.

Suppose a permanent negative shock to productivity occurs in period $t$. Initially, the shock is not perceived as permanent. We know from the discussion of prices, unemployment, and inflation that a shock of this kind initially causes the unemployment rate to increase and the price level to rise. The measured rate of price change is positive. Because the reduction in $u_t$ is treated as temporary, the public expects future prices to be lower and future employment to be higher.

Because people do not correctly perceive the permanence of the productivity shock, they consume at levels more nearly consistent with past than future values of $y^p$. Real wages fall on impact but not enough to prevent unemployment. The unemployed seek work at a real wage $w^p$ that is not fully adjusted to the permanently lower level of productivity in the economy. Workers reject offers of employment at the current wage. Because everyone believes that the economy can sustain a real wage higher than the current wage, the workers' response is rational.

Output declines first because of the permanent reduction in productivity and second because labor withdraws some of its services. Since aggregate demand initially declines just a bit, there is excess demand in the commodities market and upward pressure on the price level. Thus a large permanent negative productivity shock increases on impact the rates of both price change and unemployment.

Persistence of the negative productivity shock erodes the belief that the shock is transitory. $Eu_t^p$ declines and the initial responses of employment, output, and measured inflation are reversed. Real wages decline further, and perceived permanent real wages fall. People accept employment at lower real wages. The level of unemployment and the measured rate of inflation fall.

The speed of adjustment to a permanent productivity shock and the persistence of stagflation depend on the relative variance of permanent and transitory shocks. Infrequent permanent shocks lengthen the period of stagflation following a particular shock. Because people are unaccustomed to permanent shocks, they take longer to believe that the productivity shock is permanent after it occurs. As the frequency of shocks increases, the variance of the permanent component rises and the speed of adjustment increases.

A permanent negative productivity shock appears capable of generating the pattern of responses popularly called stagflation. Stagflation results from the inability to accurately separate permanent and transitory components of a productivity shock in a world of uncertainty. Rational responses in a world of uncertainty with prices and quantities at market-clearing values appear to be consistent with the pattern described as stagflation.

The sequence of events following a permanent productivity shock resembles the response to the 1973–4 oil shocks and the resulting stagflation. The actual sequence was, of course, a mixture of the shock and the responses to fiscal and monetary policies.

## 6 Conclusion

To generate sequences of persistent unemployment, we have used a standard equilibrium model in which all expectations are rational and all markets clear instantaneously. The distinctive feature of the theory is that the permanent and transitory components of the shocks that affect the economy are not known in advance and are not revealed for some time after they occur. People must solve an inference problem to distinguish the permanent and transitory components of the data they observe. Long after shocks occur, even rational individuals using all available information can remain uncertain about the persistence of shocks.

Individuals' decisions depend on their belief about the permanent values, so they forecast these values. Because the permanent components of past shocks have some elements in common with the current permanent component, optimal forecasts of permanent values use observed values of past and current shocks.

Although the adjustment paths in the model depend on a relatively simple stochastic structure, the qualitative implications for stagflation are more general. Rising prices and rising unemployment – stagflation – are consistent with the model under conditions that appear to have been realized in the recent past. The main implications of this chapter may be briefly summarized as follows.

A large permanent reduction in productivity increases unemployment on impact. This is because perceptions of the permanence of the lower level of productivity form slowly. Real wages decline on impact but do not fully respond to the shock until the permanence of the shock is recognized. During the transition, the labor market clears at the prevailing real wage, but the level of employment remains below the level at which anticipated and actual wages are equal.

Persistent unemployment does not depend on an accelerator as in Lucas (1975). Persistence increases (adjustment slows) as the variance of permanent shocks decreases relative to the variance of transitory shocks. Slow adjustment implies that *at times* unemployment appears to be serially correlated. Evidence of serial correlation in a finite sample can be observed by looking backward. At the time that the unemployment occurs, unemployment rates appear to be serially uncorrelated.

The theory implies that a reduction in permanent productivity raises the price level at the same time that the level of unemployment increases and subsequently lowers the real wage. On impact, the measured rate of inflation rises. As perception of the permanence of the shock grows, the measured rate of inflation declines and real wages converge to their lower permanent value.

The framework presented in this chapter also illustrates that rational expectations can be consistent with a slow revision of expectations. Much of our quantitative knowledge about the economy comes from studies that use distributed lags to obtain expected values as a weighted average of past values. Poole (1976) argues that such estimates produce lag structures that are too long to be consistent with rational expectations. This criticism seems too sweeping. If the fundamental inference problem in a world of uncertainty is judging the persistence of shocks, distributed lags are not just an acceptable procedure, they are an optimal means of forecasting. [B. M. Friedman (1979) makes a similar point with a single-equation model.] The particular form taken by the optimal predictor here is a consequence of the particular stochastic form assumed for the permanent and transitory components of the shocks. For other assumptions the optimal predictor will not necessarily be of the Koyck type; however, it will usually be a distributed lag because it is generally optimal to use *all* past information when the inference problem involves the separation of permanent from transitory changes.

# CHAPTER 10

# Permanent–transitory confusion: implications for monetary policy and the efficiency of the price system

## 1 Introduction[1]

This chapter explores the implications of the confusion between temporary and permanent changes in the relative demands for monetary policy and for the allocative efficiency of the price system. We saw in Chapter 9 that confusion between permanent and transitory changes in the level of aggregate productivity can produce the symptoms of stagflation. The confusion between permanent and transitory changes in relative prices also has implications for the allocation of resources across sectors in the economy. This is because producers usually gear their production levels to what they perceive to be permanent relative prices. Erratic monetary policy introduces transitory distortions in relative prices and makes it more difficult for producers to make accurate forecasts of the permanent values of relevant relative prices.[2]

More generally, frequent uncertain shifts in the structure of relative demands and relative supplies make it more difficult to plan production optimally. These effects and others cannot be investigated within the framework of an aggregate model of the type presented in Chapter 9 because they work by reallocating resources across sectors. We therefore move back to a multimarket equilibrium model similar in spirit to the models presented in Chapter 6. Because the discussion here focuses on the permanent–transitory confusion rather than on the aggregate–relative confusion, however, individuals in all sectors are endowed with the *same* current information.

A formal multimarkets equilibrium model incorporating the permanent–transitory confusion is presented in Section 2. Section 3 demonstrates that expectations about future relative prices may be formed adaptively and be rational at the same time. The implications for monetary policy and for the allocative efficiency of the price system are explored in Section 4, using the variance of actual around full current information output as a measure of the inefficiency of the price system.

Section 5 shows that for a given level of exogenous uncertainty, individuals choose a coefficient of adaptation of expectations that maximizes the allocative efficiency of the price system. The effect of the production lag on the allocative efficiency of the price system is investigated in Section 6 by using the divergence between actual output and full *future* information output as a measure of the allocative inefficiency of the price system.

## 2     Model

### 2a     *Supplies and demands*

The economy is composed of a large number of markets for different goods. All markets are competitive and clear instantaneously. Production takes one period, so suppliers of any given good have to decide today how much they will put on the market in the next period. Suppliers make output decisions on the basis of what they believe the relative price of their product will be in the next period.

More precisely, the supply of a good $v$ is given by

$$y_t^s(v) = \beta_v t + \gamma_v [E_{t-1} p_t(v) - E_{t-1} Q_t] \tag{10.1}$$

where $y_t^s(v)$ is the logarithm of output of good $v$ supplied at time $t$ and $E_{t-1} p_t(v)$ and $E_{t-1} Q_t$ are expected values (conditional on information up to and including period $t-1$) of the logarithms of the price of good $v$ in period $t$ and of the general price level in period $t$, respectively. The term $\gamma_v$ measures the *positive* supply elasticity of good $v$ with respect to the next period's expected relative price. The term $\beta_v t$ measures increases known with certainty to be permanent in the production of good $v$.

The demand for good $v$ at time $t$ is given by

$$y_t^d(v) = \psi_v [n_t(v) - p_t(v)] \tag{10.2}$$

where $y_t^d(v)$ is the logarithm of the demand for good $v$ at time $t$, $p_t(v)$ is the logarithm of the actual price of good $v$ at time $t$, $-\psi_v$ is the (negative) elasticity of demand with respect to its own price, and $n_t(v)$ is a shift parameter directly related to the logarithm of nominal income that people desire to spend on good $v$ at time $t$.[3] This parameter reflects changes in the aggregate level of demand as well as changes specific to the demand for good $v$. More specifically,

$$n_t(v) = x_t(v) + \delta t + m_t + \epsilon_t(v) \tag{10.3}$$

where for all $v$,

$$x_t(v) = x_t^p(v) + x_t^q(v); \qquad \Delta x_t^p(v) \sim N(0, \sigma_{xp}^2); \qquad x_t^q(v) \sim N(0, \sigma_{xq}^2)$$

$$(10.3a)$$

$$\epsilon_t(v) \sim N(0, \sigma_\epsilon^2) \qquad\qquad (10.3b)$$

and

$$\Delta m_t \sim N(0, \sigma_m^2) \qquad\qquad (10.3c)$$

The expression $\delta t + m_t + \epsilon_t(v)$ summarizes all the influences of money on the level of demand for good $v$. The coefficient $\delta$ is the part of the permanent rate of growth in the money supply that is known with certainty in advance. The term $m_t$ is the stochastic part of the money supply and is specified as a nonstationary stochastic process whose first difference has an expected value of zero and a constant variance. In addition to the term $\delta t + m_t$, which reflects that the money supply affects the total planned nominal spending on all goods in an identical manner, there is a term $\epsilon_t(v)$, which states that a given monetary impulse does not affect all markets with the same contemporaneous intensity. Some markets are affected sooner and others later. As a result the total monetary impact on the demand for a particular good may differ *temporarily* from its impact on the demand for other goods. This differential impact is captured by the transitory differential monetary noise $\epsilon_t(v)$, whose distribution is given in Equation (10.3b).

The size of the variance $\sigma_\epsilon^2$ probably depends on the degree to which the demands that face the various sectors of the economy have developed similar institutional characteristics to incorporate monetary growth. At both high and low inflation, $\sigma_\epsilon^2$ will probably be relatively low: At high inflation all sectors would have introduced devices to incorporate the effect of monetary change quickly; at low inflation none would have introduced such devices. In both cases, $\sigma_\epsilon^2$ will therefore be relatively low because most sectors respond uniformly to monetary expansion. At intermediate rates of inflation, however, some sectors are already adjusted to inflation, whereas others are not. In this range the differential impact of monetary growth in the short run is relatively high and therefore the variance $\sigma_\epsilon^2$ should be relatively large. Different costs of developing mechanisms that incorporate monetary expansion swiftly have a stronger differential impact at intermediate rates of inflation. A stylized way of expressing this is to make $\sigma_\epsilon^2$ an inverted U function of the average rate of inflation. For the range of rates of inflation actually experienced by industrialized countries, $\sigma_\epsilon^2$ is probably an increasing function of the rate of inflation.

Note from Equation (10.2) and footnote 3 that, except for differential transitory monetary noise $\epsilon_t(v)$, money is neutral in the sense that a given increase in $\delta t + m_t$ that is matched by an increase of equal size in $p_t(v)$ for all $v$ values does not affect demand in any market in the economy.

The term $x_t(v)$ expresses a real relative shock to the demand in market $v$. It contains both permanent $[x_t^p(v)]$ and transitory $[x_t^q(v)]$ effects on the demand for good $v$ whose distributions are common to all $v$ values and are given in Equation (10.3a). This specification says that even in the absence of monetary shocks, relative demands are continuously reallocated across markets in the economy in a random fashion. These relative changes in demand are partially permanent and partially temporary, and individuals never know for sure the degree of permanence of any given change.

The terms $\Delta x_t^p(v)$, $x_t^q(v)$, $m_t$, and $\epsilon_t(v)$ are all serially and mutually uncorrelated. Although the distributions of the components of $x_t(v)$ are the same for all $v$ values, the realizations of these random variables across different markets usually differ.

## 2b     *Equilibrium*

Output decisions for period $t$ are made on the basis of the relative price of good $v$ expected in period $t-1$ for period $t$. These decisions, together with the outcomes of the demand shocks $x_t(v)$ and the monetary shock $m_t + \epsilon_t(v)$, determine the equilibrium price $p_t(v)$ of good $v$ at time $t$. Formally, the equilibrium price may be obtained by equating (10.1) and (10.2), using (10.3), and solving for $p_t(v)$:

$$p_t(v) = \left( \delta - \frac{\beta_v}{\psi_v} \right) t + x_t(v) + m_t + \epsilon_t(v) - \frac{\gamma_v}{\psi_v} [E_{t-1} p_t(v) - E_{t-1} Q_t]$$

$$(10.4)$$

Not surprisingly, the equilibrium price in market $v$ is an increasing function of the total monetary impact on this market and a decreasing function of the perceptions of producers in the previous period about their permanent relative price. The higher the perceived permanent relative price is, the more they decide to produce and the larger the supply of good $v$ is in the current period. As a result the equilibrium price of the good in period $t$ is lower.

## 2c     *General price level*

The general price level is defined as a fixed-weight index of the individual prices:

$$Q_t \equiv \sum_v u(v) p_t(v) \geqslant 0; \qquad \sum_v u(v) = 1 \qquad (10.5)$$

The weight assigned to any one good is taken to be small in comparison to the sum of the weights because the number of goods in the economy is large.

## 2d    Structure of information

All individuals in the economy have access to the *same* current information. They all know the deterministic and stochastic structures of the economy and the current prices on all markets. The production decisions of individual producers depend on what they currently believe about next period's relative prices of the goods they are selling. A rational forecast as of period $t-1$ of the relative price of the good for period $t$ is the part of the actual relative price that is believed to be permanent given the information available in period $t-1$. The part of $p_{t-1}(v) - Q_{t-1}$ believed to be transitory is not relevant for forecasting $p_t(v) - Q_t$ because it will have vanished by the time the next period unfolds.[4]

The best forecast as of period $t-1$ of $p_t(v)$ is, by definition, $E_{t-1}p_t(v)$. To calculate this forecast, individuals use the knowledge that the equilibrium price is generated by Equation (10.4). So they substitute $E_{t-1}p_t(v)$ into this equation instead of $p_t(v)$ and solve for $E_{t-1}p_t(v)$ in terms of the perceived permanent values of the various shocks and their perception about the permanent value of the general price level. The result is

$$E_{t-1}p_t(v) = (1-d_v)[\delta t + E_{t-1}x_t(v) + E_{t-1}m_t] - \frac{\beta_v t}{\psi_v + \gamma_v} + d_v E_{t-1}Q_t \tag{10.6}$$

where $d_v \equiv \gamma_v/(\psi_v + \gamma_v)$. In the derivation of this equation, use has been made of the fact implied by (10.3b) that $E_{t-1}\epsilon_t(v) = 0$.

To form a perception about the permanent value of the general price level, individuals substitute Equation (10.6) for each $v$ into the definition of the general price level in (10.5), put $Q_t$ equal to $E_{t-1}Q_t$, and solve for $E_{t-1}Q_t$. The result appears as Equation (10.7):

$$E_{t-1}Q_t = \delta t + E_{t-1}m_t + \sum_v w(v)\psi_v E_{t-1}x_t(v) - \sum_v w(v)\beta_v t \tag{10.7}$$

where $\bar{d} \equiv \sum_v u(v)d_v$, $w(v) \equiv [1/(1-\bar{d})][u(v)/(\psi_v + \gamma_v)]$, and use has been made of the fact that

$$\sum_v w(v)\psi_v = \sum_v u(v) = 1 \tag{10.8}$$

$E_{t-1}x_t(v)$ and $E_{t-1}m_t$ are, respectively, the best forecasts, given the information available in period $t-1$, of the permanent level of real relative demand in market $v$ and of the permanent level of the stochastic component of money supply. Equations (10.6) and (10.7) express $E_{t-1}p_t(v)$ and $E_{t-1}Q_t$ in terms of these perceptions about permanent variables. We turn now to the characterization of the formation of these perceptions.

In period $t-1$, all people in the economy have observations about the money supply up to and including period $t-1$ from which they can deduce $m_{t-1}, m_{t-2}, \ldots$. They also have observations on prices in all markets up to and including period $t-1$. Because the expectation $E_{t-2}p_{t-1}(v)$ $-E_{t-2}Q_{t-1}$ held in the past is known in period $t-1$, an observation of $m_{t-1}$ and $p_{t-1}(v)$ amounts, through Equation (10.4) lagged one period, to an observation of the sum $O_{t-1}(v) \equiv x_{t-1}(v) + \epsilon_{t-1}(v)$. Previous values of $O(v)$ can be deduced from values of prices and quantities in preceding periods in a similar manner. The upshot is that observations of money and prices up to and including period $t-1$ are equivalent to observations of

$$m_{t-1}, m_{t-2}, \ldots, \ldots, O_{t-1}(v), O_{t-2}(v), \ldots \qquad (10.9)$$

from which people can derive optimal forecasts of the permanent values of $x_{t-1}$ and $m_{t-1}$. [The information in Equation (10.9) is denoted, for future reference, by $I_{t-1}$.] Equation (9.15) together with (10.3a) implies that the optimal forecast of the permanent value of $x_{t-1}$ is

$$E_{t-1}x_t(v) = \theta \sum_{i=0}^{\infty} (1-\theta)^i O_{t-1-i}(v) \qquad (10.10)$$

where

$$\theta = \left[ \frac{\sigma_{xp}^2}{\sigma_q^2} + \frac{1}{4} \left( \frac{\sigma_{xp}^2}{\sigma_q^2} \right)^2 \right]^{1/2} - \frac{1}{2} \frac{\sigma_{xp}^2}{\sigma_q^2}; \qquad \sigma_q^2 \equiv \sigma_{xq}^2 + \sigma_\epsilon^2 \qquad (10.11)$$

which is a geometrically declining distributed lag of the observed sums $O_t(v) \equiv x_t(v) + \epsilon_t(v)$. Because permanent changes are observed together with transitory noise, people learn about such changes by observing whether or not they persist through time. The higher the coefficient of adaptation $\theta$, the more weight is given to current information and the quicker individuals learn about any given permanent change. The value of $\theta$ is a monotonically increasing function of the ratio of variance $\sigma_{xp}^2/\sigma_q^2$. As this ratio varies from zero to infinity, the coefficient of adaptation varies from zero to one (a fuller account of those properties and some proofs appear in Chapter 9, Section 3). Note that although the expectation on the left-hand side of Equation (10.10) concerns the future value of the relative demand shock $x_t(v)$, actual values of $O(v)$ rather than of $x(v)$ are used to form this expectation. The reason is that $x(v)$ is never observed separately. The sum

$$O_{t-1}(v) = x_{t-1}(v) + \epsilon_{t-1}(v) = x_{t-1}^p(v) + O_{t-1}^q \qquad (10.12)$$

where $O_{t-1}^q \equiv x_{t-1}^q(v) + \epsilon_{t-1}(v)$ is observed instead. Because observations on $O(v)$ contain information about $x_t^p(v)$, these observations are used to generate $E_{t-1}x_t(v)$. However, since the transitory noise in Equation (10.12) includes not only the real transitory relative demand shock $x_t^q(v)$ but also the differential monetary noise $\epsilon_t(v)$, the variance of the transitory component of $O_{t-1}(v)$ is equal to $\sigma_q^2 \equiv \sigma_{xq}^2 + \sigma_\epsilon^2$. It can be seen from Equation (10.11) that the differential monetary noise $\epsilon_t(v)$ makes learning about real relative permanent changes in demand slower by decreasing the coefficient of adaptation $\theta$. This monetary noise makes it more difficult for producers to detect real permanent changes in the demand for their product.

The relative price expected for period $t$ as of period $t-1$ can now be calculated by subtracting Equation (10.7) from (10.6):

$$E_{t-1}p_t(s) - E_{t-1}Q_t = (1 - d_s)\left[ E_{t-1}x_t(s) - \sum_v w(v)\psi_v E_{t-1}x_t(v) \right]$$
$$- \frac{1}{\psi_s + \gamma_s}\left[ \beta_s - \psi_s \sum_v w(v)\beta_v \right]t \qquad (10.13)$$

This expression can be stated in terms of only observables by substituting $E_{t-1}x_t(v)$ from Equation (10.10) into (10.13). Note that the expected relative price does not depend on the expected permanent value of the money supply. This is a reflection of the fact that perceived money is neutral and people know it. Equation (10.13) states that the expected relative price is an increasing function of the perceived permanent relative demand for good $s$ and a decreasing function of the perceived permanent relative productivity of good $s$. It follows that when the relative demand for good $s$ changes permanently, perceptions about this change adjust only gradually. Because these perceptions affect actual prices through (10.4), it follows that the equilibrium price in any market responds gradually to permanent changes in the relative demand. In addition, the perceived relative price is affected by random deviations of the realization of differential monetary noise in market $s$ from a weighted average of the differential monetary noise over markets.

This can be seen more precisely by noting that the term $Ex_{t-1}(s) - \sum_v w(v)\psi_v Ex_{t-1}(v)$ on the right-hand side of Equation (10.13) may be rewritten, using (10.10), as

$$\theta \sum_{i=0}^{\infty}(1 - \theta)^i\{[x_{t-1-i}(s) - \bar{x}_{t-1-i}] + [\epsilon_{t-1-i}(s) - \bar{\epsilon}_{t-1-i}]\} \qquad (10.13a)$$

where

$$\bar{\epsilon}_{t-1-i} \equiv \sum_v w(v)\psi_v \epsilon_{t-1-i}(v); \qquad \bar{x}_{t-1-i} \equiv \sum_v w(v)\psi_v x_{t-1-i}(v)$$

for all $i$ and $t$; $w(v), \psi_v \geq 0$; and the sum of $w(v)\psi_v$ over all markets is equal, by (10.8), to 1.

Equation (10.13a) suggests that both current and past deviations of the differential monetary noise in market $s$ from its economy-wide average affect the current perceptions about the next period's relative price and therefore current production decisions. [Note that although the expected values of both $\epsilon_t(s)$ and $\bar{\epsilon}_t$ are zero, their realizations in any given period differ in general from zero.] Positive deviations will cause, ceteris paribus, an overestimate of next period's relative price and therefore a higher level of output in industry $s$. Note also that past such deviations also have an effect on today's planned output; however, the effect of any given past deviation on current output decisions diminishes as the period in which it occurred recedes into the past. This suggests that differential monetary noise has persistent but not permanent effects on the composition of output.

Although individuals have full current information on actual relative prices, which they use together with the known structure of the model to form rational forecasts, they are still subject to informational limitations for three reasons:

1. The realization of shocks in period $t$ is not known in period $t-1$.
2. Even with information about actual relative prices for period $t$, they are not able to disentangle perfectly the permanent and transitory components of the relative price.
3. Individuals cannot distinguish perfectly between changes in relative prices caused by differential monetary noise and changes caused by real demand factors.

## 3    Adaptive nature of relative price forecasts

We saw that the quantity of a good that will be produced for marketing in the next period depends on today's perception about the relative price of the good in the next period. As shown in Section A1 of the Appendix to this chapter, it is possible to write the forecast of the relative price as

$$E_t p_{t+1}(s) - E_t Q_{t+1}$$
$$= \theta(1-d_s)[p_t(s) - Q_t] + [1-\theta(1-d_s)][E_{t-1}p_t(s) - E_{t-1}Q_t]$$
$$+ \theta \frac{1-d_s}{1-\bar{d}} \sum_v u(v)d_v\{p_t(v) - Q_t - [E_{t-1}p_t(v) - E_{t-1}Q_t]\} - C_s$$

$$(10.14)$$

where $C_s$ is a constant combination of parameters whose explicit form appears in Section A2 of the Appendix. It is nonzero only because the rates of technological progress $\beta_v$ and demand elasticities $\psi_v$ differ across markets. The penultimate term arises only because supply and demand elasticities differ among markets (see Section A2 of the Appendix). Specializing Equation (10.14) to the case of identical rates of technological improvement ($\beta_v = \beta$ for all $v$) and identical demand and supply elasticities ($\psi_v = \psi$, $\gamma_v = \gamma$ for all $v$), we obtain

$$E_t p_{t+1}(s) - E_t Q_{t+1}$$

$$= \theta \frac{\psi}{\gamma + \psi} [p_t(s) - Q_t] + \left(1 - \theta \frac{\psi}{\gamma + \psi}\right)[E_{t-1} p_t(s) - E_{t-1} Q_t]$$

$$\text{(10.14a)}$$

In this case, the relative price expected for the next period is simply a weighted average of the previous expectation and the current actual value of the relative price. The adaptive forecasting of relative demand shocks carries over to the forecasting of relative prices.

Intuitively, because relative price movements are caused by both transitory and permanent shocks, the optimal forecasts of the permanent component of a relative price gives some weight to current relative prices but also to preconceptions about permanent relative prices. The weight given to the current relative price is bounded between zero and one and is an increasing function of both $\theta$ and the size of the elasticity of demand in comparison to the elasticity of supply in market $s$. The value of $\theta$ is high when the variance of permanent shocks is large in comparison to the variance of transitory shocks. In this case it makes good sense to give a large weight to actual movements in relative prices. When this variance is small in comparison to the variance of transitory shocks, actual movements in relative prices reflect mostly temporary effects. In this case it pays to stick to preconceptions.

For given supply and demand elasticities and given values of the permanent and transitory variances of relative demand shocks, Equation (10.14a) gives the optimal combination of current information and past preconceptions to forecast the next period's relative price. Because both pieces of information are used, it implies that individuals underestimate purely permanent changes and interpret purely transitory changes in relative prices as being partially permanent. This implies through Equation (10.1) that production decisions overreact to purely transitory changes and underreact to purely permanent changes in relative demands.

When elasticities and rates of technological progress differ across markets, the simple adaptive scheme of (10.14a) is supplemented by the two last terms on the right-hand side of (10.14). The first arises because the effect of a given demand shock on the general price level will depend on the market in which it is realized. This is a direct consequence of different supply and demand elasticities in different markets. The last term, $C_s$, reflects that differential rates of technological progress affect relative prices. In addition the weights on the current and the previously predicted relative prices become dependent on the market indexes.

The precise adaptive structure in Equations (10.14) and (10.14a) is a consequence of the particular stochastic assumptions made about the distributions of the permanent and transitory components of the various shocks. However, the result – that confusion between transitory and permanent changes causes perceptions about permanent magnitudes to adjust slowly even when *all* past information is used – transcends the particular stochastic structure used here.[5]

## 4    Effects of erratic monetary policy and other uncertainties on the efficiency of relative prices as signals for production decisions

Ideally, producers would like to gear their production to the actual relative price of their good in the period in which they sell it. This is not feasible for two reasons: First, they do not know what shocks are going to materialize in the future. Secondly, even in the present period, they have only partial knowledge of the permanence of the current relative price. Hence in each industry, the actual output will generally deviate from the output that producers would have been producing if they had more information. Following Barro (1976), we refer to this level of output as *full information output.*[6]

In the present context, two alternative concepts of full information output can be distinguished. The first is the level of output that would be produced if producers knew in period $t$ the true decomposition of the current relative price into its permanent and transitory components. We refer to this level of output as *full current information output* because it arises when individuals have full current information about the permanence of current shocks but no information beyond the structure of the model about shocks that will materialize in the future. The second concept, which we shall call *full future information output,* is the level of output that would have been produced if the actual relative price that will prevail in period $t+1$ were known in period $t$. This concept endows individuals not only with perfect knowledge about the composition of shocks that have occurred but also with perfect foresight about the next period's shocks. If we take the view that full information can refer to only the components of shocks that have already materialized, the first concept is the relevant one.[7] Full current information output $y_t^*(s)$ can be calculated from Equation (10.1) as

$$y_t^*(s) = \beta_s t + \gamma_s [p_{t-1}^p(s) - Q_{t-1}^p]$$ (10.15)

where $p_{t-1}^p(s) - Q_{t-1}^p$ is the best forecast of the relative price for period $t$ as of period $t-1$, provided the true values of the permanent levels of relative demand shocks in period $t-1$ are known in that period. Subtracting Equation (10.15) from (10.1), we obtain the difference between actual and full current information output as

$$D_c(s) = y_t(s) - y_t^*(s)$$

$$= \gamma_s \{ E_{t-1} p_t(s) - E_{t-1} Q_t - [p_{t-1}^p(s) - Q_{t-1}^p] \}$$ (10.16)

This suggests that the actual output is larger (smaller) than the full current information output if the price believed to be the permanent relative price of the previous period is larger (smaller) than the actual permanent relative price of that period. By going through a calculation analogous to that which led to Equation (10.13), but with true permanent values replacing perceptions about permanent values, it is possible to express $p_{t-1}^p(s) - Q_{t-1}^p$ as a function of the true permanent values of the shocks in period $t-1$. Substituting this expression as well as (10.13) into (10.16) and rearranging, we get

$$D_c(s) = \frac{\gamma_s \psi_s}{\psi_s + \gamma_s} \left\{ \left[ 1 - u(s) \frac{1 - d_s}{1 - \bar{d}} \right] [E_{t-1} x_t(s) - x_{t-1}^p(s)] \right.$$

$$\left. - \sum_{v \neq s} u(v) \frac{1 - d_v}{1 - \bar{d}} [E_{t-1} x_t(v) - x_{t-1}^p(v)] \right\}$$ (10.17)

By substituting Equation (10.10) into (10.17), we can ascertain that the unconditional expected value of (10.17) is zero. Rearranging after this substitution so that the terms in (10.17) are all mutually uncorrelated, it is possible to compute the variance of $D_c(s)$ as the sum of the variances of those terms (as shown in Section A3 of the Appendix). The result appears in Equation (10.18).

$$V[D_c(s)] = (\psi_s d_s)^2 \left[ 1 - u(s) \frac{1 - d_s}{1 - \bar{d}} \right]^2$$

$$+ \sum_{v \neq s} \left[ u(v) \frac{1 - d_v}{1 - \bar{d}} \right]^2 G(\sigma_q^2, \sigma_{xp}^2, \theta)$$ (10.18)

where

$$G(\sigma_q^2, \sigma_{xp}^2, \theta) \equiv \frac{\theta^2 \sigma_q^2 + (1-\theta)^2 \sigma_{xp}^2}{\theta(2-\theta)}$$

Equation (10.18) gives the variance of actual around full current information output. As we have seen, the variance is positive because people confuse permanent and transitory movements in relative demands. If producers had known the actual permanent value of relative demands in each period, it would have been zero. Because such perfect information is unavailable, however, actual output usually deviates from $y_t^*(s)$. The variance in Equation (10.18) is a quantitative measure of the extent of this deviation. We take it as a measure of the signaling efficiency of relative prices for production decisions. The larger the variance is, the less efficient is the price system in generating optimal production decisions and the more costly is the permanent–transitory confusion for the economy. M. Friedman (1977: 467) suggests that an increased volatility of inflation makes market prices less efficient coordinators of economic activity. The model presented here makes it possible to formalize and quantify these costs by using measures like that in (10.18).

It is interesting to inquire how the variance of actual around the full current information output is affected by various factors. It is apparent that this variance is affected by either $\sigma_{xp}^2$ or $\sigma_q^2$ only through its dependence on the term $G(\cdot)$ on the right-hand side of Equation (10.18). Differentiating $G$ partially with respect to $\sigma_{xp}^2$ and $\sigma_q^2$, we get

$$\frac{\partial G(\cdot)}{\partial \sigma_{xp}^2} = \frac{(1-\theta)^2}{(2-\theta)^2 \theta^3}; \qquad \frac{\partial G(\cdot)}{\partial \sigma_q^2} = \frac{\theta}{2-\theta} \qquad (10.19)$$

Because $0 < \theta < 1$, both partial derivatives are positive. Hence an increase in either the variance of transitory relative demand shocks or the variance of permanent relative excess demand shocks, whether caused by real or monetary factors, causes an increase in the variance of the deviation of actual output from the full current information output. Recall from Equation (10.11) that $\sigma_q^2 \equiv \sigma_{xq}^2 + \sigma_\epsilon^2$; the variance $\sigma_q^2$ is thus partly induced by the variance of the differential monetary noise $\sigma_\epsilon^2$. This implies that for a fixed $\sigma_{xq}^2$, the larger the variance of differential monetary noise, the lower is the allocative efficiency of the price system.

The policy prescription that emerges from this result is that the variance of differential monetary noise should be kept as low as possible.[8] If this variance and the rate of monetary expansion are positively related (as conjectured in Section 2 for low and intermediate rates of monetary inflation), this would also imply that the rate of monetary expansion should be kept as low as possible. Because this relationship has not yet been investigated empirically, however, the last conclusion can be only tentative. More generally, to the extent that government can decrease the real variances of relative demand shocks ($\sigma_{xp}^2, \sigma_{xq}^2$) by promoting stable policies in other areas, this is desirable as well. Policies that increase these variances make it more difficult for producers to adapt their production decisions to those irreducible variations in relative demands and productivity that are caused by nature.

## 5    Additional aspect of the optimality of forecasts

It seems intuitively plausible that by decreasing the amount of "noise" in the economy, a lower $\sigma_q^2$ will decrease the dispersion of actual around the full current informaton output. It is less clear why a decrease in $\sigma_{xp}^2$ has the same effect, because by decreasing the coefficient of adaptation $\theta$, the detection of permanent changes becomes more difficult.

The answer to this seeming paradox is that a decrease in $\theta$ also reduces the amount of unnecessary transitory noise that the expectations formation process in Equation (10.10) picks up. Taken in isolation this effect should decrease $V(D_c)$ {for notational convenience, the index $s$ of $V[D_c(s)]$ is sometimes deleted}. It turns out that these two conflicting effects of a change in $\theta$ on $V(D_c)$ exactly cancel each other, leaving only the direct positive effect of $\sigma_{xp}^2$ on $V(D_c)$. The reason for this is brought out more clearly in the following proposition.

**Proposition 1:** *For given values of $\sigma_{xp}^2$ and $\sigma_q^2$, the value of the coefficient of adaptation $\theta$ that minimizes the variance of actual around the full current information output is given by Equation (10.11).*

*Proof:* $V[D_c(s)]$ is minimized for the value of $\theta$ that minimizes the expression $G(\cdot)$ on the right-hand side of Equation (10.18). The first and second partial derivatives of $G(\cdot)$ with respect to $\theta$ are

$$\frac{\partial G}{\partial \theta} = \frac{2[\theta^2 \sigma_q^2 - (1-\theta)\sigma_{xp}^2]}{(2-\theta)^2 \theta^2}$$

and

$$\frac{\partial^2 G}{\partial \theta^2} = \frac{2\{[(2-\theta)\theta + 4(1-\theta)^2]\sigma_{xp}^2 + \theta^3 \sigma_q^2\}}{[(2-\theta)\theta]^3} \tag{10.20}$$

respectively. Because the second partial is positive for any $\theta$, it follows that $G(\cdot)$ will be minimized by the value of $\theta$ for which the first partial is zero. Solving for this value of $\theta$ from (10.20), we find that it is equal to the expression for $\theta$ in (10.11).    □

For the individual producer, $\sigma_{xp}^2$ and $\sigma_q^2$ constitute exogenous data, but producers are free to use the data they observe in any way they choose. Proposition 1 suggests that they use the available information to minimize the variance of the deviation beteween actual output and the output they would be producing if they had full current information. Intuitively the individual increases $\theta$ up to the point at which the marginal decrease in $V(D_c)$ due to a quicker detection of permanent changes is equal to the marginal increase in $V(D_c)$ caused by the fact that the higher $\theta$ also picks up more of the transitory noise. Because, at the margin, $\theta$ has no net effect on $G(\bullet)$, the total effect on $V(D_c)$ of a change in $\sigma_{xp}^2$ or $\sigma_q^2$ reduces to the direct effect of such a change, which is always positive.

## 6     Alternative measure for the efficiency of the price system and the effect of the production lag

We focus in this section on an alternative measure of the efficiency of the price system based on a comparison of actual output with full future information output. Full future information output is what a producer would have decided to produce had he or she known at the time of the production decision the actual relative price at the time of sale. The deviation $y_t^{**}(s)$ between the actual level of output and the full future information (or perfect foresight) output is another measure of the extent to which the price system gives the producer erroneous signals.

A natural, nonstochastic measure of the average deviation of actual from the perfect foresight output is the variance of the deviation $D_f(s) \equiv y_t(s) - y_t^{**}(s)$. In this section this variance is computed and its dependence on various underlying parameters is characterized. To evaluate the effect of the length of the production lag on the uncertainty faced by the individual producer, the production lag is parametrized explicitly. More precisely, it is assumed that the production decision must be made $k$ periods before the good is supplied on the market. One advantage of $D_f(s)$ over $D_c(s)$ as a measure of the uncertainty imposed on producers by the price system is that it is sensitive to the length of the production period, whereas $D_c(s)$ (which depends only on the difference between *today's* belief about the relative permanent excess demands and today's true values of relative permanent excess demands and not on the realizations of future relative excess demand shocks) is not.

The production lag is now $k$ periods. The supply in period $t$ will therefore depend on what producers believe in period $t-k$ about the permanent relative price of their good because this is the best forecast, as of $t-k$, of their relative price for period $t$. Consequently the supply function (10.1) is replaced by

$$y_t(s) = \beta_s t + \gamma_s [E_{t-k} p_t(s) - E_{t-k} Q_t]  \qquad (10.21)$$

The full future information output is given by

$$y_t^{**}(s) = \beta_s t + \gamma_s [p_t(s) - Q_t]  \qquad (10.22)$$

By subtracting Equation (10.22) from (10.21), we get the difference between the output of perfect foresight and actual output as

$$D_f(s) = y_t(s) - y_t^{**}(s)$$
$$= \gamma_s \{E_{t-k} p_t(s) - E_{t-k} Q_t - [p_t(s) - Q_t]\} \quad (10.23)$$

from which it follows that actual output will be higher or lower than it would have been if producers had perfect foresight because the relative price anticipated in period $t-k$ for period $t$ is higher or lower than the relative price that is eventually realized in period $t$.

As shown in Section A4 of the Appendix, by going through a calculation similar to that which led to Equation (10.18), the unconditional expected value of $D_f(s)$ is zero and its unconditional variance is

$$V[D_f(s)] = \gamma_s^2 \left\{ [1 - u(s)]^2 + \sum_{v \neq s} [u(v)]^2 \right\} [\sigma_q^2 + k\sigma_{xp}^2 + G(\bullet)] \quad (10.24)$$

This expression suggests that the variance of the deviation of actual output from the output of perfect foresight is an increasing function of $\sigma_{xp}^2$, $\sigma_{xq}^2$, and particularly $\sigma_\epsilon^2$.

The implications for monetary and other policies are similar to those reached in the previous section. Note that these variances affect $V[D_f(s)]$ not only through the function $G(\bullet)$, as was the case with $V[D_c(s)]$, but also through the term $\sigma_{xq}^2 + k\sigma_{xp}^2$. This is a direct consequence of the fact that in comparison to the forecast in period $t-k$, actual prices in period $t$ are subject to a transitory variance as well as to $k$ times the variance of the change in the permanent component. Because each addition to the number of production periods increases the variability of the permanent component of relative demands by $\sigma_{xp}^2$, the variance $V[D_f(s)]$ is an increasing function of $k$. This suggests that the longer the production lag, the greater is the uncertainty that has to be borne by producers and therefore the less efficient is the price system in performing its signaling function. Moreover, by differentiating Equation (10.24) partially with respect to $\sigma_{xp}^2$, it can be seen that the resulting expression is an increasing function of $k$. Hence, the longer the production lag, the more a given increase in $\sigma_{xp}^2$, whether exogenous or policy induced, will increase uncertainty and the inefficiency of the price system.

This suggests that in a model with nonuniform production lags across industries, the increase in uncertainty caused by a given increase in the permanent variances does not fall evenly on all industries. Those with longer production lags will experience greater increases in uncertainty. For a uniform degree of risk aversion across industries, this could explain the higher volatility of long-term investments.

Finally, for given values of the exogenous variances and $k$, the variance of $D_f(s)$ will be larger in industries with a larger supply elasticity $\gamma_s$. Intuitively, any given error in forecasting relative prices causes a larger deviation of the actual output from the output of perfect foresight, the larger the elasticity of supply.

Another point worthy of note is that for given values of the variances $\sigma_{xp}^2$ and $\sigma_q^2$ and any $k$, the value of $\theta$ from Equation (10.11) minimizes $V[D_f(s)]$ as well as $V[D_c(s)]$. This is a direct corollary of Proposition 1; that is, by minimizing the variance of output around the full current information output, the variance of output around the full future information output is minimized as well. Intuitively, in period $t-k$ there are two sources of uncertainty about the relative price in $t$. One is that even with all the information up to and including period $t-k$ there is no certainty about the permanent relative price in period $t-k$. The other is the unknown (as of period $t-k$) realizations of shocks between $t-k$ and $t$. The term $V[D_c(s)]$ is nonzero only because of the first element, whereas $V[D_f(s)]$ is nonzero because of both. Since the variance of only the first element is affected by the choice of $\theta$, the value of $\theta$ that minimizes $V[D_c(s)]$ also minimizes $V[D_f(s)]$.

Finally, the length of the production lag is, in general, probably not independent of the degree of uncertainty that producers have to bear until they sell the product. When this uncertainty as measured by $V[D_f(s)]$ increases, producers will try to shorten the production lag. This effect has not been investigated explicitly here because the length of the production lag was specified exogenously. Even without a formal discussion, however, it is easy to see that when the production lag is sensitive to the degree of uncertainty, an increase in the differential monetary noise $\sigma_t^2$ or in $\sigma_{xp}^2$ and $\sigma_{xq}^2$ will reduce the average production lag. Furthermore, other things being equal, industries with less flexibility in the choice of the production lag will be hurt more by a given increase in uncertainty.

## 7    Remark on generality

The focus of this chapter has been on the interaction of the permanent–transitory confusion with monetary policy, but uncertainty about the permanence of changes in relative productivities introduces an additional reason for sluggish relative prices. To keep the amount of required technicalities at a reasonable level, the effects of the permanent–transitory confusion on changes in the productive capacity have been abstracted from. For a fuller analysis, the reader is referred to Cukierman (1982a).

**Appendix**

A1     *Derivation of Equation (10.14)*

Substituting Equation (10.4) into (10.5) and subtracting the resulting expression from (10.4), we get

$$Rp_t(s) \equiv p_t(s) - Q_t$$

$$= O_t(s) - \sum_v u(v) O_t(v) - E_{t-1} R_t(s) - K_s t \qquad \text{(A10.1)}$$

where

$$E_{t-1} R_t(s) \equiv \frac{\gamma_s}{\psi_s} [E_{t-1} p_t(s) - E_{t-1} Q_t]$$

$$- \sum_v u(v) \frac{\gamma_v}{\psi_v} [E_{t-1} p_t(v) - E_{t-1} Q_t] \qquad \text{(A10.2)}$$

and

$$K_s \equiv \frac{\beta_s}{\psi_s} - \sum_v u(v) \frac{\beta_v}{\psi_v}$$

Taking expected values of both sides of Equation (A10.1) conditioned on $I_{t-1}$, we get

$$E_{t-1} Rp_t(s) = E_{t-1} p_t(s) - E_{t-1} Q_t$$

$$= E_{t-1} x_t(s) - \sum_v u(v) E_{t-1} x_t(v) - E_{t-1} R_t(s) - K_s t$$
$$\text{(A10.3)}$$

Similarly, the forecast of the relative price for period $t+1$ given the information of period $t$ can be obtained by leading Equation (A10.1) by one period and taking the expected value of both sides of (A10.1) conditioned on $I_t$:

$$E_t Rp_{t+1}(s) \equiv E_t p_{t+1}(s) - E_t Q_{t+1}$$

$$= E_t x_{t+1}(s) - \sum_v u(v) E_t x_{t+1}(v) - E_t R_{t+1}(s) - K_s(t+1)$$
$$\text{(A10.4)}$$

Subtracting Equation (A10.3) from (A10.4), we get

$$A_t(s) \equiv E_t Rp_{t+1}(s) - E_{t-1} Rp_t(s)$$

$$= E_t x_{t+1}(s) - E_{t-1} x_t(s) - \sum_v u(v) [E_t x_{t+1}(v) - E_{t-1} x_t(v)]$$

$$- [E_t R_{t+1}(s) - E_{t-1} R_t(s)] - K_s \qquad \text{(A10.5)}$$

Because the optimal forecast in Equation (10.10) is adaptive,

$$E_t x_{t+1}(v) - E_{t-1} x_t(v) = \theta[O_t(v) - E_{t-1} x_t(v)] \tag{A10.6}$$

for all $v$. Substituting Equations (A10.2), (A10.6), and (A10.2) again, but led by one period into (A10.5), using the definition of $A_t(v)$ in (A10.5) for any $v$, and solving for $A_t(s)$, we get

$$A_t(s) = \frac{\psi_s}{\psi_s + \gamma_s} \left( \theta \left\{ O_t(s) - E_{t-1} x_t(s) - \sum_v u(v)[O_t(v) - E_{t-1} x_t(v)] \right\} \right.$$

$$\left. + \sum_v u(v) \frac{\gamma_v}{\psi_v} A_t(v) - K_s \right) \tag{A10.7}$$

Multiplying both sides of Equation (A10.7) by $u(s)(\gamma_s/\psi_s)$, summing over all $s$, and solving for $\sum_v u(v)(\gamma_v/\psi_v) A_t(v)$, we obtain

$$\sum_v u(v) \frac{\gamma_v}{\psi_v} A_t(v)$$

$$= \frac{\theta}{1-\bar{d}} \sum_v u(v) d_v \left\{ O_t(v) - E_{t-1} x_t(v) \right.$$

$$\left. - \sum_v u(v)[O_t(v) - E_{t-1} x_t(v)] \right\} - \bar{K} \tag{A10.8}$$

where $\bar{K} \equiv -\sum_v u(v) d_v K_v/(1-\bar{d})$. Substituting Equation (A10.8) into (A10.7), using the definition of $A_t(s)$, and rearranging, we get

$$E_t Rp_{t+1}(s) = \theta(1-d_s) \left\{ O_t(s) - E_{t-1} x_t(s) - \sum_v u(v)[O_t(v) - E_{t-1} x_t(v)] \right\}$$

$$+ \theta \frac{1-d_s}{1-\bar{d}} \sum_v u(v) d_v \left\{ O_t(v) - E_{t-1} x_t(v) \right.$$

$$\left. - \sum_v u(v)[O_t(v) - E_{t-1} x_t(v)] \right\}$$

$$+ E_{t-1} Rp_t(s) - C_s \tag{A10.9}$$

where $C_s \equiv (1-d_s)(K_s + \bar{K})$. Subtracting Equation (A10.3) from (A10.1), we get

$$Rp_t(s) - E_{t-1} Rp_t(s) = O_t(s) - E_{t-1} x_t(x)$$

$$- \sum_v u(v)[O_t(v) - E_{t-1} x_t(v)] \tag{A10.10}$$

Substituting (A10.10) into the right-hand side of (A10.9), we get

$$E_t Rp_{t+1}(s) = \theta(1-d_s)[Rp_t(s) - E_{t-1}Rp_t(s)] + E_{t-1}Rp_t(s)$$

$$+ \theta \frac{1-d_s}{1-\bar{d}} \sum_v u(v)d_v[Rp_t(v) - E_{t-1}Rp_t(v)] - C_s$$

$$(\text{A10.11})$$

Equation (10.14) in the text follows by rearranging the right-hand side of (A10.11).

## A2    Derivation of Equation (10.14a)

By definition,

$$C_s = (1-d_s)\left\{ \frac{\beta_s}{\psi_s} - \sum_v u(v)\frac{\beta_v}{\psi_v} + \frac{1}{1-\bar{d}} \sum_v u(v)d_v\left[ \frac{\beta_v}{\psi_v} - \sum_j u(j)\frac{\beta_j}{\psi_j} \right] \right\}$$

For $\beta_s = \beta$ and $\psi_s = \psi$ for all $s$, this term vanishes. When $\psi_s = \psi$ and $\gamma_s = \gamma$ for all $s$, $d_s = \bar{d} \equiv d$ for all $s$. It follows that the penultimate term in Equation (10.14) becomes

$$\theta d\left\{ \sum_v u(v)p_t(v) - Q_t - \left[ \sum_v u(v)E_{t-1}p_t(v) - E_{t-1}Q_t \right] \right\}$$

which is obviously zero.

When $\psi_s = \psi$ and $\gamma_s = \gamma$ for all $s$, $1-d_s = \psi/(\gamma+\psi)$ for all $s$. Equation (10.14a) follows by substituting those results into (10.14).

## A3    Derivation of Equation (10.18)

From Equation (10.10), it follows that for any $v$,

$$E_{t-1}x_t(v) - x_{t-1}^p(v)$$

$$= \theta \sum_{i=0}^{\infty} (1-\theta)^i O_{t-1-i}(v) - x_{t-1}^p(v)$$

$$= -\theta \sum_{i=0}^{\infty} (1-\theta)^i [x_{t-1}^p(v) - x_{t-1-i}^p(v) - x_{t-1-i}^q(v) - \epsilon_{t-1-i}(v)]$$

$$= \theta[x_{t-1}^q(v) + \epsilon_{t-1}(v)] - \theta \sum_{i=1}^{\infty} (1-\theta)^i [\Delta x_{t-1}^p(v) + \cdots + \Delta x_{t-i}^p(v)]$$

$$- \sum_{i=1}^{\infty} (1-\theta)^i [x_{t-1-i}^q(v) + \epsilon_{t-1-i}(v)] \qquad (\text{A10.12})$$

The middle term on the extreme right-hand side of (A10.12) can be rewritten as

$$-\theta\{(1-\theta)[1+(1-\theta)+(1-\theta)^2+\cdots]\Delta x_{t-1}^{\mathrm{p}}(v)$$

$$+(1-\theta)^2[1+(1-\theta)+(1-\theta)^2+\cdots]\Delta x_{t-2}^{\mathrm{p}}(v)+\cdots\}$$

$$=-(1-\theta)\Delta x_{t-1}^{\mathrm{p}}(v)+(1-\theta)^2\Delta x_{t-2}^{\mathrm{p}}(v)+(1-\theta)^3\Delta x_{t-3}^{\mathrm{p}}(v)+\cdots$$

$$\text{(A10.13)}$$

Substituting Equation (A10.13) into (A10.12), we get

$$E_{t-1}x_t(v)-x_{t-1}^{\mathrm{p}}(v)$$

$$=\theta\left\{x_{t-1}^{\mathrm{q}}(v)+\epsilon_{t-1}(v)-\sum_{i=1}^{\infty}(1-\theta)^i[x_{t-1-i}(v)+\epsilon_{t-1-i}(v)]\right\}$$

$$-(1-\theta)\Delta x_{t-1}^{\mathrm{p}}(v)+(1-\theta)^2\Delta x_{t-2}^{\mathrm{p}}(v)+(1-\theta)^3\Delta x_{t-3}^{\mathrm{p}}(v)+\cdots$$

$$\text{(A10.14)}$$

By Equation (10.3), the unconditional expected value of each of the terms in (A10.14) is zero. Because all the terms on the right-hand side of (A10.14) are mutually uncorrelated, the variance of the expression in (A10.14) is, using (10.3),

$$\theta^2\sigma_{\mathrm{q}}^2\sum_{i=0}^{\infty}(1-\theta)^{2i}+(1-\theta)^2\sigma_{xp}^2\sum_{i=0}^{\infty}(1-\theta)^{2i}=\frac{\theta^2\sigma_{\mathrm{q}}^2+(1-\theta)^2\sigma_{xp}^2}{\theta(2-\theta)}$$

$$\text{(A10.15)}$$

Equation (10.18) follows by taking the variance of (10.17) and using (A10.15).

A4     *Derivation of Equation (10.24)*

From Equation (10.4) in the text, the expected value as of $t-k$ of $p_t(s)$ is

$$E_{t-k}p_t(v)=\left(\delta-\frac{\beta_v}{\psi_v}\right)t+E_{t-k}x_t(v)+E_{t-k}m_t$$

$$-\frac{\gamma_v}{\psi_v}[E_{t-k}p_t(v)-E_{t-k}Q_t] \qquad\text{(A10.16)}$$

Subtracting Equation (A10.16) from (10.4), we get

$$p_t(v)-E_{t-k}p_t(v)=O_t(v)-E_{t-k}x_t(v)+m_t-E_{t-k}m_t \qquad\text{(A10.17)}$$

Using Equation (A10.17) in (10.23), this last equation can be rewritten as

$$D_f(s)=-\gamma_s[p_t(s)-E_{t-k}p_t(s)-(Q_t-E_{t-k}Q_{t-k})]$$

$$=-\gamma_s\left\{O_t(s)-E_{t-k}x_t(s)-\sum_v u(v)[O_t(v)-E_{t-k}x_t(v)]\right\}=$$

$$= -\gamma_s \Big\{ [1 - u(s)][O_t(s) - E_{t-k}x_t(s)]$$

$$- \sum_{v \neq s} u(v)[O_t(v) - E_{t-k}x_t(v)] \Big\} \qquad \text{(A10.18)}$$

But for any $v$,

$$O_t(v) - E_{t-k}x_t(v) = \epsilon_t(v) + x_t^q(v) + \Delta x_t^p(v) + \cdots + \Delta x_{t+1-k}^p(v)$$

$$+ x_{t-k}^p(v) - E_{t-1}x_{t-k}(v) \qquad \text{(A10.19)}$$

From Equations (10.3) and (A10.14), it follows that the unconditional expected value of (A10.19) is zero. Because all the terms on the right-hand side of (A10.19) are mutually uncorrelated, it follows from (10.3) and (A10.15) that the variance of (A10.19) is

$$\sigma_q^2 + k\sigma_{xp}^2 + \frac{\theta^2 \sigma_q^2 + (1-\theta)^2 \sigma_{xp}^2}{\theta(2-\theta)} \qquad \text{(A10.20)}$$

Because all the terms on the right-hand side of Equation (A10.18) are mutually uncorrelated, the variance of this expression can be computed as the weighted sum of the variances of the individual stochastic terms. Each of those terms has a variance given by (A10.20), however. It follows, therefore, from (A10.18) and (A10.20) that

$$V[D_f(s)] = \gamma_s^2 \Big\{ [1 - u(s)]^2 + \sum_{v \neq s} [u(v)]^2 \Big\} \{ \sigma_q^2 + k\sigma_{xp}^2 + G(\cdot) \}$$

which is Equation (10.24) in the text.

CHAPTER 11

# Permanent–transitory confusion: implications for relative price variability and inflation

## 1    Introduction[1]

Chapter 10 showed how the confusion between permanent and transitory changes makes it more difficult for producers to make optimal production decisions. The same confusion also contributes to relative price dispersion across sectors in the economy. The differing persistence of relative demand shocks across markets combined with the permanent–transitory confusion leads to differing interpretations of the permanence of shocks and hence to different supply responses and price changes in different markets. This effect is illustrated in Section 2.

Using a sample of 15 countries, Glejser (1965) investigated the relationship between the standard deviation of a relative price change on one hand and the rate of inflation and productivity change in those countries on the other. He found that the standard deviation of a relative price change is positively related across countries with the rate of inflation and the rate of increase in productivity. Taken together with the substantial body of evidence suggesting that the level and the variance of inflation are positively related both over time and cross sectionally,[2] this suggests that relative price variability and inflation variance are positively related across countries. Most of the remainder of this chapter proposes an explanation for this. Each country is taken to be characterized by a different stochastic regime, reflected in different values of the variances $\sigma_{xp}^2$, $\sigma_{xq}^2$, and $\sigma_\epsilon^2$ from Equations (10.3a) and (10.3b). The positive relationship observed between inflation variance and relative price variability is then explained by showing that under plausible circumstances any change in $\sigma_{xq}^2$, $\sigma_{xp}^2$, or $\sigma_\epsilon^2$ changes the variance of inflation and the relative price variability in the same direction. The formal model used is the same as that of Chapter 10.[3]

The last section of the chapter gives a tentative explanation for the widely observed positive relationship between the rate and the variance of inflation.

## 2        Effect of the permanent–transitory confusion on relative price variability

To illustrate the effect of the permanent–transitory confusion on relative price variability in isolation, this section considers the particular case in which all supply and demand elasticities are identical for all goods ($\gamma_v = \gamma$ and $\psi_v = \psi$ for all $v$) and rates of technological progress are also the same for all goods ($\beta_v = \beta$ for all $v$). For this case, $\psi_v w(v) = u(v)$, and Equations (10.3) and (10.4) reduce, respectively, to

$$E_{t-1} p(s) - E_{t-1} Q_t = \frac{\psi}{\psi + \gamma} \left[ E_{t-1} x_t(s) - \sum_v u(v) E_{t-1} x_t(v) \right] \qquad (11.1)$$

$$p_t(s) = \left( \delta - \frac{\beta}{\psi} \right) t + m_t + O_t(s) - \frac{\gamma}{\psi} [E_{t-1} p_t(s) - E_{t-1} Q_t] \qquad (11.2)$$

Substituting Equation (11.2) into the definition of the general price level from (10.5) and subtracting the resulting expression from (11.2), we get

$$p_t(s) - Q_t = O_t(s) - \sum_v u(v) O_t(v) - \frac{\gamma}{\psi} [E_{t-1} p_t(s) - E_{t-1} Q_t] \qquad (11.3)$$

Substituting Equation (11.1) into (11.3) and rearranging, we get

$$p_t(s) - Q_t = O_t(s) - dE_{t-1} x_t(s) - \sum_v u(v)[O_t(v) - dE_{t-1} x_t(v)] \qquad (11.4)$$

where $d \equiv \gamma/(\psi + \gamma)$. To bring into focus the effect of the permanent–transitory confusion, it will be further assumed that the permanent components of the relative demand shocks are the same in all markets and periods; that is,

$$x_t^p(v) = x^p \qquad (11.5)$$

for all values of $v$ and $t$. It is useful to first consider the case of no permanent–transitory confusion as a benchmark: Individuals know that Equation (11.5) is the true state of the world. Therefore $E_{t-1} x_t(v) = x^p$ for all $v$, and the relative price in (11.4) becomes

$$p_t(s) - Q_t = x_t^q(s) + \epsilon_t(s) - \sum_v u(v)[x_t^q(v) + \epsilon_t(v)] \qquad (11.6)$$

So the relative price in market $s$ reflects just the transitory deviation of real and monetarily induced shocks in market $s$ from a weighted average of such shocks over markets. There is no persistence at all in relative prices because the right-hand side of Equation (11.6) depends on only purely transitory shocks that are all serially uncorrelated. It follows from Equations (10.3a) and (10.3b) that in this case the variance of relative prices is

$$V_{\text{NC}}[p_t(s) - Q_t] = \left\{ [1 - u(s)]^2 + \sum_{v \neq s} [u(v)]^2 \right\} \sigma_q^2 \tag{11.7}$$

where $\sigma_q^2 \equiv \sigma_{xq}^2 + \sigma_\epsilon^2$. The variance of relative prices is in this case induced entirely by differential realizations of transitory real relative demand shocks across markets and by the differential monetary noise.

When there is some confusion between permanent and transitory shocks, however, individuals do not forecast $x^p$ perfectly. Because the realizations of the transitory shocks in period $t - 1$ and previous periods differ among markets, the degree of confusion between permanent and transitory shocks varies from market to market depending on the size of the transitory shocks in the different markets. More precisely, in this case the relative price in Equation (11.4) becomes

$$p_t(s) - Q_t = x_t^q(s) + \epsilon_t(s) + \sum_v u(v)[x_t^q(v) + \epsilon_t(v)]$$

$$- d\left[ E_{t-1} x_t(s) - \sum_v u(v) E_{t-1} x_t(v) \right] \tag{11.8}$$

The first three terms on the right-hand side of Equation (11.8) can be recognized as being equal to the relative price of good $s$ in the absence of any confusion [compare the right-hand side of (11.6)]. The remaining terms reflect the difference between a measure of the error in forecasting the permanent level of demand in market $s$ and the average of the same measure over all markets. These terms are directly traceable to the permanent–transitory confusion. Although the true permanent level of demand is the same by construction, the errors in forecasting its level for the different markets are not the same because of different current and past realizations of transitory shocks in the various markets. Because of the adaptive nature of forecasts, the last bracketed expression on the right-hand side of Equation (11.8) displays more persistence than the terms preceding it and can therefore explain serial correlation in a given relative price over time.

Note the difference between this theory of relative price variability and that presented in Chapter 6. Here all individuals have the *same* perceptions about the permanent general price level as well as about permanent relative prices. Perceptions about permanent relative prices for different markets differ, however, even if true permanent levels of demand do not. This difference in perceptions may cause persistent deviations in relative prices even though the actual levels of permanent relative demand do not justify such deviations. Equation (11.8) suggests that the permanent–transitory confusion introduces additional sources of variability into relative prices. Because the last two terms on the right-hand side of (11.8) are uncorrelated with the first three, the variance of the relative price in this case is

$$V_{PTC}[p_t(s) - Q_t] = \left\{ [1 - u(s)]^2 + \sum_{v \neq s} [u(v)]^2 \right\} [\sigma_q^2 + G(\bullet)]$$

$$= V_{NC}[p_t(s) - Q_t] + \left\{ [1 - u(s)]^2 + \sum_{v \neq s} [u(v)]^2 \right\} G(\bullet) \tag{11.9}$$

where $G(\bullet) \equiv G(\sigma_q^2, \sigma_{xp}^2, \theta)$, whose explicit form appears in Equation (10.18), is the variance of the forecast error in the permanent component of demand in any given market. It is apparent from Equation (11.9) that a confusion between permanent and transitory shocks introduces additional variability in relative prices over and above the variability present in the absence of such a confusion. Because, from Equation (10.19), $G(\sigma_q^2, \sigma_{xp}^2, \theta)$ is an increasing function of both $\sigma_q^2$ and $\sigma_{xp}^2$, it follows that the higher any of the variances $\sigma_{xq}^2$, $\sigma_{\epsilon}^2$, and $\sigma_{xp}^2$ are, the greater the dispersion in relative prices will be.

Differences in supply and demand elasticities and in rates of technological progress over markets are additional factors that tend to increase relative price variability across markets.

## 3    General rate of inflation and its variance

By definition, the general rate of inflation is

$$\pi_t \equiv Q_t - Q_{t-1} = \sum_v u(v)[p_t(v) - p_{t-1}(v)] \tag{11.10}$$

where the second equality in Equation (11.10) follows from (10.5). Substituting (10.13) into (10.4), substituting the resulting expression into (11.10), using (10.12) and (10.10), and rearranging, we obtain

$$\pi_t = B + \Delta m_t + \sum_v u(v)[\Delta x_t^p(v) + O_t^q(v)] - \sum_v u(v)\left(1 + \theta \frac{d_v - \bar{d}}{1 - \bar{d}}\right) O_{t-1}^q(v)$$

$$+ \sum_v u(v)\left(\frac{\bar{d} - d_v}{1 - \bar{d}}\right) \left\{ \theta \sum_{i=0}^{\infty} (1 - \theta)^i \Delta x_{t-1-i}^p(v) \right.$$

$$\left. - \theta^2 [O_{t-2}^q(v) + (1 - \theta) O_{t-3}^q(v) + \cdots] \right\} \tag{11.11}$$

where it will be recalled from Chapter 10 that

$$d_v \equiv \gamma_v/(\gamma_v+\psi_v); \qquad \bar{d} \equiv \sum_v u(v)d_v; \qquad O_t^q(v) \equiv x^q(v)+\epsilon_t(v)$$

and $B$ is some combination of parameters of no particular interest.

Equation (11.11) expresses the rate of inflation as a function of the rate of growth of the money supply and of the weighted sum, over goods, of the first differences of specific demand factors. The general rate of inflation also depends on the weighted sum over markets of the first differences of perceptions about the permanent levels of specific demand factors. The expression for these perceptions, as embodied in Equation (10.10), gives rise to the dependence of (11.11) on past permanent and transitory shocks to demands. The unconditional expected value of $\pi_t$ is $B$, because by Equations (10.3a)–(10.3c) the unconditional expected value of each of the other terms on the right-hand side of (11.11) is zero. Noting that each of the stochastic terms on the right-hand side of (11.11) is uncorrelated with each of the other stochastic terms and using (10.3a)–(10.3c), we can calculate the unconditional variance of $\pi_t$ as

$$V(\pi) = \sigma_m^2 + \sigma_q^2 \sum_v [u(v)]^2 \left[ 1 + \frac{\theta^3}{2-\theta}\left(\frac{\bar{d}-d_v}{1-\bar{d}}\right)^2 + \left(1+\theta\,\frac{d_v-\bar{d}}{1-\bar{d}}\right)^2 \right]$$

$$+ \sigma_{xp}^2 \sum_v [u(v)]^2 \left[ 1 + \frac{\theta}{2-\theta}\left(\frac{\bar{d}-d_v}{1-\bar{d}}\right)^2 \right] \tag{11.12}$$

from which it follows that the variance of the rate of inflation depends on $\sigma_m^2$, $\sigma_{xp}^2$, and $\sigma_q^2 = \sigma_{xq}^2 + \sigma_\epsilon^2$.

It is obvious from Equation (11.12) that the variance of the general rate of inflation is an increasing function of the variance of the rate of increase of the money supply $\sigma_{mp}^2$. The effects of the other variances are less immediately clear because changes in $\sigma_{xp}^2$ and $\sigma_q^2$ affect $V(\pi)$ directly but also through the coefficient of adaptation $\theta$. Proposition 1 gives rather weak sufficient conditions for $V(\pi)$ to increase in all the underlying variances.

### Proposition 1:[4]

(a)  *The variance of the rate of inflation increases in $\sigma_m^2$.*

(b)  *Provided the nonstochastic distributions of $u(v)$ and $d_v$ are independent or have a positive correlation, the variance of the rate of inflation increases in $\sigma_{xp}^2$ and $\sigma_q^2$, and particularly in $\sigma_\epsilon^2$.*

Note that $u(v)$ is the weight assigned to market $v$ in the computation of the general price index. The term $d_v \equiv \gamma_v/(\psi_v+\gamma_v)$ is the ratio of the supply elasticity of good $v$ to the sum of the (absolute value of the) demand elasticity and supply elasticity of that good. We refer to $d_v$ as the relative supply elasticity of good $v$. Proposition 1 requires either that there be no systematic relationship between the weights $u(v)$ and the relative supply elasticities $d_v$ across goods, or that there be a positive association between them. This seems a reasonably weak condition. In any case it is only sufficient but not necessary. Even if it does not hold, there is a good chance that the results of Proposition 1 hold.

## 4      Relative price change and its variance

By definition, the change in the relative price of good $s$ is

$$RPC_t(s) \equiv p_t(s) - Q_t - [p_{t-1}(s) - Q_{t-1}] \tag{11.13}$$

Substituting Equation (10.13) into (10.4), substituting the resulting expression into (11.13), using (10.10), and rearranging, the relative price change of good $s$ can be expressed in terms of only actual, current, and past shocks as

$$RPC_t(s) = C + [\Delta x_t^p(s) + O_t^q(s)][1 - u(s)] - \sum_{v \neq s} u(v)[\Delta x_t^p(v) + O_t^q(v)]$$

$$- A(s)\left\{ \theta \sum_{i=0}^{\infty} (1-\theta)^i \Delta x_{t-1-i}^p(s) \right.$$

$$\left. - \theta^2 [O_{t-2}^q(s) + (1-\theta) O_{t-3}^q(s) + \cdots] \right\}$$

$$+ \sum_{v \neq s} \frac{u(v)}{1-\bar{d}} B(s,v) \left\{ \theta \sum_{i=0}^{\infty} (1-\theta)^i \Delta x_{t-1-i}^p(v) \right.$$

$$\left. - \theta^2 [O_{t-2}^q(v) + (1-\theta) O_{t-3}^q(v) + \cdots] \right\}$$

$$- [1 - u(s) + \theta A(s)] O_{t-1}^q(s)$$

$$+ \sum_v u(v)\left[ 1 + \theta \frac{B(s,v)}{1-\bar{d}} \right] O_{t-1}^q(v) \tag{11.14}$$

where

$$B(s,v) \equiv 1 - \bar{d} - (1-d_v)(1-d_s); \quad A(s) \equiv d_s - u(s)B(s,s)/(1-\bar{d})$$

and $C$ is a known combination of parameters of no particular interest for our discussion.

The unconditional expected value of $RPC_t(s)$ is equal to $C$ because the unconditional expected value of all the other terms on the right-hand side of Equation (11.14) is zero.[5] Noting that each of the stochastic terms in Equation (11.14) is uncorrelated with each of the other stochastic terms and using Equations (10.3a)–(10.3c), we can calculate the unconditional variance of $RPC_t(s)$ as

$$
\begin{aligned}
V[RPC(s)] = \sigma_{xp}^2 \Bigg( & [1-u(s)]^2 + \sum_{v \neq s} [u(v)]^2 \\
& + \frac{\theta}{2-\theta} \left\{ [A(s)]^2 + \sum_{v \neq s} \left[ \frac{u(v)B(s,v)}{1-\bar{d}} \right]^2 \right\} \Bigg) \\
+ \sigma_q^2 \Bigg( & [1-u(s)]^2 + \sum_{v \neq s} [u(v)]^2 \\
& + \frac{\theta^3}{2-\theta} \left\{ [A(s)]^2 + \sum_{v \neq s} \left[ \frac{u(v)B(s,v)}{1-\bar{d}} \right]^2 \right\} \\
& + [1-u(s)+\theta A(s)]^2 \\
& + \sum_{v \neq s} [u(v)]^2 \left[ 1+\theta \frac{B(s,v)}{1-\bar{d}} \right]^2 \Bigg)
\end{aligned}
\tag{11.15}
$$

Although this expression looks rather formidable, it turns out that under relatively weak conditions it is unambiguously increasing in all the underlying variances. The details appear in the following proposition.

**Proposition 2:**

(a)  *If the following conditions are satisfied*

   (i)          $d_s > u(s)$

   (ii)        $\dfrac{1-\bar{d}}{1-d_s} > \tfrac{1}{2} > u(s)$

   (iii)      $\displaystyle\sum_{v \neq s} [u(v)]^2 > \frac{1-d_s}{1-\bar{d}} \sum_{v \neq s} [u(v)]^2 (1-d_v)$

   *the variance of the relative price change is an increasing function of $\sigma_{xp}^2$, $\sigma_{xq}^2$, and $\sigma_\epsilon^2$.*

(b)  *The variance of the relative price change does not depend on the aggregate monetary variance $\sigma_m^2$.*

Part (b) of Proposition 2 follows immediately from the fact that $\sigma_m^2$ does not appear in Equation (11.15). The proof of part (a) is omitted.[6]

Condition (i) of Proposition 2 states that the size of the supply elasticity of good $s$ relative to the sum of the absolute values of its demand and supply elasticities must exceed the weight of good $s$ in the general price index. Because this weight is small and most supply and demand elasticities do not take the extreme values of zero or infinity, this condition is quite likely to be fulfilled. The part $\tfrac{1}{2} > u(s)$ of condition (ii) is just a restatement of the idea that $u(s)$ is small. The first inequality of condition (ii) restricts the relative demand elasticity of good $s$, $1 - d_s$, to be no larger than twice the average relative demand elasticity in the economy.

For any $s$ whose relative demand elasticity is equal to or less than the average relative demand elasticity in the economy, condition (iii) is always fulfilled because $1 - d_v < 1$ for all values of $v$. It will also be fulfilled for markets where the relative demand elasticity is greater than the average, provided $1 - d_s$ exceeds $1 - \bar{d}$ by an amount that is not too large and whose exact form can be derived from condition (iii). In any case, all three conditions are only sufficient conditions. Equation (11.15) suggests that even when one or more of these conditions are violated it is still likely that Proposition 2(a) holds.

It should be noted that the aggregate monetary variance $\sigma_m^2$ does not affect the variance of the relative price change. This is a consequence of the underlying monetary neutrality of the model and the fact that people are subject to only the permanent–transitory confusion and not the aggregate–relative confusion.[7] However, the differential (across markets) transitory monetary noise $\sigma_\epsilon^2$ affects the variance of the relative price change directly through $\sigma_q^2$ and indirectly by affecting the coefficient of adaptation $\theta$. Proposition 2(a) suggests that the total effect of an increase in $\sigma_\epsilon^2$ is to increase the variance of the relative price change.

Note that the variances of the relative price change of different goods differ even though the stochastic structure of all markets is identical. This is a consequence of the differences in elasticities across markets.

## 5     Cross-sectional relationship between the variance of inflation and the variance of relative price change

Proposition 3 is a direct consequence of Propositions 1(b) and 2(a).

    **Proposition 3:** *Under the conditions of Propositions 1 and 2, changes in the variance of permanent relative real demand shocks $\sigma_{xp}^2$, the variance of transitory relative real demand shocks $\sigma_{xq}^2$, the variance of the differential monetary noise $\sigma_\epsilon^2$, or some combination of them cause a positive relationship between the variance of the relative price change and the variance of the rate of inflation.*

This proposition implies that there should be a positive relationship between the variance of the relative price change and the variance of the rate of inflation in a cross section of countries, each with its own set of exogenous variances that is constant over time. This is in principle an empirically testable proposition. It is indirectly supported by the work of Glejser (1965), who found a cross-sectional positive relationship between the variance of the relative price change and average inflation. This finding, together with the widely documented positive relationship between the variance and the level of inflation, gives empirical support to Proposition 3. The positive over-time relationship that Vining and Elwertowski (1976) found between the variance of the relative price change and the variance of inflation is also suggestive in this context. It is not quite a test of Proposition 3, however, because it is done over time, whereas the proposition applies to different regimes for which data across countries are a better approximation.

## 6    Conjecture on the relationship between the rate of inflation and the variance of inflation

Recent empirical literature suggests that the level and the variance of inflation are positively related both cross sectionally and over time (Gordon 1971, Okun 1971, Logue and Willet 1976, Jaffee and Kleiman 1977, Foster 1978, Blejer 1979). Although the model presented here does not directly explain this relationship, when used in conjunction with additional information it may be able to offer some potentially fruitful explanations. One potential explanation is that an increase in the rate of monetary expansion is accompanied by an increase in the variance of money. Such a relationship will hold if governments tend to use stop–go policies more and with a higher frequency when the rate of inflation is higher. This could be because the government tends to attempt more unrealistic stabilization programs at higher rates of inflation. In terms of the model, a positive relationship between the variance $\sigma_m^2$ and the rate of monetary inflation immediately implies, through Equation (11.12), a positive relationship between the level and the variance of the rate of inflation. This conjecture can be easily tested empirically.

Another possibility is that the average rate of monetary expansion and the variance of the differential monetary noise $\sigma_\epsilon^2$ are positively related. At least for low and medium rates of inflation such as those experienced by Western economies, this seems to be a reasonable conjecture because at medium rates of inflation, it pays some sectors to make institutional adjustments to the inflationary environment but does not pay others. Past a high enough inflation threshold, however, all sectors will introduce the institutional adjustments. In that range, we should probably expect a negative relationship or no relationship between the rate of inflation and the variance $\sigma_\epsilon^2$. For the low and medium inflation countries, a positive relationship between the rate of inflation and $\sigma_\epsilon^2$ could provide another reason for the positive relationship observed (mostly in such countries) between the variance and the rate of general inflation.

# Notes

## General overview

1. Although the rational expectations concept was first proposed by Muth (1961) in the context of a single industry, Lucas (1972a, 1972b, 1973) was the first to apply it to macroeconomics.
2. The distinction between monetarists and Keynesians has meant different things at different times. The distinction drawn here is a description of some current basic differences between the two groups.
3. Examples of this approach are described by Gray (1976), Fischer (1977), Phelps and Taylor (1977), Cukierman (1980), and Taylor (1980).
4. Such a relationship is documented in Vining and Elwertowski (1976). Cukierman (1979b) provides an explanation for the observed relationship between relative price and general price level variability, and Parks (1978) and Hercowitz (1981) explain the observed relationship between relative price variability and unanticipated inflation.
5. These results are derived and documented empirically in Cukierman and Wachtel (1979, 1982a, 1982b). An integrated approach appears in Cukierman (1983). Note that inflation variance and inflation uncertainty are not necessarily identical.
6. See also Cukierman (1981a) for an investigation of the effects of the permanent–transitory confusion on fluctuations in the real rates of interest.
7. See Jaffee and Kleiman (1977), Leijonhufvud (1977), and Fischer and Modigliani (1978) for systematic surveys of the costs of inflation. An attempt to quantify those costs for the U.S. economy is made in Fischer (1981).
8. Some of those implications are derived by Barro (1976) and Cukierman (1979a, 1982a).

## Asymmetric information in economics and the information conveyed by prices and other signals

1. Stiglitz (1974) investigates the effect that the signaling function of education has on the demand for education.
2. Productivity is positively correlated with intelligence and intelligence is negatively related to the costs of education, which include direct costs as well as negative costs that are due to the consumption aspects of education.
3. A general analysis of the efficiency of competitive responses to signals appears in Spence (1974).

175

4. Invertibility is not always satisfied. Kihlstrom and Mirman (1975) present conditions on the utility function that assure invertibility.
5. The model also features $F$ firms with state-dependent production functions from which we abstract for simplicity.
6. Strictly speaking this theorem requires a few additional technical assumptions such as nonsatiability and differentiability of all utility functions, and that for each $y$, $\Pi_i(y) > 0$ for $i = 1, \ldots, n$.
7. This section is based on Grossman (1977).
8. More precisely it reveals the conditional expected value of the price in the second period given $\theta$.
9. This statement is strictly true only in competitive markets in which the single individual knows that he or she does not have any effect on market prices and therefore on the information that is revealed by those prices.
10. This subsection is based on Grossman and Stiglitz (1980). See also Grossman and Stiglitz (1976).
11. Such a case arises in the context of the present model when the information of the informed is perfect ($\sigma_\epsilon^2 = 0$) or when there is no noise; that is, the variance of the current supply is zero.

**Aggregate–relative confusion: implications for the Phillips curve**

1. Friedman chose this terminology by analogy to Wicksell's "natural rate of interest," whose distinguishing feature is that it is independent of monetary factors. Similarly, the natural rate of unemployment is the level of unemployment that will prevail when the temporary influence of unexpected changes in monetary policy on employment has vanished; in other words, when workers do not make errors about their real wage rate. Obviously there is nothing "natural" or God given about the natural rate of unemployment; it is natural only in the sense that it is independent of unanticipated changes in the price level.
2. Some indirect evidence on this for the United States can be obtained by comparing the Livingston survey of inflationary expectations with the University of Michigan Survey Research Center data on inflationary expectations. In both surveys, respondents are asked directly what they expect the future rate of inflation to be. The first survey includes mostly business people and may therefore be taken to represent the views of employers. The second survey is more widely based and may therefore be taken to represent more closely the views of workers. Comparison of the inflationary expectations from those two surveys suggests that the business people do not systematically outperform the general public in forecasting ability. (As a matter of fact, had we assumed that workers' expectations adapt to actual inflation quicker than employers' expectations do, a positively sloped short-run Phillips curve would have emerged.)
3. This goes back to Phelps et al.'s (1970) notion that information flows are costly. In an earlier paper, Lucas (1972a) presents a similar mechanism in the context of a pure consumption loan model in which the confusion is between

real and nominal changes. The earlier paper has more explicit utility-based microeconomic foundations than the one on which the discussion in the text is based.

4. For further extensions of the disequilibrium view of the Phillips curve, see Tobin (1972) and Baumol (1978).

5. This can be seen from the following: Denoting by the corresponding upper-case letters the antilogs of the variables in Equation (3.4), we can rewrite the demand function as

$$Y_t^d(v)P_t(v) = X_t W_t(v)$$

Summing this expression over markets, we get

$$\sum_{v=1}^{N} Y_t^d(v)P_t(v) = X_t \sum_{v=1}^{N} W_t(v)$$

which is like an equation of exchange. It says that the total nominal income (on the left-hand side) is equal to the quantity of money $X_t$ multiplied by the expression $\sum_{v=1}^{N} W_t(v)$, whose precise value depends on the (stochastic) distribution of $w_t(v)$. The term $\sum_{v=1}^{N} W_t(v)$ can be interpreted as the velocity of the circulation of money.

6. By definition, $x_t = x_{t-1} + \Delta x_t$, so that $x_t$ follows a random walk.

7. The version presented here differs from Lucas's (1973) version in two respects: First, equilibrium conditions are imposed at the level of each market rather than at the level of the whole economy. Second, the lagged cyclical output term that is featured in Lucas's model to catch persistence has been deleted for simplicity. The basic results, however, remain the same.

8. This procedure requires that the model's solution be known in advance. A procedure based on the method of undertermined coefficients, which does not require such advance knowledge, can also be used to obtain the solution for this model when supply elasticities vary across markets. See Section 5 and the Appendix of Chapter 6 for details. The cumbersome notation $p_t[w_t(v)]$ is used provisionally to stress that prices will differ across markets only if the realizations of the market-specific demand shocks differ across markets. The reason for this result is explained more fully at the beginning of Section 3b.

9. For further details and additional problems of estimation, the reader is referred to the empirical section of Lucas (1973) as well as to Arak (1977) and Lucas (1976, 1977).

10. As in Lucas (1973), Froyen and Waud feature an additional lagged cyclical output term in the supply function (3.28a). This term is important for the empirical estimation because it catches serially correlated movements in deviations of output from trend. As mentioned at the outset, however, because it is not needed for understanding the basic point of the model, it does not appear in the analytical presentation in the text.

11. Since $\sigma_u^2$ and $\sigma_x^2$ enter into Equations (3.29b) and (3.29c) in exactly the same way, the proof that $V(\pi)$ increases in $\sigma_u^2$ is identical to the proof that $V(\pi)$ increases in $\sigma_x^2$. The proof of the last relationship appears in Section A4 of the Appendix to Chapter 4.

## Aggregate-relative confusion: implications for the distribution of inflationary expectations and for inflation uncertainty

1. The discussion in this and the following section and Section 5 draws on Cukierman and Wachtel (1979).
2. The discussion in this section is partially based on Mitchell and Taylor (1982).
3. For a proof, see Appendix C of Cukierman and Wachtel (1979). More information on the variances $\sigma^2$ and $\tau^2$ can be found in Section 3 of Chapter 3.
4. This section is partially based on Mitchell and Taylor (1982).
5. This section is partially based on Cukierman and Wachtel (1982b).
6. See footnote 5 of Cukierman and Wachtel (1982a) for details. Recall that this condition is needed only to assure the positive relationship between the SRC variance and the moving variances of inflation and of the rate of change in nominal income. It is *not* needed for the implication that the Livingston variance and the moving variances are positively correlated.
7. For a different approach to the modeling of individual expectations from the Livingston survey, see Figlewski and Wachtel (1981).

## Implications of inflation uncertainty and differential inflationary expectations for the bond market and its allocative efficiency

1. The first two sections of this chapter and part of the third are adapted from Cukierman (1978).
2. The assumption of a uniformly held expectation in the context of bond market equilibrium and inflation is almost universal. It is originally due to Fisher (1896). Work by Gibson (1972), Fama (1976), Feldstein (1976), Sargent (1976), Feldstein and Summers (1978), and Friedman (1978, 1980) constitute but a small sample of the literature in which Fisher's uniformity assumption is maintained.
3. At the risk of elaborating the obvious, it should be stressed that all real rates here are ex ante perceived rates rather than actually realized ex post real rates. Only ex ante real rates determine lending and borrowing decisions, which is why the discussion focuses on them.
4. The usual caveats concerning the use of consumer surplus seem to be less important in the present context, since the shaded areas in Figure 1 may be interpreted as losses in physical outputs or returns. This will be strictly so if the supply curves of funds reflect only alternative real portfolio investment opportunities and no subjective time preference. Once risk aversion is reckoned with, however, a subjective element is reintroduced into the analysis.
5. The interpretation of the results obtained here in terms of the model of Chapter 4 is strictly legitimate provided the observation on the economy-wide interest rate does not provide individuals in localized markets with additional information about the current monetary shock. If it does, the rational expectations equilibrium of Chapters 3 and 4 has to be reworked to incorporate this information. Further details appear in Chapter 7.

6. There may, however, be a fully expected redistribution because of nominal taxation (Feldstein 1976, Birati–Cukierman 1979). Also the nominal rate may fail to adjust because of usury laws or other reasons. The statement in the text abstracts from these considerations.

### Aggregate–relative confusion: implications for relative price variability

1. For earlier accounts of and explanations for this relationship, see Cairnes (1873), Graham (1930), and Mises (1953). Jaffee and Kleiman (1977) also investigate this relationship, but their evidence is somewhat mixed. More precisely, they find that the constant in a regression of the coefficient of variation of relative price variability on the reciprocal of the general rate of inflation is insignificant. This implies that there is no relationship between relative price variability and inflation. This result should be taken with some caution, however, owing to possible biases created by their procedure, which involves dividing both the dependent and the independent variable by the general rate of inflation.
2. This section is adapted from Cukierman (1979b).

### Place of the aggregate–relative confusion within the economics of asymmetric information: some concluding reflections

1. The idea that equilibrium has to be self-fulfilling is shared by the signaling literature. See, for example, Spence (1973).
2. When individuals observe less than all prices but more than one, a residual confusion between aggregate and relative shocks obviously remains. This confusion decreases monotonically with the number of markets that individuals are allowed to sample. An analysis of the case in which individuals decide how many markets to sample appears in Cukierman (1979a).
3. This point as well as the general ideas in this section are due to Karni (1980, 1981). See also Barro (1980).
4. The main argument does not depend on this restriction as long as $\eta$ is not equal to either zero or infinity.

### Permanent–transitory confusion and other reasons for persistence: overview

1. Perceptions of permanent income are central to Friedman's (1957) permanent income hypothesis. Beliefs about permanent wages play an important role in the determination of the current labor supply. See Lucas and Rapping (1969) and Brunner and Meltzer (1978).
2. For a lucid discussion of the permanent–transitory confusion in terms of the distinction between risk and uncertainty, see Meltzer (1982).
3. A more general formulation of time-dependent disutility from work appears in Kydland and Prescott (1980, 1982).

### Permanent–transitory confusion: implications for stagflation and the persistence of unemployment

1. This chapter draws heavily on Brunner et al. (1980) with the permission of the *Journal of Monetary Economics*.
2. For alternative hypotheses that explain stagflation, see Friedman's Nobel lecture (1977).
3. For a derivation of a similar labor supply function from a microeconomic model, see Lucas and Rapping (1969). For computational convenience, $\eta \log \delta$ is used here as the normalizing constant in the labor supply.
4. The model does not rule out the possibility that some synchronization of expenditures to permanent income is achieved by changing the excess demand for bonds. As a matter of fact, the constraint $g < 1$ originates in the requirement that the excess demand for bonds is an increasing function of actual income and a decreasing function of permanent income.
5. It is possible to allow for varying degrees of persistence of the transient component by specifying it as a general linear stationary autoregressive moving average (ARMA) stochastic process [see Beveridge and Nelson (1981)]. The formulation in the text is used for simplicity.
6. This is the fundamental thesis of Brunner and Meltzer (1978). If the shock is permanent, it becomes relevant for predicting the future course of the economy. If it is transitory, it is irrelevant for predicting the future. The oil shocks of the seventies, changes in rainfall, and the famous disappearance of the Peruvian anchovies are examples of real shocks that cannot be accurately labeled as permanent or transitory when they occur.
7. For the particular stochastic process used here, the predictor in Equations (9.15) is also the minimum-variance estimator of the *actual* value of $x$ for period $t + 1$, given the information set $I_t$. This can be seen by noting that by Wold's decomposition theorem (Sargent 1979: Chapter XI, Section 11), $\Delta x_{t+1}$ can be expressed as the first-order moving average process $\Delta x_{t+1} = \gamma_{t+1} - (1-\lambda)\gamma_t$, where $\gamma_t$ is white noise. Expressing $\gamma_{t+1}$ as an infinite lag on values of $\Delta x$ up to and including period $t$ (the set $I_t$) by using the lag operator and rearranging, we can see that the best prediction of $x_{t+1}$ given $I_t$ is also given by Equations (9.15). Note that this feature is specific to the particular stochastic process used here.
8. Inspection of (9.15b) shows that for any $\infty > h \geqslant 0$, $0 \leqslant \lambda < 1$. Hence whatever the ratio between $\sigma_{xp}^2$ and $\sigma_{xq}^2$, the expression in (9.15a) is a Koyck distributed lag with a sum of weights that is equal to one.
9. This can be seen by noting that $S_n = 1 - (1-\lambda)^n$. Because $\lambda < 1$, this implies that $S_n$ increases with $\lambda$. Differentiating (9.15b) with respect to $h$, we obtain

$$\frac{\partial \lambda}{\partial h} = \frac{1}{2}\left\{\left[\left(\frac{1+h+h^2/4}{h+h^2/4}\right)\right]^{1/2} - 1\right\}$$

which must be positive. It follows that

$$\frac{\partial S_n}{\partial h} = \frac{\partial S_n}{\partial \lambda}\frac{\partial \lambda}{\partial h} > 0$$

10. In fact, additional permanent shocks will continue to affect the economy according to the stochastic process in Equations (9.11) and (9.12). However, if the permanent shock to productivity that occurs in period $t$ is large in comparison to $\sigma_{up}^2$, it will dominate the economy for a while. See also the discussion at the end of Section 5b.

11. Equation (9.19) can be derived as follows: Rewrite (9.15a) as

$$Ex_{t+j}^p = \lambda \sum_{i=0}^{j} (1-\lambda)^i x_{t+j-i} + (1-\lambda)^{j+1} Ex_{t-1}$$

for $x = u$, substitute the result into (9.16b), and use the assumption in (9.17) and the fact that $u_{t+s}^p = u^p$ for $s < 0$ and $u_{t+s}^p = u^p + Du^p$ for $s \geqslant 0$.

12. Details appear in Cukierman and Meltzer (1982). They show that in the presence of the permanent–transitory confusion, forecast errors taken from *finite* samples following a large permanent shock will show evidence of serial correlation, although there is no such serial correlation in the population.

13. The qualitative results are unaffected if we allow the money stock to grow secularly.

**Permanent–transitory confusion: implications for monetary policy and the efficiency of the price system**

1. This chapter draws heavily on Cukierman (1982a) with the permission of the *Journal of Monetary Economics*.

2. For a thought-provoking discussion along those lines, see Friedman (1977).

3. This can be seen by noting that Equation (10.2) is equivalent to

$$Y_t^d(v) = [N_t(v)/P_t(v)]^{\psi_v}$$

where the uppercase letters are the antilogs of the corresponding lowercase letters in (10.2).

4. For the particular stochastic structure postulated here, the best forecast of the following period's relative price is identical to the current perception of the current permanent relative price. For more general stochastic processes, this is not necessarily the case. The specification adopted here is used because of its simplicity and the clear-cut intuitive distinction that it provides between permanent and transitory shocks. For more general specifications, see Beveridge and Nelson (1981).

5. For example, if for any stochastic process whose first difference is a stationary process of the ARMA type, the perception of the permanent component is defined as the predicted value of the process as the forecast horizon goes to infinity, this perception is usually a distributed lag of many past realizations of the process (Beveridge and Nelson 1981).

6. In Barro's model, however, the informational confusion is between aggregate and relative price movements, and it is assumed that all markets have identical demand and supply functions.

7. Both Barro (1976) and Cukierman (1979a) use the full current information output as a benchmark. Because a comparison of actual and the full future

information output is of independent interest, however, the implications of a measure based on the full future information output are presented in Section 6.

8. By contrast, similar investigations within the framework of the aggregate–relative confusion come up with the result that the variance of aggregate monetary shocks should be kept at zero (Barro 1976, Cukierman 1979a). In the present framework this variance, which is summarized by $\sigma_m^2$, does not affect the allocative efficiency of the price system because the aggregate–relative confusion has been assumed away.

### Permanent–transitory confusion: implications for relative price variability and inflation

1. This chapter is partly based on Section II of Cukierman (1982a) with the permission of the *Journal of Monetary Economics*.
2. See Gordon (1971), Okun (1971), Logue and Willet (1976), Jaffee and Kleiman (1977), Foster (1978), and Blejer (1979).
3. This model features real relative shocks to demand (some of which are monetarily induced) but no exogenous stochastic shocks to supply. All the qualitative results presented here, however, carry over to the case of stochastic shocks to both relative supplies and relative demands (Cukierman 1982a).
4. The proof appears in Part A of the Appendix to Cukierman (1982a).
5. For $\psi_v = \psi$, $\gamma_v = \gamma$, and $\beta_v = \beta$ for all values of $v$, $C$ is equal to zero.
6. The proof appears in Appendix B of Cukierman (1982a).
7. By contrast, in models that deal exclusively with the aggregate–relative confusion (like that of Chapter 6), the variance of the relative price change does depend on the aggregate monetary variance.

# Glossary of symbols

Symbols are listed by chapter or by groups of chapters as follows:

Chapter(s) 2
    3, 4, 6, and 7
    5
    9
    10 and 11

Within each list, symbols are alphabetized, reading from left to right, regardless of meaning or capitalization. Greek terms are similarly alphabetized following Roman ones.

## Chapter 2

$a$   Unknown random quality parameter

$c$   Cost of obtaining an observation on $\theta$

$d$   Coefficient of absolute risk aversion

$P_0$   Price of risky asset in period 0

$P_1$   Yield in period 1 of risky asset

$P^a(y)$   Walrasian equilibrium price vector of contingent consumption under symmetric information

$P^0(y)$   Rational expectations equilibrium price vector of contingent consumption under asymmetric information

$PR^i$   Subjective probability distribution of agent $i$ about $a$

$r$   $\equiv \sigma_\theta^2/\sigma_\epsilon^2$

$S$   Current supply of risky asset

$s_i$   State of nature $i$, $i = 1, \ldots, n$

$u$   Random return on a risky asset

$u_y$   Posterior (after $y$ has been observed) probability distribution

$y$   Stochastic variable observed by agent 1

$y$   $\equiv (y^1, \ldots, y^H)$   Vector of private information, where $H$ is the number of individuals

$\tilde{y}$   $\equiv (\tilde{y}^1, \ldots, \tilde{y}^H)$

$y^h$   Specific realization of $\tilde{y}^h$

$\tilde{y}^h$   Random variable observed by individual $h$ that is correlated with the distribution of next period's state

$y_i$   $= P_1 + \epsilon_i$   Stochastic variable that is observed by agent $i$ in period 0

183

$\epsilon_i$    White noise process

$\theta$    Privileged information variable

$\lambda$    Proportion of informed inviduals

$\Pi_i(y)$    Conditional probability that state $i$ realizes given $y$

$\Pi_i^h(y^h)$    Conditional probability that individual $h$ assigns to state $i$ after observing $y^h$

$\rho_\theta$    Coefficient of correlation between $\theta$ and the market price

$\sigma_s$    Variance of $S$

$\sigma_\epsilon^2$    Variance of $\epsilon$

$\sigma_\theta^2$    Variance of $\theta$

## Chapters 3, 4, 6, and 7

$a$    $\equiv \gamma\theta/(1+\gamma\theta)$    Trade-off coefficient

$B_t$    Mean bias of expected inflation

$B_t^d(v)$    $\equiv B_t^d[w_t(v)]$    Demand for bonds by all individuals in market $v$ at time $t$

$EQ_t$    Expected value of $Q_t$

$E_w \pi_L^*(w_t)$    Mean expected inflation over the distribution of $w_t$

$f$    Positive coefficient

$FE_t$    Inflation forecast error

$F(v)$    $\equiv [\bar\gamma - \gamma(v)]/[1+\gamma(v)]$

$I_t(v)$    $\equiv I_t[w_t(v)] \equiv I_t(w_t)$    Information available in market $v$ at time $t$

$k(s)$    $\equiv 1/[1+\gamma(s)]$

$m_t$    Number of respondents to Livingston survey in period $t$

$N$    Number of markets in the economy

$n_t$    Nominal interest rate on a one-period loan contracted in period $t$ to be repaid in period $t+1$

$P_t(v)$    Price in market $v$ at time $t$

$p_t(v)$    $= p_t[w_t(v)] = p_t(w_t)$    log of price in market $v$ at time $t$

$p_t(v, w_t)$    Log of price in market $v$ when supply elasticities differ across markets

$Q_t$    Log of the (geometric) average price level at time $t$

$\bar Q_t$    Expected value of general price level in period $t$ given information until and including period $t-1$

$Q_t^*(v, w_t)$    Log of general price level as perceived in market $v$ when supply elasticities differ across markets

$Q_t^*(w_t)$    $\equiv Q_t^*[w_t(v)] \equiv E[Q_t/I_t(w_t)] \equiv E[Q_t/I_t(v)]$    Conditional expected value of $Q_t$ given $I_t(v)$

$Q_{t+1}^*(w_t)$    $\equiv E[Q_{t+1}/I_t(w_t)]$

$r$    $\equiv \sigma^2/\tau^2$

$s_t$    $\equiv \epsilon_t + w_t$

$t$    Time index

$u_t$    Random shock to aggregate productivity

$u(v)$    Weight of $p_t(v)$ in average price index

$v$    Market index

| | |
|---|---|
| $V(B)$ | Variance of mean bias |
| $V(FE)$ | Variance of forecast error or inflation uncertainty |
| $\bar{V}_t(FE)$ | Estimate of $V(FE)$ for period $t$ |
| $V(\pi)$ | Variance of rate of inflation |
| $V(\pi^R)$ | Cross-sectional variance of relative price change |
| $V(\pi^*)$ | Variance of $\pi^*$ across markets |
| $V(\pi_L^*)$ | Variance of $\pi_L^*$ across markets |
| $W_t(v)$ | Relative demand shock in market $v$ at time $t$ |
| $w_t(v)$ | Log of relative demand shock in market $v$ at time $t$ |
| $X_t$ | Aggregate money stock at time $t$ |
| $x_t$ | Log of the aggregate money stock at time $t$ |
| $y_{ct}$ | Average cyclical component of output in the economy in log form |
| $y_{ct}(v)$ | Log of cyclical component of output in market $v$ at time $t$ |
| $y_{ct}(v, w_t)$ | Log of cyclical component of output in market $v$ when supply elasticities differ across markets |
| $y_{ct}^d(w_t)$ | Log of demand for the cyclical component of output in a market that sustains the shock $w_t$ |
| $Y_t^d(v)$ | Output demanded in market $v$ at time $t$ |
| $y_t^d(v)$ | Log of output demanded in market $v$ at time $t$ |
| $y_t^d(w_t)$ | Log of demand in a market that sustains the shock $w_t$ |
| $y_{nt}$ | Normal or trend output at time $t$ |
| $y_t^s(v)$ | Log of total output supplied in market $v$ at time $t$ |
| $z[w_t(v)]$ | Relative price in market $v$ at time $t$ |
| $\alpha$ | Productivity level at time 0 |
| $\beta$ | Rate of growth of productivity |
| $\gamma$ | Elasticity of output supplied with respect to perceived relative |
| $\bar{\gamma}$ | Weighted mean value of $\gamma(v)$ over markets |
| $\gamma(v)$ | Elasticity of supply in market $v$ |
| $\delta$ | Mean rate of growth of $x$ |
| $\Delta x_t$ | First difference of $x_t$ |
| $\epsilon_t$ | $=\Delta x_t - \delta$  Random shock to the rate of growth of the money supply |
| $\eta$ | Elasticity of demand for bonds with respect to real rate of interest |
| $\theta$ | $\equiv \sigma_w^2/(\sigma_w^2 + \sigma_x^2)$ |
| $\theta(v)$ | $\equiv \theta(1+\bar{\gamma})/[(1+\theta\bar{\gamma}+(1-\theta)\gamma(v)]$ |
| $\lambda(\theta)$ | $\equiv 1/(1+\bar{\gamma}\theta)$ |
| $\pi_i(s)$ | Undetermined coefficients for market $s$, where $i = 0, 1, \ldots, 4$ (see Appendix to Chapter 6) |
| $\bar{\pi}_{Lt}(i)$ | Mean, over individuals, inflation forecast from the Livingston survey in period $t$ |
| $\pi_{Lt}^*(i)$ | Inflation forecast of individual $i$ in Livingston's survey made in period $t$ |
| $\pi_t$ | $\equiv Q_t - Q_{t-1}$  Rate of inflation |
| $\pi_t^R(v)$ | Relative price change in market $v$ between time $t-1$ and time $t$ |

$\pi^*(w_t)$    Rate of inflation expected at time $t$ to occur between period $t$ and period $t+1$ in a market that sustains the shock $w_t$

$\pi_L^*(w_t)$    Rate of inflation expected at time $t$ to occur between period $t-1$ and period $t+1$ in a market that sustains the shock $w_t$

$_{t-1}\pi_{t+1}$    Actual inflation between period $t-1$ and period $t+1$

$\rho$    Coefficient of correlation between $\epsilon$ and $u$

$\rho_{Q_t p_t(v)}$    Coefficient of correlation between $Q_t$ and $p_t(v)$

$\rho_{\epsilon_t s_t}$    Coefficient of correlation between $\epsilon_t$ and $s_t$

$\sigma^2$    $\equiv \sigma_{Q_t}^2$    Variance of $Q_t$

$\sigma_a^2$    $\equiv \sigma_x^2 + \sigma_u^2 - 2\rho\sigma_x\sigma_u$

$\sigma_{p_t(v)}$    Standard deviation of $p_t(v)$

$\sigma_u^2$    Variance of $u_t$

$\sigma_w^2$    Variance of $w_t(v)$ for all $t$ and $v$

$\sigma_x^2$    Variance of $\Delta x_t$ for all $t$

$\tau^2$    Variance of $z[w_t(v)]$

$\phi_t$    Exogenous shock to excess demand for bonds

# Chapter 5

$a_s, b_s$    Positive parameters characterizing the demand or supply of trader $s$ in the bond market

$\mathrm{Cov}(\pi^*)$    Covariance between the expectations of different traders

$\mathrm{Cov}(\pi, \pi^*)$    Covariance between actual and expected inflation rates

$E\pi$    Unconditional expected value of the rate of inflation

$E\pi^*$    Overall mean expected inflation across time and individuals

$I_B$    Real stock demand for funds of borrower $B$

$I_L$    Real stock supply of funds of lender $L$

$I_A^i$    Actual quantity of funds borrowed or lent by trader $i$ through the bond market

$I_O^i$    Quantity of funds trader $i$ would have borrowed or lent through the bond market if $r$ was known in advance

$L$    $= \Sigma_i L_i$

$L_i$    Consumer or producer's surplus lost by trader $i$

$n$    Nominal rate of interest

$R$    $= n - \pi^*$   Ex ante real rate of interest when expectations are uniform

$r$    $= n - \pi$   Ex post real rate of interest

$r_i$    Real rate of interest of trader $i$ when expectations differ across traders

$UG_i$    Unexpected gains of trader $i$

$v_s$    $\equiv (1/b_s)/[\Sigma_s (1/b_s)]$

$V(\pi^*)$    Variance of inflationary expectations over individuals

$V_0(\pi^*)$    Overall variance of inflationary expectations

$V_\epsilon(\pi^*)$    Over-time variability of inflationary expectations

$\mathrm{Var}\, I_i$    Variance of the $i$th trader position in the bond market

$\pi$    Actual rate of inflation

$\pi*$   Rate of inflation expected by all individuals when expectations are uniform

$\bar{\pi}*$   Weighted mean expected inflation rate across traders when expectations differ

$\pi*(j)$   Rate of inflation expected by individual $j$; $j = L, B$

$\rho$   Coefficient of correlation between the expectations of different traders

# Chapter 9

$A$   $\equiv \omega\eta/(\eta + \omega)$

$B, b, g, \theta$   Fixed parameters of money demand function

$Du^p$   Maintained large change in $u^p$

$E_q u_{t-1}$   Unconditional expected value of $u_{t-1}$ over the distribution of $u_{t-1}^q$

$e_t$   Log of aggregate demand

$Eu_t^p$   $\equiv E(u_t^p/I_t)$   Optimal predictor of $u_t^p$ given $u_t, u_{t-1}, \ldots$

$Ex_t^p$   Optimal predictor of $x_t^p$ given $x_t, x_{t-1}, \ldots$

$E\epsilon_t^p$   $\equiv E(\epsilon_t^p/I_t)$   Optimal predictor of $\epsilon_t^p$ given $\epsilon_t, \epsilon_{t-1}, \ldots$

$E\psi_t^p$   $\equiv E(\psi_t^p/I_t)$   Optimal predictor of $\psi_t^p$ given $\psi_t, \psi_{t-1}, \ldots$

$h$   $\equiv \sigma_{xp}^2/\sigma_{xq}^2$

$I_t$   Information set of individuals in period $t$; includes $x_t$ and all previous values of $x$

$k, \alpha, \beta$   Fixed parameters of the aggregate demand function

$L_t$   Labor input

$l_t^d$   Log of labor demand

$l_t^p$   Log of permanent employment

$l_t^s$   Log of labor supply

$m$   Parameter of money supply function

$m_t^d$   Money demand in nominal terms

$m_t^s$   Log of money supply in nominal terms

$n_t$   Percentage of unemployment

$p_t$   Log of price level

$p_t^p$   Log of permanent price level

$_t p_{t+1}^*$   Log of price level expected for period $t+1$ in period $t$

$r_t$   Nominal rate of interest

$r_t^p$   Permanent nominal interest rate

$S_n$   $\equiv \lambda \sum_{i=0}^{n-1} (1-\lambda)^i$

$t$   Time index

$u_t$   Aggregate productivity shock

$u_t^p$   Random walk component of $u_t$

$u_t^q$   White noise component of $u_t$

$w_t$   Log of real wage rate

$w_t^p$   Log of permanent wage rate

$x_t$   $\equiv x_t^p + x_t^q$   Sum of random walk and white noise processes

$x_t^q$     White noise process
$Y_t$     Aggregate output
$y_t$     Log of current output
$y_t^p$     Log of permanent income
$\delta$     Elasticity of production function with respect to labor
$\Delta x_t^p$     First difference of a random walk
$\epsilon_t$     Aggregate demand shock
$\epsilon_t^p$     Random walk component of $\epsilon_t$
$\epsilon_t^q$     White noise component of $\epsilon_t$
$\eta$     $\equiv 1/(1-\delta)$
$\lambda$     $\equiv (h + \frac{1}{4}h^2)^{1/2} - \frac{1}{2}h$
$\lambda_u$     $= [\sigma_{up}^2/\sigma_{uq}^2 + (\sigma_{up}^2/4\sigma_{uq}^2)^2]^{1/2} - \sigma_{up}^2/2\sigma_{uq}^2$
$\sigma_{up}^2$     Variance of $\Delta x_t^p$
$\sigma_{uq}^2$     Variance of $x_t^q$
$\sigma_{xp}^2$     Variance of $\Delta x_t^p$
$\sigma_{xq}^2$     Variance of $x_t^q$
$\psi_t$     Random shock to money supply
$\psi_t^p$     Random walk component of $\psi_t$
$\psi_t^q$     White noise component of $\psi_t$
$\omega$     Elasticity of labor supply with respect to the actual real wage rate

## Chapters 10 and 11

$C_s$     Constant combination of parameters of market $s$
$\bar{d}$     $\equiv \sum_v u(v)d_v$
$D_c(s)$     Difference between full current information output and actual output in market $s$
$D_f(s)$     Difference between full future information output and actual output in market $s$
$d_v$     $\equiv \gamma_v/(\psi_v + \gamma_v)$    "Relative elasticity of supply"
$E_{t-k}p_t(v)$     Expected log of price of good $v$ for period $t$ conditioned on information available at time $t-k$
$E_{t-k}Q_t$     Expected log of general price level for period $t$ conditioned on information available at time $t-k$
$E_{t-1}m_t$     Expected value of $m_t$ conditioned on information available in period $t-1$
$E_{t-1}x_t(v)$     Expected value of $x_t(v)$ conditioned on information available at time $t-1$
$E_{t-1}\epsilon_t(v)$     Expected value of $\epsilon_t(v)$ conditioned on information available in period $t-1$
$G(\sigma_q^2, \sigma_{xp}^2, \theta)$     $\equiv [\theta^2\sigma_q^2 + (1-\theta)^2\sigma_{xp}^2]/[\theta(2-\theta)]$
$m_t$     Shock to money supply that affects all markets identically
$n_t(v)$     $\equiv x_t(v) + \delta t + m_t + \epsilon_t(v)$
$N_t(v)$     Antilog of $n_t(v)$
$O_t(v)$     $\equiv x_t(v) + \epsilon_t(v)$

| | |
|---|---|
| $P_t(v)$ | Price of good $v$ |
| $p_t(v)$ | Log of price of good $v$ |
| $p^p_{t-1}(s)$ | Log of actual permanent price of good $s$ in period $t-1$ |
| $Q_t$ | Log of general price level |
| $Q^p_{t-1}$ | Log of actual permanent value of general price level in period $t-1$ |
| $Rp_t(s)$ | $\equiv p_t(s) - Q_t$  Actual relative price of good $s$ |
| $RPC_t(s)$ | Change in the relative price of good $s$ between $t-1$ and $t$ |
| $t$ | Time index |
| $u(v)$ | Weight of good $v$ in general price index |
| $V[D_c(s)]$ | Variance of $D_c(s)$ |
| $V[D_f(s)]$ | Variance of $D_f(s)$ |
| $V_{NC}[p_t(s)-Q_t]$ | Variance of relative price levels in the absence of the permanent–transitory confusion |
| $V_{PTC}[p_t(s)-Q_t]$ | Variance of relative price levels in the presence of the permanent–transitory confusion |
| $V[RPC(s)]$ | Variance of relative price change |
| $V(\pi)$ | Variance of the rate of inflation |
| $w(v)$ | $\equiv \{1/(1-\bar{d})\}[u(v)/(\psi_v + \gamma_v)]$ |
| $x^p$ | Value of $x^p_t(v)$ when $x^p_t(v) = x^p$ for all $v$ |
| $\bar{x}_t$ | Weighted mean of $x_t(v)$ over goods |
| $x_t(v)$ | $= x^p_t(v) + x^q_t(v)$  Total demand for good $v$ |
| $x^p_t(v)$ | Permanent (random walk) component of demand for good $v$ |
| $x^q_t(v)$ | Transitory (white noise) component of demand for good $v$ |
| $Y^d_t(v)$ | demand for good $v$ |
| $y^d_t(v)$ | Log of demand for good $v$ |
| $y^s_t(v)$ | Log of supply of good $v$ |
| $y^*_t(s)$ | Full current information output in market $s$ |
| $y^{**}_t(s)$ | Full future information output in market $s$ |
| $\beta_v$ | Rate of change of productivity in industry $v$ |
| $\gamma$ | Value of $\gamma_v$ for the case of uniform supply elasticities |
| $\gamma_v$ | Supply elasticity of good $v$ with respect to its perceived relative price |
| $\delta$ | Mean value of rate of monetary growth |
| $\bar{\epsilon}_t$ | Weighted mean of $\epsilon_t(v)$ over goods |
| $\epsilon_t(v)$ | Monetarily induced shock that affects only market $v$ |
| $\theta$ | $\equiv [\sigma^2_{xp}/\sigma^2_q + (\sigma^2_{xp}/4\sigma^2_q)^2]^{1/2} - \sigma^2_{xp}/2\sigma^2_q$ |
| $\pi_t$ | Rate of inflation |
| $\sigma^2_m$ | Variance of $m_t$ |
| $\sigma^2_q$ | $\equiv \sigma^2_{xq} + \sigma^2$ |
| $\sigma^2_{xp}$ | Variance of $\Delta x^p_t$ |
| $\sigma^2_{xq}$ | Variance of $x^q_t$ |
| $\sigma^2_\epsilon$ | Variance of $\epsilon_t(v)$ |
| $\psi$ | Value of $\psi_v$ for the case of uniform demand elasticities |
| $\psi_v$ | Demand elasticity of good $v$ with respect to its perceived relative price |

# References

Akerlof G.A. 1970. "The market for 'lemons': quality uncertainty and the market mechanism," *Quarterly Journal of Economics* 84:488-500.

Almon S. 1965. "The distributed lag between capital appropriations and expenditures," *Econometrica* 33:178-96.

Amihud Y. and H. Mendelson. 1982. "Relative price dispersion and economic shocks: an inventory adjustment approach," *Journal of Money, Credit and Banking* 14:390-8.

Anderson R.M. and H. Sonnenschein. 1982. "On the existence of rational expectations equilibrium," *Journal of Economic Theory* 26:261-80.

Arak M.J. 1977. "Some international evidence on output–inflation tradeoffs: comment," *American Economic Review* 67:728-30.

Arrow K.J. 1973. "Higher education as a filter," *Journal of Public Economics* 2: 193-216.

Bach G.L. and A. Ando. 1957. "The redistributional effects of inflation," *The Review of Economics and Statistics* 39:1-13.

Bach G.L. and J.B. Stephenson. 1974. "Inflation and the redistribution of wealth," *The Review of Economics and Statistics* 56:1-13.

Barro R.J. 1976. "Rational expectations and the role of monetary policy," *Journal of Monetary Economics* 2:1-32.

1977. "Long term contracting, sticky prices and monetary policy," *Journal of Monetary Economics* 3:305-16.

1980. "A capital market in an equilibrium business cycle model," *Econometrica* 48:1393-417.

Barro R.J. and H.I. Grossman. 1976. *Money, Employment, and Inflation.* New York: Cambridge University Press.

Baumol W. 1978. "On the stochastic unemployment distribution model and the long-run Phillips curve," in A.R. Bergstrom et al. (eds.), *Stability and Inflation, Essays in Honour of Professor A.W. Phillips.* New York: Wiley.

Beja A. 1977. "The limits of price information in market processes," W.P. No. 78-19 Graduate School of Business Administration, New York University. Revised, December.

Beveridge S. and C.R. Nelson. 1981. "A new approach to decomposition of economic time series into permanent and transitory components with particular attention to measurement of the business cycle," *Journal of Monetary Economics* 7:151-74.

190

Birati A. and A. Cukierman. 1979. "The redistributive effects of inflation and of the introduction of a real tax system in the U.S. bond market," *Journal of Public Economics* 12:125–39.

Blejer M.J. 1979. "Inflation variability in Latin America – a note on the time-series evidence," *Economics Letters* 2:37–41.

1981. "The dispersion of relative commodity prices under very rapid inflation," *Journal of Development Economics* 9:347–56.

Blejer M.J. and L. Leiderman. 1980. "On the real effects of inflation and relative price variability: some empirical evidence," *Review of Economics and Statistics* 62:539–44.

1982. "Inflation and relative price variability in the open economy," *European Economic Review* 18:387–402.

Blinder A. and S. Fischer. 1981. "Inventories, rational expectations, and the business cycle," *Journal of Monetary Economics* 8:277–304.

Bordo M.D. 1980. "The effects of monetary change on relative commodity prices and the role of long-term contracts," *Journal of Political Economy* 88: 1088–109.

Brunk, H.D. 1965. *An Introduction to Mathematical Statistics,* 2d ed. Waltham, Toronto; London: Blaisdell Publishers Company.

Brunner K. and A.H. Meltzer. 1978. "Monetary theory." Unpublished.

Brunner K., A. Cukierman, and A.H. Meltzer. 1980. "Stagflation, persistent unemployment and the permanence of economic shocks," *Journal of Monetary Economics* 6:467–92.

1983. "Money and economic activity, inventories and business cycles," *Journal of Monetary Economics* 11:281–319.

Burger A.E. 1969. "The effects of inflation (1960–68)," *Federal Reserve Bank of St. Louis Monthly Review* 51:25–36.

Cagan P. 1972. *The Channels of Monetary Effects on Interest Rates.* New York: National Bureau of Economic Research.

Cairnes J.E. 1873. *Essays on Political Economy: Theoretical and Applied.* London: Macmillan.

Carlson J. 1977. "A study of price forecasts," *Annals of Economic and Social Measurement* 6:27–56.

Cukierman A. 1977. "A test of expectational processes using information from the capital market – the Israeli case," *International Economic Review* 18: 737–53.

1978. "Heterogeneous inflationary expectations, Fisher's theory of interest, and the allocative efficiency of the bond market," *Economics Letters* 1: 151–6.

1979a. "Rational expectations and the role of monetary policy: a generalization," *Journal of Monetary Economics* 5:213–29.

1979b. "The relationship between relative prices and the general price level: a suggested interpretation," *American Economic Review* 69:444–7.

1980. "The effects of wage indexation on macroeconomic fluctuations – a generalization," *Journal of Monetary Economics* 6:147–70.

192　　**References**

1981a. "Interest rates during the cycle, inventories and monetary policy – a theoretical analysis," in K. Brunner and A.H. Meltzer (eds.), *The Costs and Consequences of Inflation, Carnegie Rochester Conference Series on Public Policy* 15, Autumn. Amsterdam: North-Holland.

1981b. "Relative price uncertainty and the theory of indexed bonds." Unpublished.

1982a. "Relative price variability, inflation and the allocative efficiency of the price system," *Journal of Monetary Economics* 9:131–62.

1982b. "Wage indexation and the theory of indexed bonds," in M. Sarnat and G. Szego (eds.), *Saving, Investment and Capital Markets in an Inflationary Economy*. Cambridge, Mass.: Ballinger.

1983. "Relative price variability and inflation: a survey and further results," in K. Brunner and A.H. Meltzer (eds.), *Carnegie Rochester Conference Series on Public Policy* 19, Autumn. Amsterdam: North-Holland.

Cukierman A. and A.H. Meltzer. 1982. "What do tests of market efficiency in the presence of the permanent–transitory confusion show?" Unpublished.

Cukierman A. and P. Wachtel. 1979. "Differential inflationary expectations and the variability of the rate of inflation: theory and evidence," *American Economic Review* 69:595–609.

1982a. "Relative price variability and nonuniform inflationary expectations," *Journal of Political Economy* 90:146–57.

1982b. "Inflationary expectations and further thoughts on inflation uncertainty," *American Economic Review* 72:508–12.

Diamond D.W. and R.E. Verrecchia. 1981. "Information aggregation in a noisy rational expectations economy," *Journal of Financial Economics* 9:221–35.

Engle R.F. 1980. "Estimators of the variance of U.S. inflation based upon the ARCH model." Economics Department, working paper, University of California, San Diego.

Fama E.F. 1970. "Efficient capital markets: a review of theory and empirical work," *Journal of Finance* 25:383–417.

1976. "Inflation uncertainty and expected returns on treasury bills," *Journal of Political Economy* 84:427–48.

Feldstein M. 1976. "Inflation, income taxes and the rate of interest: a theoretical analysis," *American Economic Review* 66:809–20.

Feldstein M. and L. Summers. 1978. "Inflation, tax rules, and the long-term interest rate." Discussion paper no. 606, March, Harvard Institute of Economic Research, Cambridge, Mass.

Figlewski S. and P. Wachtel. 1981. "The formation of inflationary expectations," *The Review of Economics and Statistics* 63:1–10.

Fischer S. 1977. "Long-term contracts, rational expectations and the optimal money supply rule," *Journal of Political Economy* 85:191–205.

1981a. "Relative shocks, relative price variability and inflation," *Brookings Papers on Economic Activity,* No. 2, 381–431.

1981b. "Towards an understanding of the cost of inflation: II," in K. Brunner and A. Meltzer (eds.), *The Costs and Consequences of Inflation, Carnegie*

*Rochester Conference Series on Public Policy* 15, Autumn. Amsterdam: North-Holland.

1982. "Relative price variability and inflation in the U.S. and Germany," *European Economic Review* 18:171–96.

Fischer S. and F. Modigliani. 1978. "Towards an understanding of the real effects and costs of inflation," *Weltwirtschaftliches Archiv,* Band 114:810–33.

Fisher I. 1896. "Appreciation and interest," *Publications of the American Economic Association,* 3d series II:331–442.

Foster E. 1978. "The variability of inflation," *Review of Economics and Statistics* 60:346–50.

Friedman B.M. 1978. "Who puts the inflation premium into nominal rates?" *Journal of Finance* 33:833–45.

1979. "Optimal expectations and the extreme information assumptions of 'rational expectations' macromodels," *Journal of Monetary Economics* 5: 23–42.

1980. "Price inflation, portfolio choice, and nominal interest rates," *American Economic Review* 70:32–48.

Friedman M. 1957. *A Theory of the Consumption Function.* New York: National Bureau of Economic Research.

1959. "The demand for money: some theoretical and empirical results," *Journal of Political Economy* 67:327–51.

1968. "The role of monetary policy," *American Economic Review* 58:1–17.

1969. *The Optimum Quantity of Money and Other Essays.* Chicago: Aldine.

1977. "Nobel lecture: inflation and unemployment," *Journal of Political Economy* 85:451–72.

Froyen R.T. and R.N. Waud. 1980. "Further international evidence on output–inflation tradeoffs," *American Economic Review* 70:409–21.

Gibson W. 1972. "Interest rates and inflationary expectations," *American Economic Review* 62:854–65.

Glejser H. 1965. "Inflation, productivity and relative prices – a statistical study," *Review of Economics and Statistics* 47:761–80.

Gordon R.J. 1971. "Steady anticipated inflation: mirage or oasis," *Brookings Papers on Economic Activity* 2:499–510.

Gould J.P. 1968. "Adjustment costs in the theory of investment of the firm," *The Review of Economic Studies* 35:47–56.

Graham F.D. 1930. *Exchange, Prices, and Production in Hyperinflation: Germany 1930.* Princeton, N.J.: Princeton University Press.

Gray J.A. 1976. "Wage indexation: a macroeconomic approach," *Journal of Monetary Economics* 2:221–35.

Graybill F.A. 1961. *An Introduction to Linear Statistical Models,* vol. 1. New York: McGraw-Hill.

Grossman S.J. 1976. "On the efficiency of competitive stock markets where traders have diverse information," *The Journal of Finance* 31:573–85.

1977. "The existence of future markets, noisy rational expectations and informational externalities," *The Review of Economic Studies* 44:431–49.

194     **References**

1981. "An introduction to the theory of rational expectations under asymmetric information," *The Review of Economic Studies* 48:541-59.

Grossman S.J. and J.E. Stiglitz. 1976. "Information and competitive price systems," *American Economic Review* 66:246-53.

1980. "On the impossibility of informationally efficient markets," *American Economic Review* 70:393-408.

Haberger A.C. 1963. "The dynamics of inflation in Chile," in C. Christ (ed.), *Measurement in Economics and Econometrics*. Stanford, Calif.: Stanford University Press.

Hall R.E. 1977. "Expectation errors, unemployment and wage inflation." Manuscript, Center for Advanced Study in the Behavioral Sciences.

1978. "Stochastic implications of the life cycle-permanent income hypothesis: theory and evidence," *Journal of Political Economy* 86:971-88.

Hellwig M.F. 1980. "On the aggregation of information in competitive markets," *Journal of Economic Theory* 22:477-98.

1982. "Rational expectations equilibrium with conditioning on past prices: a mean-variance example," *Journal of Economic Theory* 26:279-312.

Hercowitz Z. 1981. "Money and the dispersion of relative prices," *Journal of Political Economy* 89:328-56.

1982. "Money and price dispersion in the United States," *Journal of Monetary Economics* 10:25-38.

Hirschleifer J. and J.G. Riley. 1979. "The analytics of uncertainty and information – an expository survey," *Journal of Economic Literature* 17:1375-421.

Ibrahim J.B. and R. Williams. 1978. "Price unpredictability and monetary standards: a comment on Klein's measure of price uncertainty," *Economic Inquiry* 16:431-7.

Jaffee D.M. and E. Kleiman. 1977. "The welfare implications of uneven inflation," in E. Lundberg (ed.), *Inflation Theory and Anti-Inflation Policy*. London: Macmillan.

Jaffee D.M. and T. Russell. 1976. "Imperfect information, uncertainty, and credit rationing," *Quarterly Journal of Economics* 90:651-66.

Jordan J.S. and R. Radner. 1982. "Rational expectations in microeconomic models: an overview," *Journal of Economic Theory* 26:201-23.

Jorgenson D.W. 1965. "Capital theory and investment behavior," *American Economic Review* 53:247-59.

Juster F.T. and R. Comment. 1978. "A note on the measurement of price expectations." Unpublished paper, Institute for Social Research, University of Michigan.

Karni E. 1980. "A note on Lucas' equilibrium model of the business cycle," *Journal of Political Economy* 88:1231-6.

1981. "Equilibrium business cycle theory with centralized trading in some assets," in M.J. Flanders and A. Razin (eds.), *Development in an Inflationary World*. New York: Academic.

Kihlstrom R.E. and L.J. Mirman. 1975. "Information and market equilibrium," *The Bell Journal of Economics* 6:357-76.

Klein B. 1975. "Our new monetary standard: the measurement and effects of price uncertainty, 1880-1973," *Economic Inquiry* 13:461-83.

Kydland F.E. and E.C. Prescott. 1980. "A competitive theory of fluctuations and the feasibility and desirability of stabilization policy," in S. Fischer (ed.), *Rational Expectations and Economic Policy.* Chicago: University of Chicago Press.

1982. "Time to build and aggregate fluctuations," *Econometrica* 50:1345-70.

Laidler D. 1966. "The rate of interest and the demand for money - some empirical evidence," *Journal of Political Economy* 74:543-55.

Leijonhufvud A. 1977. "Costs and consequences of inflation," in G. Harcourt (ed.), *The Microeconomic Foundations of Macroeconomics.* London: Proceedings of an IEA conference.

Levi M. and J. Makin. 1980. "Inflation uncertainty and the Phillips curve: some empirical evidence," *American Economic Review* 70:1022-7.

Lintner J. 1969. "The aggregation of investors diverse judgements and preferences in purely competitive security markets," *Journal of Financial and Quantitative Analysis* 4:347-400.

Lipsey R. 1960. "The relation between unemployment and the rate of change of money wage rates in the United Kingdom, 1862-1957: a further analysis," *Economica* (NS) 27:1-31.

Liviatan N. and D. Levhari. 1977. "Risk and the theory of indexed bonds," *American Economic Review* 64:366-75.

Logue D.E. and T.D. Willet. 1976. "A note on the relation between the rate and the variability of inflation," *Economica* 43:151-8.

Lucas R.E. Jr. 1967. "Adjustment costs and the theory of supply," *Journal of Political Economy* 75:321-34.

1972a. "Expectations and the neutrality of money," *Journal of Economic Theory* 4:103-24.

1972b. "Econometric testing of the natural rate hypothesis," in Otto Eckstein (ed.), *The Econometrics of Price Determination Conference.* Washington D.C.: Board of Governors of the Federal Reserve System.

1973. "Some international evidence on output inflation tradeoffs," *American Economic Review* 63:326-35.

1975. "An equilibrium model of the business cycle, *Journal of Political Economy* 83:1113-44.

1976. "Errata," *American Economic Review* 66:985.

1977. "Some international evidence on output-inflation tradeoffs: reply," *American Economic Review* 67:731.

Lucas R.E. Jr. and L. Rapping. 1969. "Real wages, employment and inflation," *Journal of Political Economy* 77:721-54.

MaCurdy T.E. 1981. "An empirical model of labor supply in a life-cycle setting," *Journal of Political Economy* 89:1059-85.

Meltzer A.H. 1982. "Rational expectations, risk, uncertainty and market responses," in P. Wachtel (ed.), *Crises in the Economic and Financial Structure.* Lexington, Mass.: Lexington Books.

Mises Ludwig Von. 1953. *The Theory of Money and Credit,* translated by H.E. Batson. New Haven, Conn.: Yale University Press.

Mitchell D.W. and H.E. Taylor. 1982. "Inflationary expectations: comment," *American Economic Review* 72:502–7.

Mullineaux D.J. 1980. "Unemployment, industrial production and inflation uncertainty in the United States," *The Review of Economics and Statistics* 62: 163–9.

Muth J.F. 1960. "Optimal properties of exponentially weighted forecasts," *Journal of the American Statistical Association* 55:299–306.

1961. "Rational expectations and the theory of price movements," *Econometrica* 29:315–35.

Nelson P. 1974. "Advertising as information," *Journal of Political Economy* 82: 729–54.

1975. "The economic consequences of advertising," *Journal of Business* 48: 213–41.

Oi W.Y. 1962. "Labor as a quasi fixed factor," *Journal of Political Economy* 70: 538–55.

Okun A.M. 1971. "The mirage of steady anticipated inflation," *Brookings Papers on Economic Activity* 2:485–98.

Padoa-Schioppa F. 1979. "Inflazione e pressie relativi," *Moneta e Credito* 32.

1981. "Cross sectional and intertemporal price variability," Center for Operation Research and Econometrics (CORE) Discussion Paper 8115, Louvins la Neuve, Belgium.

Parks R.W. 1978. "Inflation and relative price variability," *Journal of Political Economy* 86:79–96.

Patinkin D. 1965. *Money Interest and Prices,* 2d ed. New York: Harper & Row.

Perry G. 1966. *Unemployment, Money Wage Rates and Inflation.* Cambridge, Mass.: MIT Press.

Phelps E.S. 1967. "Phillips curves, expectations of inflation and optimal unemployment over time," *Economica* (NS) 34:254–81.

Phelps E.S. and J.B. Taylor. 1977. "Stabilizing powers of monetary policy under rational expectations," *Journal of Political Economy* 85:163–90.

Phelps E.S. et al. 1970. *Microeconomic Foundations of Employment and Inflation Theory.* New York: Norton.

Phillips A.W. 1958. "The relation between unemployment and the rate of change of money wage rates in the United Kingdom, 1861–1957," *Economica* 25: 283–99.

Poole W. 1976. "Rational expectations in the macro model," *Brookings Papers on Economic Activity* 2:463–514.

Rothschild M. and J.E. Stiglitz. 1976. "Equilibrium in competitive insurance markets: an essay on the economics of imperfect information," *Quarterly Journal of Economics* 90:629–49.

Salop J. and S. Salop. 1976. "Self selection and turnover in the labor market," *Quarterly Journal of Economics* 90:619–27.

Salop S. 1977. "The noisy monopolist: imperfect information, price dispersion and price discrimination," *The Review of Economic Studies* 44:393–406.

Samuelson P.A. and R.M. Solow. 1960. "Analytical aspects of anti-inflation policy," *Papers and Proceedings of the American Economic Association* 50:177-94.

Sargent T.J. 1973. "Rational expectations, the real rate of interest and the natural rate of unemployment," *Brookings Papers on Economic Activity* 2:429-80.

1976. "Interest rates and expected inflation: a selective summary of recent research," *Explorations in Economic Research* 3:303-25.

1978. "Estimation of dynamic labor demand schedules under rational expectations," *Journal of Political Economy* 86:1009-44.

1979. *Macroeconomic Theory.* New York: Academic.

Schultze C.L. 1959. "Recent inflation in the U.S." Study Paper No. 1 prepared for Joint Economic Committee, U.S. Congress.

Sheshinski E. and Y. Weiss. 1977. "Inflation and the costs of price adjustment," *Review of Economic Studies* 64:287-303.

Spence M. 1973. "Job market signaling," *Quarterly Journal of Economics* 87: 355-74.

1974. "Competitive and optimal responses to signals: an analysis of efficiency and distribution," *Journal of Economic Theory* 7:296-332.

Stiglitz J.E. 1974. "The demand for education in public and private school systems," *Journal of Public Economics* 3:349-85.

Stiglitz J.E. and A. Weiss. 1981. "Credit rationing in markets with imperfect information," *American Economic Review* 71:393-410.

Taylor J.B. 1980. "Aggregate dynamics and staggered contracts," *Journal of Political Economy* 88:1-23.

1981. "On the relation between the variability of inflation and the average inflation rate," in K. Brunner and A.H. Meltzer (eds.), *The Costs and Consequences of Inflation, Carnegie Rochester Conference Series on Public Policy* 15. Amsterdam: North-Holland.

1983. "Optimal stabilization rules in a stochastic model of investment with gestation lags." Unpublished.

Tobin J. 1972. "Inflation and unemployment," *American Economic Review* 62: 1-18.

Treadway A.B. 1969. "On rational entrepreneurial behavior and the demand for investment," *The Review of Economic Studies* 36:227-40.

Turnovsky S.J. 1977. "Structural expectations and the effectiveness of government policy in a short-run macroeconomic model," *American Economic Review* 67:851-66.

Verrecchia R.E. 1982. "Information acquisition in a noisy rational expectations economy," *Econometrica* 50:1415-30.

Vining D. and T. Elwertowski. 1976. "The relationship between relative prices and the general price level," *American Economic Review* 66:699-708.

Wachtel P. 1977. "Survey measures of expected inflation and their potential usefulness," in Joel Popkin (ed.), *Analysis of Inflation: 1965-74.* New York: National Bureau of Economic Research Studies in Income and Wealth, Vol. 42.

Wolff E.N. 1979. "The distributional effects of the 1969-75 inflation on holdings of household wealth in the United States," *The Review of Income and Wealth* 13:195-207.

# Index

aggregate–relative confusion, 8; aggregation of information by prices and, 107–8; causality and, 101–2; centralized bond market and, 108–11; economic theory and, 5–6; inflation and relative price changes and, 84–5; inflation uncertainty and, 61–3, 63–7; inflation variability and relative price variability and, 85–9; inflationary expectations and information and, 54–5; inflationary expectations and relative price variability and, 89–92; inflationary expectations and variance and, 61–3; inflationary expectations surveys and, 53–4; information and, 13–14; labor productivity and, 120; Lucas's model and rational expectations and equilibrium and, 40–6; monetary variability and inflationary expectations and inflation variance and, 58–61; monetary variability and price level perceptions and, 55–7; Phillips curve empirical testing and, 49–50; Phillips curve overview and, 35–8; Phillips–Lucas trade-off evidence and, 50–1; relative price determinants and, 84; relative price variability and supply elasticities and, 92–101; short-run Phillips curve and, 46–9; social costs of inflation and, 61

Akerlof, G. A., 14
Anderson, R. M., 32
Arrow, Kenneth J., 15

Barro, R. J., 48, 93, 110, 154
Beja, A., 31
Blejer, M. J., 61, 84
Blinder, A., 120
bond market, 8; aggregate–relative confusion and, 108–11; allocative efficiency and, 72–6; differential expectations of inflation and redistribution through, 78–80; equilibrium with heterogeneous expectations and, 69–71; inflation expectations and volume of trade and, 76–8; study and, *xii*
Bordo, M. D., 102
Brunner, Karl, *xiii*, 121
business cycles, 139–40

Cagan, P., 136
capital, 72, 125
capital stocks, 116–17
Carlson, John, 53, 58
causality, 89, 101–2

change, *see* permanent and temporary change
commodities market (economic model), 127–8
competition, 28
confusion, *see* aggregate–relative confusion; permanent–transitory confusion
consumer price index, 58, 64, 84
consumption, 6; information and, 20, 24–6
consumption smoothing, 117–18
contracts: contingent, 15; insurance, 17–18; staggered, 121–2
credit markets, information and, 18–19
Cukierman, A., 7, 38–9, 63–4, 89, 91, 101–2, 111, 160

demand, 108, 135; asymmetric information and market prices and, 20–2; bond market and inflationary expectations and, 70, 71; capital, 117; commodities, 125; contracts and, 121–2; inventories and, 121; Lucas's model and Phillips curve and, 38–9, 41, 45–6; model of economy and, 123–4; for money, 127; permanent-transitory confusion and, 145, 146–8; price information and, 31–2; privileged information and, 26; relative prices and, 87, 97–8, 153; work period disutility and, 119

demand shocks, 148; bond market and, 108; distribution of rate of inflation and, 60; information output and, 156; Lucas's model and Phillips curve and, 44, 46; price forecasts and, 54, 55, 57; relative prices and, 85, 88, 89, 91, 92, 98, 154, 167–9, 173

demand elasticity: relative price change and, 173; relative price forecasts and, 153

Diamond, D. W., 32, 33
disequilibrium, 3–4

Economic Cooperation and Development (OECD) countries, 84
economists, classifying, 2–3
education, screening for productive ability and, 15–16
Elwertowski, T., 84, 88, 89, 90, 91, 174
employees: Phillips curve and, 35–6; turnover and, 16–17
employers: Phillips curve and, 35–6; productive ability screening and, 15–16; turnover and, 16–17